EDUCATION FOR RURAL DEVELOPMENT

D. P. Nayar

SHIPRA

Rs. 180; US$ 9

ISBN: 978-81-7541-456-3

2014 Impression
(2009)

Education for Rural Development

Published by:
SHIPRA PUBLICATIONS
H.O.: LG 18-19, Pankaj Central Market, I.P. Ext.,
Patparganj, Delhi 110092, Ph. 22235152, 22236152
Br. Off.: 4617/18, Main Ansari Road, Daryaganj,
New Delhi 110002; Ph.9650028065, 9810522367
Email: info@shiprapublications.com
Website: www.shiprapublications.com

Acknowledgement

The study owes its genesis to the financial support provided by the Indian Council of Social Science Research (ICSSR). The office accommodation and the administrative support was provided by the National Council of Educational Research and Training (NCERT). The NCERT and the National Institute of Educational Planning and Administration (NIEPA) (now National University of Educational Planning and Administration, NUEPA) also made available their library facilities. The informal contact with the faculty of these two institutions, located in close proximity, was also of invaluable help. NUEPA, by utilizing my services now and then, as a resource person, also provided opportunities for continued contact with strategic personnel from the Education Departments of the States.

My special thanks are due to the eminent personalities in various fields who, in spite of their heavy pre-occupations, graciously gave me the opportunities to discuss with them various aspects of the complex problems discussed in the Study. I am also grateful to the officers of the Central Ministries – especially those concerned with the education, cultural and rural development – and the Planning Commission as well as those of the Haryana State. At the State level my special thanks are due to the Chief Secretary, without whose support the State level portion of the study would not have been carried out. I am also grateful to the Deputy Commissioners of Mohendergarh and Hissar districts, who with the assistance of their District and lower level officers of the various Departments helped me to study the problems faced at the district and the lower levels, not only by the official machinery but also by the local communities.

The most important support came from institutions whose response to the questionnaire was spontaneous, probably largely due to their realization of the importance of the subject of study.

Lastly, my thanks are due to my research and clerical assistants without whom the document could not have been prepared.

D. P. Nayar

New Delhi

Contents

Acknowledgements *iii*
Introduction 1

Chapter 1
Dynamics of Rural Development 9
Development Trends and their Likely Outcome, Poverty and Inequality, Regional Disparities, Population Explosion, Rural Employment, Nutrition, Human Resources Development, Agriculture, Energy, Rural Electrification, Science and Technology, Administrative Innovations

Chapter 2
Preferred Future 47
Rural Society in Transition, Preferred Future, Central Aim, Economic Order, Political Order, Cultural Dimension, Educational Support, Strategies of Development, Conclusion

Chapter 3
Educational Imperatives Processes, Programmes and Structures : 76
School Education and Non-formal Education
Methodological Imperative, Problem-Centred and Life-Centred Education, Activity-Centred Education, Production-Centred Education, Creating a Scientific Temper, Teaching the Cooperative and Democratic Way of Life, Development of Personality Traits and Leadership Qualities, Major Issues and the Content Imperatives, Energy, Ecological Balance, Population Explosion, Transfer of Technology, Building of Community Cohesion, Linking School Education to Rural Development, Pre-school Education, Elementary Education, Health, Agriculture, Cooperation, Education and Employment, Secondary Education

Chapter 4
Higher Education **115**
University Education, Over-all Constraints and Required Strategies, Location, Integration of Theory and Practice, Coordination, Clear Reiteration of the University's Responsibility, Improving General Atmosphere, Overall Programmes: Some Significant Beginnings, National Service, Continuing Education, Adult Education and Extension Work, University Involvement in Eco-development, Restructuring of Courses and Reorientation of Methodology, Specific Categories: Present Position and Further Recommendations, General Universities, Agricultural Universities, Technical Institutions, College (Arts, Science and Commerce), Engineering Colleges and Polytechnics, Conclusions

Chapter 5
Non-Formal Education and Rural Development **151**
Objectives, Suggested Criteria, Present Position: A Critical Analysis, Heavy almost sole preoccupation with literacy, Lack of a sense of direction; a consistent approach, Absence of Effective Implementation Machinery, Centrally framed and directed programmes, Lessons from Successful Experiments, An Effective Strategy

Chapter 6
Challenges of Implementation **167**
Basic Education, Education and Community Development, Rural Institutes, National Adult Education Programme (NAEP), Causes of Failure of NAEP, Lessons of the Past: Problems and Remedies, Political Factor, Technical Factor, Structural Reorientation, Central Level, Planning Commission, Ministry of Human Resource Development (M/HRD), State Level, District and Sub-District Level, Coordination

Chapter 7
Conclusions **222**
Introduction, Perspective and Priority, Educational Imperatives, Implementation Challenge, Political Factor, Technical and Administrative Factor, Central Level, State Level, District and Sub-District Level

Index **247**

Introduction

The Perspective

When statesmen all over the world are crying hoarse that the world has never been so near complete annihilation as today, the world's prime concern naturally is to avert the impending disaster. But what humanity needs is not temporary respite from conflict but an enduring peace. And peace cannot be manoeuvred, it has to be built from the base. Till recently two superpowers, each in search of superiority over the other and mortally afraid of each other, were increasing their power of destruction, completely indifferent to the cry of humanity for peace and survival. The inequalities of nations are matched – sometimes even more than matched – by inequalities within the lowest units. If the world has to be re-built, in order to survive, an exactly opposite impulse has to be generated at the bottom and made to move up with increasing acceleration and vigour. There has to be a progressive taming of the ego and selfishness in ever-widening concentric circle. As Gandhiji put it, the individual must live for the family, the family for the village, the village for the district, the district for the State, the State for the nation and the nation for the world.

The strength of the new world order will depend upon the foundations laid at individual, family and rural community levels - rural, because the vast majority of the world's population lives in rural areas. It is in this perspective that the urgency and importance of rural development emerges clearly. It is not a programme of caring for the weak, the lowly and the lost, who have been, and could still be ignored with impunity or for whom crumbs could be thrown from the dinner table. Rural development can no longer entail a residual approach. It is necessary for the very survival of the world and has to be at the heart of world development. It needs to be remembered that peace is indivisible. So is prosperity, to be durable.

The achievement of the above goal requires a revolutionary change in the attitude of the "haves", so that they do justice to the "have nots" in enlightened self-interest. This change can be forced through a violent revolution and confrontation. In this it is largely the weak who suffer far more than the strong. The control of a revolution soon passes into the hands of outsiders who exploit the weak for their own purposes. That is why Gandhiji said that the crux of the problem lay in putting the destiny of the poor in their own hands. That can only be done through education.

Education, therefore, has to be the pivotal force of development, if it is to be in the interest of the poor. It is from this fact that the theme of the study: ***"Education for Rural Development"*** derives its significance. What should be the type of education which will meet the challenge? How can it be introduced and operated in the present situation? What has been our experience in the past? What orientation is required for the future? These and a host of other related questions are sought to be answered in the present study.

In the present context, while India's development effort is very considerable and is daily mounting, her educational system represents a huge potential. There seems, at present, hardly any interaction between education and other development sectors with the result that their mutually reinforcing capabilities are not developed and exploited. The education system, by and large, creates problems rather than solves them. The present study is, in a global perspective, a country study, of the net-work of interrelationship and interactions both existing and those required to achieve the over-all objectives – between education and other development sectors and their implications in all their ramifications.

Design, Methodology and Outline of the Study

The study began as a micro study, confined to two districts of the Haryana State viz. Hissar and Mahindergarh.

It, however, soon became clear that such a study would have very limited use as most decisions were and had to be taken at the national and State levels. It was, however, realized that in any dynamic system of democratic planning, there had to be interaction between the top and the bottom through various intermediate levels and the problem of planning and implementation had to be studied all along the line. The top-most level – the national level – had to be studied in an international perspective in the context of an interdependent world.

The study falls broadly into three parts, interrelated but each distinct in character, dictating its own methodology. These are:

1. Dynamics of Rural Development;
2. Educational Imperatives: Processes, Programmes and Structures; and
3. The Implementation Challenges.

The first part is devoted to the study of forces operating in rural areas, the extent to which and the manner in which they could be manipulated to obtain the Preferred Future – the future which we could, should and were most likely to plan for. In regard to the Preferred Future, a Preliminary Statement was prepared on the basis of library study, keeping in mind the Indian Constitution, the manifestoes of the major political parties, plan documents, constraints of the existing situation and the likely denouement of the existing trends. The strategic points in this statement were identified and tested against the views of thinkers, planners, political leaders, senior administrators, educationists and others. Thirty three persons were interviewed and others sent their replies to specific questions including – both former and present – 2 Education Ministers, 3 Deputy Chairmen and 2 Education Members of the Planning Commission, 2 Chairmen and one Vice-Chairman of the University Grants Commission, 4 Vice-Chancellors of universities – including one of a premier Agricultural University – and other senior technical and administrative officers of the Government of India. A former Acting Director-General of UNESCO was also interviewed. In the light of these discussions, the Preliminary Statement was modified, where necessary, and also enriched. While each one of these distinguished personalities made a valuable contribution to the emergence of the final position embodied in this section, in the very nature of things, none of them can be held responsible for any view expressed therein. The author alone is responsible.

The second part spells out the educational imperatives or The Preferred Future, judges them against past experiences, the world trends in pedagogy etc. and suggests a course of action. It defines the methodological imperatives and the major issues in development and their contextual content imperatives. Finally, it indicates the existing and possible linkages between different stages of education and the various sectors of development. All stages of formal education, as well as non-formal education, are covered.

Apart from library research and discussion with strategically placed persons, this section is supported by studies under the following heads:

1. Rural development and universities;
2. Involvement of general colleges in rural development;
3. Involvement of engineering colleges and polytechnics in rural development;
4. National Service Scheme and rural development;
5. Analysis of the syllabi of Classes VIII and X in the schools of Haryana; and
6. 2 district studies (Mahindergarh and Hissar) in regard to linkages between school and adult education with development. Both academic and administrative aspects were studied.

The first three studies use the questionnaire method. The fourth study is based on the study of existing literature and discussions with knowledgeable persons. The last study is based on discussions and visits.

The third part is entitled: the Implementation Challenges. A forging of education as an instrument of rural development will call for many changes in the existing practices – both academic and administrative – and pose a serious challenge to our capacity for management. The chapter first analyses our experience in the management of four of our major innovative programmes launched since independence and draws from this analysis the guide-lines for future action. This is followed by a section which examines the existing structures at the Central, State, District, Block and Community levels and suggests orientation thereof if the challenge of innovation management has to be adequately met. This section draws heavily on the two district studies mentioned above, apart from the discussions with senior administrators at the Central and State levels.

Relevance to Other Developing Countries

While the study deals with India, it might have some relevance to other developing countries as well, because the situation in most developing countries is similar in certain essential respects as explained below:

1. The extreme poverty of the large mass of the people. The poverty has to be removed within the constraints of limited resources and existing inequalities, dictating the strategy of generating the maximum possible self-reliance among the people themselves through a wholly or largely self-supporting craft-centred education. This will have a triple advantage:
   - It will considerably add to the total production potential with available resources.
   - It will start and develop the process of human resource development in which the developing countries are very rich.
   - The growing economic strength of the mass of the people will start the process of establishing a more equitable relationship between various classes, through a peaceful process, with minimum of confrontation. It would strengthen national cohesion and integration within each nation and improve its relative position vis-à-vis the outside world. It is in this sense that the battle for a more effective position in the North-South dialogue has to be won by the developing countries in their own rural areas.
2. The education systems in most developing countries are still largely a continuation of the systems established during colonial days. While their irrelevance to the needs of these countries, after independence, is well recognized and time and again proclaimed, they still continue unchanged in their existing momentum

and their linkages with the existing power structure – again a hang-over of the past colonial era-which makes it extremely difficult to alter them.

3. While there are important voluntary organizations in many developing countries, the task of remodeling the education system is so large that the responsibility has mainly to be borne by the governments of the countries. The task, however, requires a development-oriented administration while the administrations, inherited, by most developing countries, have primarily law and order orientation.

While in India, the education system continues, by and large, on old lines, there is a widespread recognition of its irrelevance. India has conducted valuable experiments, though on a limited scale, which are likely to have significance not only for the future policy of this country but of other developing countries as well. India may have some relevant lessons-both positive and negative – as to how to face the tremendous challenge of forging education as an instrument of national development and social transformation.

Another use of such country studies, where educational reform is studied in relationship with the total socio-economic situation and the political as well as administrative structure, is that they are likely to throw up suggestions which may be developed and modified by other countries, viewing them against their own social, political, economic and administrative systems.

The common problems of our various countries and the fact that promising beginnings have been made to tackle them in most of these countries highlight the necessity and advantage of mutual exchange of experiences. This book aspires to be a modest effort in that exercise.

To the Educational and Over-all Planner

It is hoped that the study will be useful to students of education and educational planners, in giving them a synoptic view of development, which is becoming more and more important, as planning process becomes increasingly complex and comprehensive. A 'pure' educationist is becoming rapidly obsolete for the tasks of educational planning and implementation. It is hoped, that the book will give to the overall planner an idea of the potentiality of education as a instrument of development and the way its potential could be exploited. It could also serve to educate the public at large in regard to the needed educational reforms, which require for their successful implementation a broad understanding of the issues involved, so necessary for public cooperation.

General Approach

A word about the general approach in the document. It is a frank analysis of our weaknesses. That is not to belittle our achievements, which are considerable – almost staggering in some respects. The study is intended to be an action oriented document. For moving forward on sound lines we need a keen awareness of our weaknesses that we need to shed. I hope, India is mature enough to look at its faults steadily in the face. We learn as much from our failures as from our successes. Dressing up failure as success is easy and tempting but suicidal.

P.S. Efforts have been made by friend-colleagues of the departed soul to update the data as far as possible to further enhance the value of this publication after the demise of the author.

Chapter One

Dynamics of Rural Development

Introduction

In this inter-twined and inter-dependent world, rural development can best be studied in the perspective of national and global development. As a sector of overall development, however, rural development, is unmistakably of the highest priority, even though the large mass of people involved are not able to articulate effectively their needs and aspirations. Many outsiders support rural development only in enlightened self-interest; the politicians mouth it because of the political advantage of 'espousing' the cause of the majority who live in rural areas.

The developing nations, constituting the predominant majority of the world population, are largely rural. In India, nearly 72 per cent of the people live in rural areas (Census of India 2001). The importance of numbers is doubly enhanced in the democratic context, where the power of the vote lends their voice the added significance. It is not accidental, therefore, that the rural poor have become hot favourites of the politicians.

The rural areas provide employment to around 60 per cent of the country's labour force through agriculture.[1] Agriculture's contribution to GDP declined from 29.76 per cent during 1993-94 to 1995-96 to 23.15 per cent during 2000-2001 to 2002-03. In some backward states, contribution is close to 40 per cent. Industry, the other main source of employment, is itself considerably dependent on agriculture for its raw materials and as the consumer of industrial products like fertilizers, pesticides etc.

The development of rural areas is important to industry and the urban elite because of the vast and potential market that the rural population provides for manufactured goods. This potential demand can be converted into effective demand only by increasing the purchasing power of the rural people. This urban-rural and industry – agriculture relationship uniquely illustrates the universal principle of interdependence, which holds good both in the national and international world. They are like the spokes of a wheel, which should be of equal size for the wheel's smooth movement.

The present condition of the rural poor is desperate. At the beginning of the new millennium, 260 million people were living below the poverty line in India; of them, 75 per cent were in rural areas[2]. Their frustration and age-long resignation can at any moment turn into violence, especially when ignited by political parties. This frustration has the potentiality to destroy the very fabric of Indian society. That is why the powers that be fear the "rebellion of the poor". Further, poverty, illiteracy, ignorance and resignation of the vast majority with its state cannot provide the context for a modernizing society. Any development foisted on these people, however well designed, can only defeat the purposes aimed at. It is no wonder that our development so far has only widened the gap between the rich and the poor. Without preparing the "receiving mechanism", expansion of the "delivery system" can only increase the power of the exploiting sections of society; and if these trends continue, the consequences can be disastrous. We must act before the point of no return is reached. Within the rural areas themselves, the poor are in the grip of a small clan, who seem to be in league with the urban elite.

The traditional supports of the rural society – community cohesion, deep-rooted traditional values etc. – are being steadily eroded by the forces of pseudo modernization without anything significant replacing them. They are further being denuded of talent and enterprise, which tend to migrate to urban areas, instead of contributing to transformation of the rural society. They further accentuate the problems of poverty, unemployment, over-crowding and disease.

With the ever-increasing acceleration of modernization, it becomes much more urgent that the large majority of people, who live in rural areas, is made capable of bearing the 'shock of change'.

It is in the rural areas that major issues in the world's future development – population growth, energy, ecology, technology, etc. – present their most serious challenge not only because of the dimensions of the problems involved but also because their solutions call for innovative approaches. We are comparatively far more familiar with the problems and solutions of urban areas, whereas the problems of rural development have, by and large, remained hitherto largely neglected and unexplored.

Another very important reason for urgent attention to rural development is that, in some respects, rural areas present the most precious reservoir of our civilization. Here men do not live suffocatingly close to each other, yet are close enough to continue to have mutual relevance and mutual concern; here man is not engaged in a short-sighted fight to the finish with his best friend – nature; where nature still has a sporting chance to help humans – unsolicited and very often unrecognized; where contemplative life is still possible: where humans can still meet their basic necessities in a pure, unadulterated form; and where, in short, it is still possible to ensure the quality of life. The following words of the University Education Commission (1949) merit utmost consideration:

> "The Significance of the Indian Village – As free India begins to plan its course – a great increase of interest in village welfare is in evidence. This is important, not only for the sake of the villages, but for the destiny of India as a whole.
>
> In the course of world history, seldom has the greatness of a nation long survived the disintegration of its rural life. For untold ages, man by nature has been a villager and has not long survived in any other environment. Almost every study of the subject, which has been made in Europe and America, has revealed that, as a rule, city families survive for only a few generations. Cities grow and thrive for only as long as they are constantly replenished from the rural population. So long as a nation's rural life is vigorous, it possesses reserves of life and power. When for a long time cities draw the cream of life and culture from the villages, returning almost nothing, as has been the case in India during the last two centuries, the current village resources of culture and energy become depleted, and the strength of the nation is reduced."[2]

It is important for the survival of the human race that rural areas must survive; and for their survival rural development is essential. The size of the area and population involved in rural development is so enormous that the options exercised in their development will have a tremendous impact on world development; and, unless the options open are wisely exercised and the advanced countries lend a truly friendly helping-hand in enlightened self-interest, development may not take place in a manner which makes for a better and a more harmonious world.

While it would be difficult to question the necessity of giving the top-most priority to rural development, three factors, are likely to seriously limit its realization in practice. Firstly, the momentum of existing programmes - in which vested interests, which are deeply embedded and exert their pressure in very subtle ways–makes it very difficult for any planner at any given point of time to give to rural development the needed allocations, which alone are the acid test of the priority allotted to this sector. Secondly, while the production related programmes may get the necessary allocations, social services and human resource development do not get their due share because of the poverty and lack of organization of the poor and their consequent inability to mount the pressure required for getting their rights recognized. Thirdly, the recognition of the degree of dependence of production on the human factor is still of lesser importance among the planners.

The development of rural areas, thus, is vital to the survival of the developing world – nay, of the world as a whole. That explains the pre-occupation of the world bodies with this problem. In order to go about the job scientifically and systematically, however, the dynamics of rural development – the forces that can initiate, sustain, and manipulate it in planned directions – must be understood before one is able to design appropriate strategies for the purpose. We must study the forces already in operation in rural societies and their natural denouement and prognosis; the extent to which these forces can be manipulated to lead us to the desired goal; and the new forces that can be generated to make the situation respond to the needs of planned changes. Finally, we come to the question of the role that education can play in this process, the extent to which it is discharging that function and how it can do so more effectively.

Development Trends and their Likely Outcome

Before one can devise effective strategies to reach the desired development goals, one needs to study the present position as it has developed over the years, the various strands therein and their likely results if past trends are allowed to continue. Only such a study can reveal the possibilities and lines of fruitful intervention.

Further, for obvious reasons, it would be useful to study these trends in a global perspective. The international action can both thwart and help local and national action. Secondly, the available options open to developing countries are limited by the global situation. For example, if future development of rural areas were to depend heavily on oil, oil is simply not likely to be available on the scale needed or price that can be easily afforded. Thirdly, the strategies adopted for development of rural areas, which means the major part of the world, both spatially and population-wise, are bound to have a tremendous impact on the world as a whole. The developed countries should be interested in helping developing countries to evolve strategies, which would leaa to a better and more equitable, rather than a divided world, driven by confrontation and conflict. Fourthly, studies conducted in the global context can help to identify the common problems of developing counties, providing the foci for pooling of useful experiences in tackling them, thereby assisting the evolution of appropriate strategies and promoting cooperation among the developing countries.

Poverty and Inequality

Globally speaking, the central fact in the present position relating to rural development is the extreme poverty of vast masses of human beings. The world may be divided into high-income, middle-income and low income countries. The plight of the low-income group countries is grim and the future prospects are even grimmer. While the community of interests, between industrial countries and the oil-exporting capital surplus countries, is now well established and there is a growing realization of the importance of middle-income countries to the industrialized west, the low-income countries are left in the cold and the gap between the rich and the poor nations is going to widen further. In 1981, the World Bank summed up the situation as follows:

> "The outlook for reducing poverty has worsened along with the prospects for the poor countries. Current estimates suggest that in 1980 about 750 million people lived in absolute poverty in the developing world, i.e., about 33 per cent of its population (these estimates exclude China). If high case growth is extended to the year 2000, the proportion by them could be reduced to 18 per cent. But continued rapid population growth would mean that the absolute numbers living in poverty would still total 630 million. Under the low case at the end of a century of unprecedented economic and social advance in some parts of the world, 850 million people may still be living in absolute poverty" (*World Development Report* (WDR) 1981, pp.17-18).

The position has improved somewhat as recent estimates by the World Bank (2006) show that the proportion of the developing world's population living in extreme economic poverty – defined as living on less than a $1 per day – has fallen from 28 per cent in 1990 to 21 per cent in 2001. While there has been some improvement in reducing poverty levels, there still exist wide regional disparities. Globally, poverty reduction has been accompanied by rapid growth in China and the East Asian and the Pacific regions. Poverty also decreased in South Asia over the last two decades, but at a relatively slower pace. In Sub-Saharan Africa, where GDP per capita rose to 14 per cent; poverty rose from 41 per cent in 1981 to 46 per cent in 2001 swelling the existing number pf persons living in extreme poverty by an additional 150 million.[3]

The awareness among industrial countries of their interest in the development of the low-income countries needs to be strengthened in their own interest. The *World Development Report 1981*, while referring to the hardship of developing countries due to the population – poverty nexus points out:

> "Nor will the hardship necessarily be confined to developing countries. A world of 1.5 billion in 1950 grew to one of 4 billion by 1975 and will exceed 6 billion by the end of this

century. This pressure will bring to every country will be considerable, since all are affected by world demand for food and for finite resources, and by the dangers to clean air and oceans. Failure to slow population growth, substantially by the end of this century, means that rapid population growth will continue in the next decade and lead to an ultimate world population of 11 billion or more instead of the 8 billion at which it could be stabilized. Any residual belief that industrial countries can somehow immunize themselves from the problems faced by the developing world will then be painfully exposed."

Further:

"The developing countries increasingly act as the 'engine of growth' for the rest of the world. While the main transmission of economic activity is still from the industrial to the developing countries, the reverse effects are not negligible. Some estimates suggest that an extra percentage point on the growth rate of the developing countries will raise industrial countries growth by about 0.1 to 0.2 per cent. Another study calculated that, by sustaining their imports in the mid-1970s, while the rest of the world's slowed down, the middle-income countries had an impact on the industrial countries equivalent to a significant reflection of the economy of the Federal Republic of Germany. They prevented the recession in the industrial world from becoming over worse than it was" (*World Development Report 1981*, pp. 111-112).

Again, the Report cryptically remarks:

"It is the poor countries that emerge so vividly in this Report as being left behind by world growth, facing a further deterioration in their prospects. They remain on the periphery of the expanding trade and financial links among industrial oil-exporting and middle-income countries" (*World Development Report 1981*, p. 111).

The inequalities between developed and developing countries extend to equally glaring inequalities within developing countries themselves, where the poor are concentrated largely in rural areas. It is the weakness of these areas that constitutes the chief weakness of the developing countries because most of the export trade of these countries depends on agricultural products. Also because it is in rural areas that vast resources – both human and material – lie unexploited. That is why the key to the predominance of the developing world on the international scene lies in the development of their own rural areas.

Even, two and half decades later, global inequalities have become massive with varied trends. Global income-inequality has steadily increased over the years until the onset of rapid economic growth of India and China. The existing inequalities between and within the nations are evident from the following statement of the World Development Report (WDR) 2006:

> " ... an individual in the tenth percentile in the U.S. distribution enjoys a level of income higher than an individual earning the mean income in Brazil or Argentina. While a Chinese individual living in rural area has a mean income similar to an average Cambodian, an urban Chinese enjoys a similar income to an average Brazilian. A South African at the bottom of the income distribution in her country earns as much as the average individual in Mali while a South African at the ninetieth percentile of that income distribution enjoys a standard of living (in income) comparable to that of a median Irish individual" (p. 62).

> "...while the world got richer, income inequality - relative and absolute, international and global – increased tremendously over a long period of time (1920-1992). But the story is less clear-cut for a more recent time frame. In the post-World War II era, inter-country inequality (unweighted) has continued to increase while international inequality (weighted for population) declined. International inequality declined in the final decades of the twentieth century, because the inequality-reducing effects of income growth in China and South Asia more than offset the inequality-boosting effects of continued steady income growth in the now-developed countries and the declining incomes in Sub-Saharan Africa" (p. 65).

> "... between 1960 and 1990, however, there also were large differences by regions. Inequality between the countries of

> OECD (and the rest of Europe including Turkey) decreased by 50 per cent during this period, at the end accounting for only one-third of total inequality. During the same period, international inequality in Sub-Saharan Africa doubled, causing its share in total inequality to increase from 20 per cent to 36 per cent. In both Sub-Saharan Africa and Latin America and Caribbean, overall inequality levels remain high, while high income countries show signs of convergence (p.65).

According to WDR 2006, the absolute poverty rates have, however, declined in the past 20 years or so. "While there are roughly 400 million fewer people who live on less than $1 a day in 2001, than there were in 1981, the number of poor people in Sub-Saharan Africa almost doubled from approximately 160 million to 313 million. While some populous countries, almost exclusively in Asia, such as Bangladesh, China, India and Pakistan, made significant headway against extreme poverty, almost all increases in extreme poverty – especially in countries with high initial headcount rates – took place in Sub-Saharan Africa" (p. 66).

In India, as already stated, about 51 per cent of the population in the rural areas, about 38 per cent in the urban and about 48 per cent in the country as a whole, were estimated to live below the poverty line on the basis of the minimum calorie requirement (2400 in rural areas and 2100 in urban) and Rs. 65 per capita per month in rural areas and Rs. 75 per capita per month in urban areas at 1977-78 prices. The situation has improved considerably in the recent past. In 2004-05, 27.9 per cent of population in India (28.7 per cent of population in rural areas and 25.9 per cent in urban areas) were, however, still living below the poverty line.[4]

Explaining the rural-urban disparities in terms of consumption expenditure, Bhalla (2003) notes:

> "India has now a pretty long history of widening rural-urban disparities in consumption expenditure and judging by the most recent past, the prospects are for disparities to get worse. It is important to note that the disparities between poor and non-poor in terms of per capita consumption expenditure have also widened with great intensity during

the reform period" (Quoted from India: Rural Development Report, Rural Institutions, 2005. p.106).

Data given in Table 1.1 demonstrate the glaring differences between the rich and the poor in India in terms of household income and expenditure. In 1975-76, the share of household income of the lowest 20 per cent of the population in the total household income in the country was just 7 per cent as compared to 33.6 per cent of highest 10 per cent of population. Similarly, the highest 10 per cent of the population had 26.7 per cent share in the total household expenditure in the country in 1983. This share was as low as 8.1 per cent for the lowest 20 per cent of the population. In 1997, however, the relative share of the lowest 20 per cent of the population in the total household expenditure was the same. It had increased to 33.5 per cent for the highest 10 per cent of the population, thereby indicating increasing inequalities among households (see Table 1.1).

TABLE 1.1: Share of income and expenditure of the highest and lowest segments of population in India

Year	*Percentage Population Segment*		*Percentage Share of Household Income/Expenditure to the Total Household Income/Expenditure*
1975-76a[5]	Lowest	20	7.0
	Highest	10	33.6
1983b	Lowest	20	8.1
	Highest	10	26.7
1992c	Lowest	20	8.5
	Highest	10	28.4
1997d	Lowest	20	8.1
	Highest	10	33.5

Sources: (*a*) World Development Report, 1988, Table 24, pp.272-73.
(*b*) World Development Report, 1992, Table 30, pp.276-77.
(*c*) World Development Report, 1997, Table 5, pp.222-23.
(*d*) World Development Report, 2000-01, Table 5, pp.282-83.

If black-market money, which is estimated to be substantial, is also taken into account, the share of the national income going to the top 10 per cent would be much higher. Their share of the national assets, revealed and concealed, would not be less than 50 per cent. As regards rural areas specifically, the top 10 per cent rural households have a share of around 31 per cent in rural household incomes, according to a 1980 study of the National Council of Applied Economic Research.

According to All India Debt and Investment Survey, 1991-92, households having total assets value of less than Rs. 20,000 formed a little more than $1/4^{th}$ of all rural households, and accounted for only about 2.4 per cent of total assets of the rural households. On the other hand, households in the assets group of Rs. 2.5 lakh and above were less than $1/10^{th}$ in number but accounted for nearly 1.1 per cent of the value of total assets. In the case of urban households, more than one-third of the households in the assets classes of 'less than Rs. 20,000' accounted for only about 1.4 per cent of the total assets of all urban households. Nearly 66 per cent of the total assets of all urban households was held by 14.2 per cent of households, each reporting assets of Rs. 2.5 lakh and above'.[6]

The fact that this development is taking place in spite of the declared socialistic aims of the Indian government and society, shows that vested interests are so entrenched and work in such subtle ways that more basic and radical remedies are called for than those adopted so far. The most dangerous aspect of the arithmetic of inequality in India is the socio-political system of which the inequality is both a cause and consequence. The socio-political system provides to this inequality such entrenched power that ending it by the normal democratic processes is going to be extremely difficult though not impossible.

The inequalities in rural areas are far steeper than is represented by the fact that the top 10 per cent of the population own very much more than 51 per cent of the national wealth. The National Sample Survey revealed that only 2.3 per cent of the rural households owned 30 per cent of the land. And when we remember that land is the most important and very often the only resource in rural areas – the concentration of economic and the consequent socio-political power in rural areas can be well imagined. The inequalities, particularly in terms of concentration of land holdings, continue to be high in rural areas. The average value of the gini coefficient of land distribution is found to be very high, i.e. 0.71.[7] Gross inequalities in land ownership in rural India have persisted since independence in spite of the tendency for population pressure to bring about a more even distribution of holdings. The coefficient for land distribution in rural areas declined from 0.686 in 1953-54 to just 0.669 in 1982. This has placed India in the middle range of land inequality by international standards.[8] Small and marginal farmers with 78 per cent of land cultivate only 32 per cent of the cropped area, whereas medium and large farmers with 8.8 per cent of land holdings cultivate 47 per cent of the cropped area.[9]

Regional Disparities

Considered region-wise, the central eastern region is the most poverty-stricken region of the country, both in terms of poverty ratio as well as concentration of the poor. The group of 4 major states – Bihar, Madhya Pradesh, Orissa and Uttar Pradesh together constitute more than 61 per cent of the rural poor in India. It may be noted that the share of the rural poor was 49.8 per cent in 1983. This share increased to 55 per cent in 1993-94 and further to 61 per cent in 2004-05. Bihar and Uttar Pradesh alone constitute more than 42 per cent of the rural poor[10]. These states have much higher share in all India rural poor in comparison to their share in all India rural population. The incidence of rural poverty was the lowest (4.81 per cent) in Jammu and Kashmir, followed by Punjab (9.55 per cent), Kerala (12.27 per cent), Himachal Pradesh (12.55 per cent), Haryana (13.41 per cent), Rajasthan (18.91 per cent), and Gujarat (19.76 per cent) – mainly in the northern India.[11]

Keeping in view the need to alleviate rural poverty, the government of India has taken various steps, which include:

1. Recognizing the role of economic growth in providing more employment avenues to the population;
2. Reinforcing growth oriented approach by focusing on specific sectors, which provide greater opportunities to people to participate in growth process;
3. Internalizing progressively the various dimensions of poverty relating to health, education and other basic services in the planning process;
4. Enhancing investment in education, sanitation, agriculture, area development programmes and afforestation to provide employment to the rural poor.

5. Taking up special programmes for the traditionally deprived group like scheduled castes and tribes, the disabled and the other vulnerable groups.
6. Taking up anti-poverty programmes that seek to transfer assets and skills to people to cope with transient poverty.
7. Streamlining the targeted public/distribution system to protect the poor from the adverse effects of rise in prices.[12]

More specifically, the Ministry of Rural Develcpment has undertaken several programmes for implementation. Some of these programmes are as follows:

- The Sampoorna Grameen Rozgar Yojna (SGRY): it was launched in September, 2001. The scheme promises 100 days of employment in a financial year to every household.
- National Food for Work Programme (NFWP): the scheme introduced in November, 2004 is operative only in most backward areas. Under this scheme the workers get wages both in cost and food grains.
- Pradhan Mantri Sadak Yojna (PMSY): the scheme was introduced in December 2000. it is intended to connect villages and urban areas by all weather roads by the end of the Tenth Five Year Plan. All habitations having population of 500 and more will be covered under this scheme. In case of desert and hill areas or difficult regions, the habitation with 250 people or more will get the same treatment.
- National Rural Employment Guarantee Act, 2005 (NREG): under this scheme, employment would be provided to every rural household whose adult member volunteers to do unskilled manual work. The scheme is operative in 200 districts and would become operative in the whole of India from 2010.
- Indira Awas Yojna (IAY): the scheme is meant to provide houses to weaker sections of the society living in rural areas. The government will build about 60 lakhs houses under this scheme by 2010.

Population Explosion

Apart from inequality, another major cause of poverty is the fast increasing population. The close link between rapid population growth and poverty has been clearly established by various studies. In fact, the world faces one of the most serious challenges to growth and development from an exploding population. It took 35 years for the world population to grow from 2 billion to 4 billion. The other 2 billion were estimated to be added in 25 years only. It was projected that, with appropriate action, it could be possible to stabilize world population at 8 billion. It has been further estimated that, given the existing growth rate, population in India would become 1.1 billion or more in the twenty first century (World Development Report, 1981).

India's population increased from 547.95 million in 1971 to 1028 million in 2001 (532.4 million males and 496.4 million females)[13]. The Technical Sub-Group on Rural Development of the Futurology Panel of the NCST estimated[14] that, even on the Medium-2 projections of the Registrar General, the country would need to produce in the year 2000, 100 million tonnes of food grains more than it produced in 1975 in order to give to the population the minimum desirable nutritional standards (2400-3100 calories) – a task which would be impossible of accomplishment by stepping up indigenous production, even with a reduction in the existing consumption standards which would imply "a step towards starvation" for large segment of population. Even if one were not to accept this pessimistic view because of the progress achieved between 1960-61 and 1975-76 when some of the crops achieved fantastic results[15] – wheat increased by 162 per cent, Bajra 73 per cent and Maize 78 per cent – the serious challenge to our technological competence and skill to manage our limited land and water resources is unmistakable. This will lead to increased demand for employment, education, health services etc. In the context of the constraint of resources, the standard, in all these services, may fall.

With 1028 million people, India became the second country in the world after China to cross the one billion mark in population. It is estimated that by 2050, India will, most likely, overtake China to become the most populous country in the world[17]. Though in absolute terms, 180.6 million persons have been added during the last decade (i.e. 1991-2001), the net growth rate in population has witnessed a declining trend over the decades starting from 1961. The decline in the decadal growth rate of population during the last decade was the sharpest since independence. The average growth rate during 1991-2001 declined to 1.93 per cent per annum, indicating that the country is entering a phase of rapidly declining fertility. Nine states and union territories, including Kerala, Tamil Nadu and Punjab, which account for 15 per cent of the total population, have reportedly already reached the replacement level of fertility. Other states such as Bihar, Haryana, Uttar Pradesh, Sikkim, Nagaland, Delhi, Chandigarh and Gujarat have shown an increase in the population growth rate during this period. 11 states and union territories including some of the most populous states like Uttar Pradesh, Rajasthan, Bihar and Madhya Pradesh may not be able to reach the fertility replacement level by 2010.[18]

Various studies have established the causes of rapid population growth; lack of education, especially among women; inadequate health facilities, which does not ensure the survival of children born; early marriage; etc. So it covers practically the entire gamut of development and the answer to rapid population growth is nothing short of all-round development. And as the population problem is much more acute in rural areas, rural development gains urgency and priority from this point of view as well.

Rural Employment

Different rounds of N.S.S. provide four sets of data on rural unemployment. The data on unemployed based on female (CDS approach) indicate that "in most states and at all India level, female rural unemployment rate is higher than that of the male one. Further, during the period 1983 to 1994 as also over the reform period of 1994-2000, rural unemployment rates, both for male and females, are not only high but are also rising in many states, which is the reverse of the trend of rural poverty. This is disturbing".

Further: "Despite several steps taken by the government of India to provide regular and productive employment in rural areas, the rural employment situation was far from satisfactory. Most workers in rural areas are engaged in low-paid agricultural activities, either as self employed or casual labour. In many regions, in view of the low absorption capacity of subsistence agriculture and in the absence of any major organized sector industry, there was distress and diversification of work force to unorganized, non-agricultural activities...."[19]

Keeping in view the rampant unemployment among the rural population, rural poverty alleviation programmes have been revamped to enhance their effectiveness. Programmes that provide self employment and wage employment to the poor are proposed to be implemented with greater vigour during the Tenth Five Year Plan:

1. The Swaran Jayanti Gram Swrozgar Yojana (SGSY) would provide opportunities for self-employment to the rural poor. The programme would shift to a process-oriented approach in four states:
   - Social mobilization for formation of self help groups;
   - Savings among the group and initial lending among its members and provision of a revolving fund;
   - Micro finance; and
   - Micro enterprise development.
2. Network institutions that promote self help movement would be created;
3. Special attention would be given to providing technical support; upgrading technology and standardization of products.[20]

Nutrition

A consequence of rapid population growth and existing social and economic inequalities, unemployment and under-employment present an even greater challenge than food production, as it affects the purchasing power of the rural masses and restricts severely their ability to improve their condition through self effort. Science and technology may be able to meet the challenge of increased food production required for feeding the world's increasing population, but it may not be able to effect its distribution in a manner as would ensure its reaching the vast masses who need it most but may not have the money – because of lack of adequate employment – to buy it and there may be starvation in the midst of plenty. The World Development Report 1981 of the World Bank states as follows:

> "Globally, the food production has grown marginally faster than population. Consumption per person has been increasing in most parts of the developing world, with sub-Saharan Africa and parts of Asia the major exceptions" (p. 101).
>
> "...While there is no evidence that outright starvation has become more pervasive, nonetheless the number of malnourished people has probably increased and the position of particular groups and certain areas may have deteriorated seriously. Most of the under-nourished live in the country-side" (p. 101).

That the position has not shown much improvement would be evident from the following statement:

> "Today, nearly half of the world's population – nearly three billion — live on less than $2 a day. Approximately 790 million people in the developing world are still chronically undernourished, almost two-thirds of whom reside in Asia and the Pacific. According to UNICEF, 30,000 children die each day due to poverty. "One child out of every six born in the least developed countries dies before the age of five, compared with one child out of every 167 born in rich countries. On average, a child from the poorest 20 per cent of the population in a developing country is at least twice as likely to die before the age of five as a child from the richest 20 per cent. The most impoverished – usually rural areas – have few or no health-care facilities and few means of transporting people for medical assistance."[21]

India accounts for 57 million of the world's 146 million malnourished children. It has the same rate of malnutrition as Ethiopia (47 per cent), Nepal and Bangladesh (48 per cent). This is in stark contrast with the figures for China (eight per cent), Thailand (18) and even Afghanistan (39).[22] "At the current rate of progress, the millennium development goal to halve child hunger by 2015 will not be reached till 2025.[23] Severe malnutrition is more frequent among girls (19.1 per cent) than boys (16.9 per cent). Malnutrition rates among children of 0-3 years vary greatly across states, from Madhya Pradesh (55.1 per cent), Bihar (54.4), Orissa (54.4), Uttar Pradesh (51.7) and Rajasthan (50.6) to Goa (28.6), Manipur (27.5) and Kerala (26.9). Nearly half of all children in India under three are underweight, a quarter of all children are born with low weight, and three quarters of under-three children and half of adult women are anaemic. Malnutrition is not only about hunger; its effect is compounded by early marriage and consequent early motherhood, lack of adequate sanitation. Insufficient quantity of food is less to blame for child under-nutrition than poor food quality and safety, and women's low social status.

It is ironical that people who produce food should themselves be on the verge of starvation.

Indian planners have no doubts about the capacity of the country to produce sufficient food but feel nervous on its distribution; among others, lack of adequate purchasing power among the large number of the unemployed and the under-employed, especially in the rural areas is a principal reason. While rural population has declined from 80 per cent of the total population in 1971 to 72.22 per cent in 2001, in absolute numbers it has increased from 438.85 million to 741. 66 million.[24] While the share of the labour force employed in agriculture has decreased from 72.5 per cent in 1971 to 59.7 per cent in 1999-2000, the absolute numbers employed in agriculture have increased from 211.2 million in 1971 to 237 million in 1999-2000.[25] The pressure on the already hard pressed land has increased, thus aggravating further the existing unemployment and under-employment of people. Further, improvement of agriculture and diversification of the rural economy is perhaps one of the most serious challenges that will have to be faced. Unemployment is the greatest insult to man's self-respect, who is rejected as useless, and the worst form of inequity and injustice. The situation is rendered even more tragic as the economically inactive population has increased from 53.17 per cent in 1971 to 56.9 per cent in 2001,[26] indicating more people finding it to difficult to secure gainful employment.

Human Resources Development

The developing world is full of the teeming millions, the disinherited of the earth. They need to be fed, housed, educated and trained, provided with work opportunities, primary health care and family welfare information and facilities before this vast liability can be turned into the most precious asset. Faced with the constraint of resources, the comparatively long-term character of the programmes of human development and lacking appropriate strategies to make them cost effective shortening the period of return from investment, reducing their cost by creating maximum self-reliance of the people etc., most developing countries have adopted the 'Social Service' strategy which is, in a way, a residual approach to programmes of human development. And yet recent history has shown that resources spent on development of human resources are a profitable and inevitable investment for growth. Timely action on broad-based development, including humane formation of capital, has brought many poor countries in two decades to their present middle-income status (World Development Report 1981).

In India, the general features of the situation are similar. While there has been considerable expansion of social services in rural areas, their coverage and quality is far from satisfactory. It is doubtful whether the deficiencies will ever be made up in the foreseeable future unless new and more innovative strategies are developed. These strategies will have to depend largely upon self-help, using governmental assistance as a catalyst. They will have the additional advantage of organizing communities and building their capacity for self-help. In this development orientation of social services, education at all levels will need to provide the necessary transforming force. This will require reorientation of education, making it environment and problem centred, using creative methodologies which would feed and sharpen curiosity, build initiative, resourcefulness, spirit of cooperation and team work, promote leadership qualities which would lead the products of the education system to make rural societies dynamic and competent, capable of standing on their own. Built around productive activities, cooperatively organized, such a system would also provide a substantial portion of its own finance. Education system will be continuously providing society, rural and urban, dynamic and committed leadership, appropriate technologies and new perspectives. That was the dream of the Father of the Nation, when he presented his scheme of *Nayee Taleem* (New Education) before the country, which was unfortunately thrown over-board! But we can always take up the thread if we have the necessary understanding and will.

Agriculture

The need to provide food to the world's increasing population at adequate nutritional standards and to increase the income of the poor are reasons enough to make enhancing agricultural production and productivity as the most important concern in rural development. While industrial growth is essential for rapid development, rapid industrialization itself has been supported in most countries by broad-based agriculture. As the World Development Report, 1981 states:

> ".... agricultural success generates domestic demand for industrial products; supplies cheap food to industrial workers, and raw materials for agro-processing; earns foreign exchange to finance imports of capital and intermediate goods for industry; and encourages labour intensive industries in small towns and villages."[27]

This observation is relevant even in the present context. Feeding a population – all sections of it, especially the poorest segment poses a three fold problem. It requires increasing domestic production, arranging imports when domestic supplies fall short, and arranging an efficient distribution system. Domestic supplies depend upon the availability of appropriate technologies, an extension system to carry them across to the people as well as the supply of required inputs. The world experience shows that technologies have to be local specific and require lot of adaptive research to make known technologies suited to the local socio-economic situation, without which very often the message of extension is rightly rejected by farmers. Appropriate agricultural policies are needed, balancing the need for incentives to farmers to increase production and the need to supply cheap food to industrial labour and weaker sections in rural areas. To ensure effective distribution, infrastructure in the form of road and rail transport, storage etc. has to be built; and the purchasing power of the poor – the most important missing link – increased. Credit facilities, cooperative organizations and an efficient administrative system are also required both for increasing production and for effective distribution, especially to ensure that supplies reach the weakest sections and the leakages in transit are eliminated. All these factors form a complex, integrated whole and failure at any point dislocates the system and seriously affects the intended goal viz. feeding of the population.

When domestic supplies fall short, they have to be supplemented by imports through trade or aid. Management of imports of the required quantities, and within the appropriate time, is much more difficult than management of domestic supplies. Trade is made more difficult through protectionist policies of developed countries adopted to protect their own producers and consumers by, among others, foreign exchange constraints. The inefficient information systems and trading mechanism and inefficient administrative structures in developing countries also place them at considerable disadvantage. The politicization of aid and its side effects on domestic production and consumption complicate aid. Moreover, availability of global supplies may not coincide with domestic shortages. For any of these factors, aid may be stopped when it is most needed, as it happened during the world food crisis of 1973-74, when food aid actually declined.[28]

In India, ever since independence, rural areas and the weaker sections have been drawing increasing attention of planners and the effort at their development has been gaining momentum, though insights and the strategies that they dictated have varied. Investment in rural areas has been increasing, production strategies have altered, the social implications of change and its management have brought about many institutional changes and the scene is anything but static. The most significant changes are those that have taken place in agriculture. For agriculture will largely determine for decades to come not only the state of the economy but also the position of rural society.

Indian agriculture, which had been stagnant for half a century, received its first challenge with the separation of areas now part of Pakistan. The earlier phase of development, however, could achieve only limited success as the technological and institutional support had yet to be forged. This took place largely after 1960-61, though the Community Development Programme, initiated in 1952, the National Extension Service that followed and implementation of the recommendations of the Balwant Rai Mehta Committee had made significant beginnings in this direction. After 1960-61, the most obvious indicator of rapid growth was increase in food production from about 82.01 million tonnes in 1960-61 to 125 million tonnes in 1977-78.[29] The increase in food production has been even more significant in recent years; it increased to 204 million tonnes in 2002-05.[30] In many crops like wheat, bajra and maize, the increases were even more significant.

To understand the significance of this big leap forward in agricultural production, one has to take a look at the history of Indian agriculture immediately preceding the bursting of the Green Revolution in the country in the years following 1960-61. India's exploding population – from 10 million at the time of Akbar to 1027 million in 2001– has always posed a serious problem for the country. The droughts and famines, which were a common feature in pre-independence days, were sought to be tackled through increasing canal irrigation as a safeguard against erratic monsoons. In spite of all these efforts, agriculture grew only at the rate of 0.11 per cent per annum. After Independence – through multi-purpose projects and increase of both canal and tube-well irrigation; land reclamation; and the large labour force, thrown up by an expanding population, energized by the inspiration of independence and the incentives provided, the growth rate during 1950-60 was stepped up to 2.8 per cent (population increase 2.1 per cent) against China's 2 per cent, in spite of the fact that some of the most fertile lands had become part of Pakistan. In reality up to 1960, was a period of preparation for the Green Revolution, which gained momentum thereafter. The Community Development movement was launched in 1952 and the National Extension Service followed closely on its heels. These prepared the people for large-scale involvement in their own improvement. The extension services forged an instrument for carrying new innovations to the people during 1960-65. The implementation of the Balwant Rai Mehta Committee's recommendations also created a climate for local involvement in development and an institutional framework for local action. The abolition of Zamidari and the land reforms that followed created a climate for a big leap forward inspite of all the shortcomings of implementation. The

Bhoodan Movement played the most significant role in revolutionizing people's idea about land, and as a matter of fact, prepared the ground for and hastened the implementation of land reforms.

The establishment and development of the agricultural universities during 1960-65 – with education, research and extension functions – prepared the country for original and adaptive research and for training of large number of scientists and extension workers that a country of India's size would require for agricultural revolution. The setting up of steel mills during the first two plans of 1951-1961 equipped the country for manufacture of new agricultural implements and machinery that would be required for the advent of new technologies (new seeds, chemical fertilizers, insecticides, etc.) which sparked off the Green Revolution. This is perhaps the most spectacular phenomenon in the history of world agriculture. The growth rate of agricultural production in Punjab exceeded that of Taiwan, which had been held up as a model of success in agriculture. "The entire history", says Dr. Randhawa, "of agriculture does not reveal an example of success as the green revolution in the Punjab". At the heart of the Green Revolution was, as Randhawa puts it, "wise planning and administration", which provided to agriculture the necessary support of credit, marketing and storage. The needs of the agricultural revolution were comprehensive and were attended to in unison.[31]

It is also important to look into the agricultural policy followed during the last five decades to understand the sources of output growth. It can be broadly divided in three phases. In the first phase (1950-51 to mid-1960s), India witnessed rapid agrarian reforms, institutional changes and development of major irrigation projects. The intermediary landlordism was abolished and tenant operations were given security of farming and ownership of land. States imposed land ceilings to eliminate large sized holdings and cooperative credit institutions were strengthened.[32] The main source of growth in the pre-green revolution period was, therefore, the expansion of area, which somehow decreased in the green revolution period.

The second phase (mid-1960s to early 1980s), which is also known as the Green Revolution period, saw a marked change in agriculture in terms of introduction of modern technology.

The main source of increase in agricultural productivity was technological breakthroughs in wheat and rice. The food crisis in early 1960s had forced policy makers to realize that continued reliance on food imports would lead to political pressure and economic instability, and there was a desperate need to increase agricultural production.[33] The country, therefore, went for the introduction of new seeds of high yielding varieties (HYV) of wheat and rice. This involved use of fertilizers and irrigation. Introduction of modern farm inputs; spread of HYV of wheat and rice; use of fertilizers; and expansion of irrigation facilities marked the new agricultural strategy in the country. This also led to expansion of agro input industry. The biggest achievement of new agricultural strategy has been the attainment of self-sufficiency in food grains. During this phase, research, extension, input supply, credit, marketing, price support, and spread of technology were the prime concern of policy makers.[34] Important institutional arrangements such as Food Corporation of India and Agricultural Prices Commission were made to ensure remunerative prices to producers, maintain reasonable process for consumers and maintain buffer stock of food grains to ensure price stability. The agrarian reforms, however, took a back seat.

The third phase in Indian agriculture began in early 1980s. With a change in the economic policy towards delicensing and deregulation in industry, agriculture policy lacked clear direction. By this time, though limited to narrow pockets, there was tremendous increase in agricultural growth accompanied by rise in real farm incomes. This led to the emergence of interest groups influencing agriculture policy. Subsidies and support to agriculture increased during this period. Public expenditure on agriculture for infrastructure development started declining in real terms, while investments by farmers kept on rising.[35] In this period, the output growth in agriculture became broad based and gained momentum. The rural economy witnessed a process of diversification with fast growth in non-food grain output like milk, fishery, poultry, vegetables, fruits, etc. leading to an accelerated growth in the contribution of agriculture to GDP in the 1980s. The development strategy adopted in agriculture was largely market driven.

Today, though green revolution has been widely diffused in irrigated areas throughout the country, the dryland areas have not benefited from technological breakthroughs. Besides, economic reforms in the 1990s created new challenges for agriculture requiring appropriate policy response. The challenges facing Indian agriculture include ensuring sustainable growth, efficiency and equity. There are also other important concerns like food security, livelihood, employment and improvement in the standard of living of agricultural population. Consequently, the Government of India came out with New Agricultural Policy in 2003. The National Agricultural Policy aims to attain:

- a growth rate in excess of 4 per cent per annum in agriculture sector;
- growth is to be based on efficient use of resources and conserves our soil, water and bio-diversity;
- growth with equity i.e. growth which is wide-spread across regions and farmers;
- growth that is demand driven and caters to domestic markets and maximizes benefits from exports of agricultural products in the face of challenges arising from economic liberalization and globalization; and
- growth that is sustainable technologically and economically[36].

Notwithstanding these laudable objectives, emerging challenges in agriculture are required to be addressed through multi-pronged strategy including appropriate incentive structure, infrastructure, technology, market development, extension, regulation, input supply, tenancy reforms and the like. However, it is critical that the country develops appropriate area specific action plans so as to effectively implement policy directions. This has to be done without any further loss of time, otherwise, the frustrated farmers will continue to commit suicides as has been happening, particularly in the Vidharbha region of Maharashtra and other areas over the last few years[37].

Energy

Rural development faces a two-fold energy crisis. It shares with industrial world the effects of oil crisis at a time when modernization of agriculture and industrialization of rural areas is in increasing need of oil for fertilizer production, agro-industries, agricultural processing industries and expanding transport facilities to service increasing trade in agricultural products. In addition, it faces the fuel-wood crisis and spreading deforestation, with disastrous effects on the local ecology and the very survival of the world's population as a whole.

The magnitude of oil crisis for the oil importing developing countries, where most of the world's rural population is concentrated, is well brought out in the World Development Report, 1981. Oil import bill of these countries rose from 2.8 per cent of their GDP in 1978 to 5.3 per cent ($ 74 billion) in 1980. In some countries like India, Brazil and Turkey, oil imports absorbed over 50 per cent of their export earnings. In such circumstances, with the pressure of demand from high-energy consumption sectors like industry, transport etc. in urban areas, availability of commercial energy for rural development is going to be very limited. That is why the World Development Report 1981 has concluded:

> "What is clear, however, is that the majority of poor rural families will remain dependent on fuel-wood and organic wastes for the foreseeable future. Unless that challenge is faced, the burden of the 'other energy crisis', on those who are least able to bear it, will continue to grow" (p. 42)

That the position has worsened further is indicated in World Trade Report 2005, according to which: "Nearly 90 per cent of the population in developing Asia lives in economies, which are net importers of fuels. Asia is the most adversely affected region by higher fuel prices in the global markets. Nepal, Mongolia, Pakistan and India spent between 20 per cent and 35 per cent of their export earnings from merchandise and commercial services on (net) imports of fuels in 2001-2003. The three biggest net importers of fuels in Asia during the same period were the Republic of Korea, India and China. During the period 1990-2003, Asian developing countries recorded the strongest expansion in energy demand and the sharpest rise in imports of fuels of all regions". [38]

To understand the nature of the fuel-wood crisis, one has to remember that over 2 billion people rely-almost entirely – for meeting their energy needs on fuel-wood and traditional fuels, animal and vegetable waste. In some developing countries, even industry relies heavily on fuel-wood. In some countries like Mali, Tanzania and Nepal traditional fuels meet over 90 per cent of their energy consumption. The Report goes on to say:

> "The quantities involved are large. . . .Perhaps as much as 930 million cubic metres of wood, 400 tons of animal waste and the same amount of crop residue are being burnt in developing countries every year. This is equivalent to almost 5 million barrels of oil per day and represents roughly one quarter of the energy used in developing countries, and just under 5 per cent of the world's energy consumption".[39]

The demand for household fuel adds to the pressure on forests, for more land required for agriculture and housing to feed and house the increasing population and the increasing world demand for paper. The rising oil prices have increased the demand for charcoal in urban areas. All this has led to large-scale deforestation and the consequent soil erosion, floods and silting of rivers. Vast areas have been turned into deserts, which further deplete the availability of fertile land. Further, land being deprived of animal and crop waste, which is burnt for fuel, becomes less and less productive, requiring more and more land being brought under the plough, leading to further cutting of forests. Agriculture is also adversely affected by cutting of receding forests in search of fuel-wood; this leaves less and less time with the poor people for agriculture. In the context of complex fuel-wood crisis, says the Development Report:

"The poorest are the worst affected, since they can least afford to buy fuel. In parts of Africa, purchasing fuel can cost a poor family 35 to 40 per cent of its income and people have been reduced to one cooked meal a day. In poor areas of Nepal and Haiti, cropping patterns have even changed in favour of foods that require less cooking". (p. 40-41).

Rural Electrification

There has been considerable expansion of the rural electrification programme since independence. In 1960-61, only 4.4 per cent of the villages had electricity. By 2001, 86.5 per cent of villages were electrified. Rural electrification has however, been uneven among states; the states of Haryana, Punjab, Kerala and Tamil Nadu achieved cent per cent village electrification in the decade of seventies itself. On the other hand, the progress of village electrification was quite slow in states of Assam, Bihar, Manipur, Meghalaya, Orissa, Rajasthan and West Bengal in the beginning of nineties. In the subsequent decade, except for Meghalaya, the performance of the rest of states improved considerably. In quite a few states (Assam, Bihar, Meghalaya, Orissa, UP and West Bengal), over 20 per cent of villages have no electricity supply.[40]

In order to provide guidance to the Electricity Regulatory Commission and the Central Electricity Authority to discharge their functions, the Government of India notified the National Electricity Policy on 12th February 2005. The policy aims at development of power sector, providing electricity to all areas and "protecting interests of the consumers and others stake holders keeping in view the availability of energy resources, technology available to exploit these resources, economics of generation using different resources and energy security issues".[41]

A mighty reforestation effort – relying largely on local community effort, whose interest in the long-term fruits thereof need to be assured to enlist their cooperation – to reverse the trend is needed so that more trees are planted than are cut. Schools and colleges also need to be drawn in for the planting and nurturing of trees by making reforestation an educational project: a centre of interest and focus for the integration of knowledge of disciplines. It is a very large force and enlisting its intelligent cooperation can make a big difference to the programme. The teaching community can provide leadership to adults also and enthuse them for the programme.

Another front on which action is needed is to increase efficiency of fuel use. The improvements required should be simple and cheap so that poor families can afford them and operate the new gadgets like the smokeless *Chulha* (oven) etc. In evolving such devices educational institutions, close to the lives of the people and aware of their socio-economic condition and constraints, can play an important part.

Fuel substitution is a third possibility to economize on fuel wood. The supply of kerosene at subsidized rates links us with the oil crisis and its complications. The most useful is *gobar* gas (gas from animal dung), which not only provides fuel from a renewable resource but also leaves the quality of manure unaffected. Such resources in developing countries are very large and need proper mapping. In course of time hydro-electric power, solar energy etc. may also provide viable alternatives on the scale needed, and their development should get high priority.

The appropriate energy policy for rural development in India is dealt with in detail in the chapter on "Mobilization of Energy for Rural Development"[42] in the book: Management of Rural Energy Systems by Satsangi (1984). What follows is largely a summary of what has been stated there.

The book focuses on energy plan for rural development and effective utilization of known resources and the discovery and development of new resources. Of known resources, oil is the most important but very little of it is used in rural areas and that also largely in the transport sector and where mechanization of agriculture and industrialization has taken place, as in the areas of the Green Revolution like the Punjab. The hike in oil prices has adversely affected the availability of oil even for the Green Revolution areas and led to what Randhawa calls the "Browning of the Green Revolution." In 1980, for example, the crisis was obtrusively presented to anyone traveling on Delhi – Chandigarh road, where farmers in sheer desperation held up buses to drain off their oil for tractors and pump sets and a long row of stranded buses met the eye. Coal is emerging as India's main source of commercial energy in place of oil. But its heavy transport cost places serious limitations on its availability in sufficient quantities in far-flung rural areas of the country. Both on grounds of availability – whether due to prices or limited reserves – and pollution effects, the fossil fuels can play only a marginal role in rural development.

Any large-scale and safe availability of energy from nuclear energy is yet a distant dream. By and large, in the foreseeable future, dependence will have to be largely on renewable sources of energy. India is rich in such resources. It has been estimated, for example, that if gas was produced from all available animal waste and crop residue, and converted into electricity at 25 per cent efficiency, the electricity produced would be three times the total electricity consumed in the country. It was estimated that the human waste and cattle dung could produce fertilizers worth over Rs. 5000 crores a year[43] at current prices, even if 50 per cent of it could be collected. In addition, this could produce *gobar*-gas in no mean quantities. There would, moreover, be considerable savings on rural sanitation. The sun's energy is sustaining the earth spontaneously in hundred and one ways: making plants grow, drying of clothes, drying of vegetables for preservation, assisting fermentation, disinfecting the country-side, keeping the balance of oxygen and carbon dioxide to make life possible etc. The energy supplied by the sun in this fashion is incalculable. India has mounted a well-directed programme of harnessing sun's rays for use at will. So far as low temperatures are concerned, India is already able to produce energy from the sun's rays for use on a commercial scale. As regards high temperatures, it is still experimenting. India's streams have considerable potential for production of large quantities of electricity. There are considerable possibilities of mini hydro-electrical projects, which have great significance for the development of cottage industries and agriculture. There is also considerable scope for harnessing the energy of the winds in hill and tides on sea coasts for generating electricity on a decentralized basis.

But perhaps the most abundant resource is the muscle and the bullock power. Human development through proper food, appropriate health measures and education to improve human ingenuity are important in the context of energy as well. The bullock, even though it shares food with man – using, however, only the poorest soils and waste lands – is one of the important means of transport and for ploughing the land in most of the country-side. It is also an important source of skins and hides. Even its droppings, if properly used, are an important source of fertilizers and *gobar* gas. A multi-purpose animal, its economy needs to be very carefully considered before it can be condemned as a voracious competitor with man in food consumption and hence deserving elimination in the prevailing food crisis and land shortages.

India has mounted a well-directed effort for the development of her energy resources. In that, the following imperatives of the characteristics and constraints of the rural situation will need to be kept in view while dealing with development of energy resources for rural areas:

Firstly, there is the poverty of the people and the resource constraint. Any relevant invention, therefore, must be cheap. Secondly, the educational level is very low and the technical know-how of the village society for working and maintaining, leave alone manufacturing of equipment, is very limited. Therefore, the relevant devices must be simple. Thirdly, the vast distances and the variety of locally available raw materials would need to be taken into consideration in devising mechanisms for energy creation. Fourthly, the new devices must be relatively simple to be within the limited managerial capacity of the Indian villager. Fifthly, it must not destroy the decentralized character of the traditional sector, which provides employment to the large majority of the people. On the contrary, the major contribution of any innovation should be to strengthen the traditional sector, without destroying its decentralized character. Otherwise, it will make the employment situation worse. Sixthly, the rural society is not a homogeneous one and so new technology must be accompanied by a suitable organisational structure so that the existing inequalities are not increased and the weakest sections of society are enabled to take advantage of the new technology. Seventhly, side by side with gradually improving technology, the educational effort, closely linked to it, must be intensified so that the people can understand, appropriate, operate and improve upon the new techniques and equipment introduced so that the village economy, instead of remaining in a stagnant state, becomes a steadily growing and improving economy. Lastly, the technology must be free from pollution. Today even the ignorant poor and the illiterate millions of India are able to lead a comparatively healthy life because of the bountiful sun and the free air. Any despoliation of the environment will spell disaster for the country-side. For even the wildest imagination cannot think of anti pollution measures on a gigantic scale that would be required if such a tragedy took place".[44]

Science and Technology

Science and technology are the two most powerful forces for development – science giving the "why" of things and phenomena, and technology giving the "how" of problems: how they are to be solved with the help of knowledge derived from science. They are relevant both for natural and social phenomena. Societies have a tendency to stagnate. For, with the passage of time, certain social norms seem to be taken for granted even though they may have lost their original rationale. It is the function of science through its eternal questioning of "the why and the wherefore" of things to stir the stagnant minds and effect the necessary modifications required by changed conditions. It is the function of technology to make necessary modifications through appropriate social engineering. Similarly, with the physical and the material world, the existing techniques and machines have to be perpetually re-examined, out-dated ones discarded and new ones invented and adopted in their place.

The Indian rural society has been stagnating for quite some time and needs to be churned so that it can adapt itself to the needs of change and development. Though some significant steps have been taken, like the introduction of the new technologies that have ushered in the Green Revolution, the change needed has to be so far more comprehensive than is indicated by the changes in production techniques. For maximum effect, change needs to be well-ordered so that changes in one area are supported by change in other areas. Otherwise, there may be wastage and misuse of the wealth created. Unsupported by a corresponding educational effort for proper utilization of investment, much of the wealth generated in the Punjab villages has gone into promoting ostentatious life styles, alcoholism and drug addiction. The studies conducted by the Punjab Agricultural University, Ludhiana indicate that comprehensive change would involve:

Inculcation of scientific temper in the people so that the rationale of every thing around them is sought, which would ultimately lead to the rationalization of every aspect of their lives: social, political and economic. The questioning spirit generated leads to the quest for progressive all-round improvement;

Development of the capacity and urge for detailed observation and exploration, which should lead to identification of new resources in the environment, as the first step towards exploiting them; and

The obtaining of technologies to improve existing ones or to solve new problems through indigenous R&D effort or borrowing as well as the designing of appropriate structures-both organizational and technical-to improve the viability of the technical innovations within the social and economic conditions of the villager.

The creation of the scientific temper, is largely the function of the methodology of education and should be a matter of concern for education – both formal and non-formal. Technological innovations on the other hand need to keep in view basic characteristics and needs of rural situation. The following points will merit special consideration in policy formulation:

1. The existing technologies, representing as they do centuries of experience and adjustment with the socio-economic environment, should receive the highest priority with a view to discovering the science behind them, thereby getting a clue to their up-gradation and improvement.
2. The technologies adopted should be relatively simple – though the experience of Punjab shows that the capacity of the rural people to adopt sophisticated technology has been under-rated – and its operation, maintenance, appropriation and improvement should be within the technical and managerial capacity – with due education and training – of the rural people.
3. For successful borrowing, a clear identification of problems and awareness of the technologies available in the international market are essential. So is a vigorous indigenous R & D effort if we are to make correct judgement and appropriate and improve upon the borrowed technology, as Japan does, and thereafter to export it. Intimate contact with the field would be necessary so that technology which is selected is appropriate to the total socio-economic situation prevailing at the field level. Moreover, when buying technology, it should be bought outright and by a team of technologists, representatives of the government and the banks etc. – in short of all interests that would be

involved in operationalizing it. Before borrowing a technology, the machinery for operationalizing it should be geared up.

4. Introduction of new technology should be preceded by a vigorous programme of suitably oriented education and skill training.
5. When new technology – indigenous or borrowed – is introduced in an area, its impact on local communities, especially the weaker sections, must be carefully assessed by technical people, social scientists and others concerned. New technology thoughtlessly introduced wreaks havoc, especially among the weaker sections. Examples are an industry set up in an *Adivasi* area, a dam built, a road constructed in a backward region etc. Project facilitating transport invites a horde of exploiters in a backward area. A multi-purpose dam displaces thousands of people, without providing them alternate residential accommodation and employment. When a technology to be introduced is likely to lead to far-reaching changes in the economic and social life of the area, the poor people must be enabled to face these changes and to exploit the new opportunities that may be opened up by the new projects.
6. Technologies adapted to upgrade the efficiency of the traditional sector must not destroy its decentralized and small-scale character, which is responsible for the large scale employment that it provides to our spread out population in the rural areas. Wherever necessary and possible, the production process must be broken into sub-processes, many of which can be decentralized as in the case of the Hero Cycle for example, where all the parts are manufactured in small decentralized units. The mother unit only assembles the parts and exercises quality control.
7. In rural development two types of activities are involved: evolution of technology and technology transfer. In the former case, the problem is to effect small improvements in existing technologies – adding a ball-bearing to the ordinary *chakki* (hand operated-grinding machine), the smokeless *chulah* (oven) and a

number of such innovations that our village and cottage industries have effected and are effecting. The significance of these small technological innovations is that they are immediately absorbed and appropriated by millions of people – given marginal help in extension and training – and the cumulative effect on the national wealth is tremendous. The improvements resulting from such innovations have the additional advantage of being effected at millions of points and the most difficult problem of distribution of created wealth does not arise.

There are, however, other types of innovations like the satellite, which affect rural development but whose control has to be at a central level. In such cases, there are various levels at which the new technology has to be managed and various levels of technological and managerial competencies are required to man various strategic points of the chain down to the village community. What is required is that when the technology reaches the people, it should be simple enough to be handled by the rural people, who should be trainable for the tasks expected of them. For example, in the above case of the Satellite, what the local people need to know is how to switch on and off the TV set and to take it to the mechanic when it goes out of order.

The former is a case of technological evolution and the latter a case of transfer. In the latter case, too, the technology must be tested for its relevance to the needs and modifications in the technology effected to adapt it to local needs. The most effective means of transfer of technology is through demonstration.

Administrative Innovations

The dynamic situation in the rural areas calls for a major administrative effort and some of the innovations that need to be introduced may be briefly mentioned:

(1) Decentralization of development effort and its concentration at the block as the focus of integration, supervision and popular participation;
(2) Creation of the National Extension Service to transfer new technology to the agriculturists;
(3) "Target Group" approach as represented by the creation of special agencies like the Small Farmers' Development

Agency (SFDA), Marginal Farmer and Agricultural Labour Development Agency (MFALD) and Tribal Development Agency (TDA); and

(4) Agencies embodying the "area approach" like those for Command Area Development, Hill Area Development, Drought Prone Area Programme etc.

These innovations and the experience they represent should be of considerable help in devising the future administrative machinery for rural development. The chief characteristic of this development is the realization of the need for micro-planning – planning on family, community and village basis – laying down action points under millions of location specific projects, which can only be handled and coordinated at the local level, through structures in which the beneficiaries are fully involved. To perfect this mechanism is the task for the future.

REFERENCES

1. Radhakrishnan, R. (2002), "Agricultural Growth, Employment and Poverty: A Policy Perspective", *Economic and Political Weekly*, January 19-25.
2. Planning Commission, Tenth Plan, (2002-2007) p.293.
   University Education Commission Report, Ministry of Education, Government of India, 1949, p. 566.
3. http://www.worldbank.org.
4. *WDR 2006*, p.278 and Himanshu: Recent Trends in Poverty and Inequality: Some Preliminary Results; *Economic and Politically Weekly*, February 10-16, 2007, p. 497.
5. Indicates percentage share of household income. For all other years, figures refer to the percentage share of household expenditure.
6. *RBI Bulletin*, May 1999.
7. Thorat, Sukhadeo (1997) "Trends in Land Ownership, Tenancy and Land Reform", in Bhupat Desai (ed.), *Agricultural Development Paradigm for the Ninth Plan under New Economic Environment*. New Delhi: Oxford & IBH.
8. Besley, Timothy, and Robin Burgess, 1998, Land Reform, Poverty Reduction and Growth: Evidence from India. Mimeo, London School of Economics, quoted in Robin Mearns in *Access to Land in Rural India: Policy Issues and Options*, http://www.worldbank.org/html/dec/Publications/Workpapers/wps2000series/wps2123/wps2123.pdf
9. Samuel, John, *Growth without Development: Rhetoric and*

Deprivation, National Centre for Advocacy Studies, www.ncasindia.org.

10. Adapted from India, Rural Development Report, op. cit. p. 106-109. The figures relate to 1999-2000.
11. S. Mahendra Dev, C. Ravi: Poverty and Inequality: All India and States 1983-2005. Published in the *Economic and Political Weekly*, February 10-16, 2007, p. 519.
12. Planning Commission, *Tenth Five Year Plan*, 2002-07, Vol. II p.293.
13. India, 2006, Ministry of Information and Broadcasting, Government of India, 2006, p. 7.
14. *An Outlook for India's Future* (2000 A.D.: Interim Report on Futurology, National Committee on Science and Technology), New Delhi, 1978, pp. 88-89.
15. *Report of the Committee on Panchayati Raj Institutions*, Government of India, Ministry of Agriculture and Irrigation, Department of Rural Development, New Delhi, 1978, p. 11.
17. *Census of India*, 2001.
18. *Fertility Estimates of the National Commission on Population*, Government of India.
19. India, Rural Development Report, (2005), op. cit. p. 124).
20. Planning Commission, *Tenth Five-Year Plan*, p. 313.
21. UNICEF, *The State of the World's Children 2005*, p. 17.
22. UNICEF, *Progress for Children: A Report Card on Nutrition, 2006.*
23. *Ibid.*
24. *Census of India, 2001.*
25. *NSS 55th Round Survey, 1999-2000.*
26. *Census of India, 2001.*
27. *World Development Report, 1981*, p. 100.
28. *Ibid*, p. 103.
29. *Report of the Committee on Panchayati Raj Institutions*, p. 14.
30. *Economic Survey, 2005-06.*
31. Randhawa, M.S. (1980), *Green Revolution in India: Progress, Problems and Prospects*, Silver Jubilee Commemoration Medal Lecture, Indian Science Academy, New Delhi.
32. Radhakrishna, R. (1993), "Indian Agriculture: Growth, Employment and Equality", in Tapas Majumdar (ed) *Nature, Man and the Indian Economy*, Oxford University Press, Delhi.
33. Rao, M.V. (1996), "Agricultural Development with a Humane Face", *Economic and Political Weekly*, 31 (26): A-50-A-62, June 29.
34. *Ibid.*
35. Chand, Ramesh (2001) "Emerging Trends and Issues in Public and Private Investments in Indian Agriculture: A State-wise Analysis, *Indian Journal of Agricultural Economics*, vol. 56, No. 2, pp. 161-184.

36. Planning Commission, *Tenth Five-year Plan* (2002-07), p.527.
37. There are alarming report of farmers Committing Suicide in Vidharbha region of Maharashtra. According to a press report 1452 farmers committed suicide in 2006. (*Times of India*, dated 14th February, 2007).
38. *World Trade Report 2005*, p. 15.
39. Ibid. (p. 40).
40. *India Rural Development Report*, (2005). National Institute of Rural Development, Ministry of Rural Development, Hyderabad.
41. *India 2006*, Publication Division, Ministry of Information and Broadcasting, Government of India, p. 260.
42. Satsangi, Prem S. and Gautam, Vinayashil, ed. (1983), *Management of Rural Energy Systems*, Galgotia Publications, New Delhi.
43. Nayar, D.P. (1983) "Mobilization of Energy for Rural Development," in Prem S. Satsangi and Vinayashil Gautam, ed, *Management of Rural Energy Systems*, op. cit.
44. Nayar, D. P., *op. cit.* pp. 99-100.

Chapter Two

Preferred Future

We have discussed the dynamics of rural development in the previous chapter. The various dimensions of the development process in rural India in the post independence period have been identified and their impact on progress of rural areas has been outlined. It has been stressed that to enable rural society to become an active partner in the development of the country, it would be necessary to bring about basic modifications in the structure and processes of rural development.

In this chapter, it is proposed to highlight broadly the goals of rural development in order to ensure preservation and development of rural areas with the avowed objective of developing an egalitarian and non-exploitative social order, where individuals are bound together by mutual respect and concern, where cooperation rather than competition is the dominating factor. Before elaborating the concept, it would be appropriate to discuss the transitional character of the rural society in present-day India.

Rural Society in Transition

A variety of extraneous factors have disturbed the centuries old peace and tranquility of the rural community, which had, by and large, remained stable through millennia of upheavals and turmoil. The first onslaught on it came in the form of cheap machine-made goods, which destroyed its prosperity and self-sufficiency, based on its handicrafts. The introduction of the Zamindari System – under which large tracts were given to some individuals in return for a fixed revenue to the British government, affected a large number who cultivated their piece for sustaining themselves. These individuals, in turn, extorted unchecked tax revenues from the peasantry and thereby weakened the farming community. The legal system introduced also destroyed the independence of local communities to settle their disputes without taking recourse to a distant legal authority and encouraged litigation amongst their members, who were subjected to law's delays. So did the police, which undermined the people's capacity and the will to stand together against internal disorder and external attack. The process of weakening the self-sufficient character of the local communities was accelerated by the expansion of the network of, and the consequent influx, of exploiting traders from urban areas. While the pace of urbanization was not as rapid as it is now, yet its disruptive effects on rural community began to be visible even before independence of the country and the advent of planned development. In spite of all these factors, rural communities still hung together and the old balance between the classes, arrived at through a sense of common destiny based on spatial contiguity, continued, though considerably weakened. The existing alignments on the basis of caste were accepted unquestioningly. The glaring inequalities were mellowed down to some extent by certain behavioural patterns, resulting from inter-dependence. The rural society was, by and large, a stable although stagnant society, glossing over many inequalities and injustices, which people had begun to take in their stride, as a part of the existing reality.

Then came the dizzy heights of independence giving rise to uninhibited hopes and aspirations of which only the sky was the limit, supreme confidence in themselves and in their leaders, undue expectations from their government, insufficient awareness of their own responsibility, almost blind faith in the power and reliability of the ballot box, mushrooming of new leadership to whip up expectations through facile promises etc. Various measures taken by popular government strengthened their confidence in a brighter future – the reorganization of the states and the weakening of the economic and political power of the princes; Zamindari abolition; abolition of untouchability through legislation; freeing of bonded labour; and so on. Apart from the plethora of legislations enacted to help the under-dog, the government launched a number of mass programmes in quick succession. These were: the adult education programme;

the Community Development and National Extension Service programme, which Nehru wanted to "spread like wild fire" in the country-side; extension of the powers and responsibilities of Panchayati Raj institutions; vast expansion of health and education; etc. and finally, the Green Revolution. These gave people the confidence that government meant business. Political leaders went to the doorsteps of the poorest and concern of the weaker sections appeared to be their constant refrain.

But sooner than later, the stark reality began to dawn on the poor – that the millennium that had come was not for them. What was happening was- what Gandhiji had apprehended and wanted to safeguard against – brown *sahebs* replacing the white *sahebs*. Pran Chopra, in a lucid article entitled "Rural-Urban Conflict and Partnership" (The Times of India of October 13, 1982) analysed this transition. According to him, with the comparatively easy elimination of the power of the Zamidars, with no mass base, so important in democracy, way opened for the middle class of land owners and self-cultivating small peasant proprietors to assume leadership in the rural areas. A partnership was forged between this leadership, which commanded the rural votes, and the urban middle class, which, because of the charismatic leadership that it threw up during the freedom struggle, also had considerable influence on the rural votes. In addition, in cooperation with industrial classes, it manipulated the sophisticated levers of political, administrative and legislative power. The institutions of independent India have grown under this joint partnership and naturally, primarily to its own advantage. A partner let the other establish its own power and prestige base within its own sphere of influence and appropriate the wealth inherited from the earlier elite: the princes and the Zamindars, and the wealth created in independent India, so long as the urban partner assured to its rural partner a reasonable price for its products and ensured a reasonable supply of the inputs required for agriculture; and the urban partner did not interfere with its rural partner's appropriation of spoils; so long as injustices perpetrated did not become so obvious and acute as to create tensions that would endanger the security of the rural vote. With the forces of law and order at the level combining with urban – rural elite, the local/ poor had no chance of getting a fair deal.

The harsh reality of the new situation soon began to dawn on the rural poor. As many studies have shown, the benefits of government schemes intended for the poor, were appropriated by the better-off classes. Any show of the emerging confidence among the poor was put down with a heavy hand and wealth created by them outside the village but brought to the village as a symbol of their newly-won economic position, was destroyed. Unfortunately, such incidents are on the increase. Similarly, local elections are still won on the basis of muscle-power and even gun-power of the elite. The rural poor have no chance of winning against the rich. Even in case of the reserved seats, the 'creamy layer' of the lower classes get them; they may not generally represent the interests of the weakest. There are also traditional linkages – for instance of caste and sub-caste – which determine the results of elections.

The above situation – expectations on the one hand and frustration due to harsh reality on the other –has created a very tense situation in the countryside. Every now and then, one comes across reports of some Harijan huts being burnt, some *Harijan* women raped, terror spread in some villages etc. They are followed by the dilatory processes of local police to punish the 'guilty', with whom they are too often in league. Votes are also won on the basis of violence or threat of violence. Even though the ballot is secret, it comes to be known, especially in local elections, who voted for whom; and if the poor have voted against the powerful, the latter have a hundred and one ways of punishing them. Many studies have borne out this brutal reality. Pran Chopra states:

> "The Socialistic Republic of India has steeper inequalities to boast of than the one reflected in the fact that 10 per cent of the population owns much more than 51 per cent of the national wealth. For example, according to the National Sample Survey, only 2.5 per cent of rural households own 50 per cent of the land. This by itself is a sharper inequality than is reflected in the top 10 per cent households having a 33.6 per cent share of the income of all households.
>
> "But the inequality reflected in the share of the top 10 per cent is more dangerous in India's socio-political circumstances because it is both more cruel, as it has already proved to be, and more difficult to remedy in the future".

There is increasing impatience with the status quo, which may at any time blow up through sheer frustration and desperation. The central issue is whether the tragedy of confrontation, spreading like wild fire through lakhs of India's villages, can be averted; whether there is any peaceful method to usher in a more just and consequently more stable order. This is also a question before the international community. The solutions we learn at home will be relevant to international situation and vice-versa.

In the meantime, certain cracks in the existing power structure are visible. Firstly, the alliance between the urban elite and the rural elite is coming under considerable strain because of increasing difficulty of keeping a mutually satisfying balance between the rural interests, requiring higher prices of agricultural produce and lower cost of inputs, on the one hand and the urban-industrial interest to keep prices of food-grains and raw materials for industry within affordable limits. The hike in oil prices resulting in general inflation affects these interests. This has hit the small farmers especially hard and they are sooner than later likely to realize that their interests are more allied to those of the landless labourers rather than the big farmers, with whom they have been aligning themselves so far for reasons of castes. This alienation and realignment is likely to increase as richer farmers more and more appropriate the benefits of government programmes intended for the small and marginal farmers. The caste alignment is also being weakened by the new political alignments that are being forged, though caste is continuing to be encouraged and exploited by political parties. Another factor which is likely to weaken bigger farmers is the cry for lowering of land ceilings and re-distribution of land as it is being increasingly realized that, given the necessary inputs, present ceilings can be considerably reduced to satisfy hunger for land in India with the added advantage of increased productivity.

One off-shoot of this mounting dissatisfaction of the under-dogs with their plight, due to the triangular linkage of caste, profession and social prestige, is the aversion to their own ancestral professions, with the system's in-built national apprenticeship under the best possible circumstances and no cost to the exchequer and which had been responsible for the quality of the traditional sector against all odds.

Apart from the divisions of the rural society according to caste, economic status and politics, there is the injustice done to women who, in spite of their very important role in agriculture, are denied their due share in decision making. Sushila Nayar, the noted social worker, and former Union Health Minister, stated:

> "In the August 1983 number of Anasuya, the Gujarati Monthly of 'SEWA', Ahmedabad, there is a graphic narration of the experience of women survey workers in some of the villages of Gujarat. The men would have liked the survey workers to talk to them rather than to their women folk. The women have no brains, according to these men. They think the women are like their cattle. Smt. Deoki Jain tells me that she has recently received reports of seven case studies from Bangalore, revealing a similar attitude on the part of men. The poor women, be they fisherwomen, agriculturists, Harijans or labourers, are largely treated as cattle by the menfolk although there are honourable exceptions.
>
> "The housewife, who labours from morning till night doing household chores, bearing and rearing children, cooking, cleaning, bringing water and firewood which may take several hours a day in many parts of the country, is not considered working women by our planners or census staff. In a particular village, I am told, the census figures recorded one hundred working women out of about 800. Were the remaining 700 or more resting on their beds? It shows the general attitude of men towards women's work. Studies have revealed that women carry two-thirds of the total work load in the country and receive not more than 10% of the total wages, out of which they probably do not get even 1% for their own use."

Another important aspect of the rural society in transition, which needs to be noted by planners of rural development, is the large-scale migration that takes place from rural to urban areas. The rural population has declined from 80.09 per cent of the total population in 1971 to 72.22 per cent in 2001.[1] This has worsened the unemployment position and over-crowding in the cities – for small and medium sized towns have been stagnating – as well as increased the costs of reaching minimum social services to these pockets of concentrated poverty. Secondly, as it is the more talented and the more adventurous who migrate, villages are further denuded of talent and enterprise, while facing an ever-increasing challenge to their capacity for production and social management.

Another aspect of the impact of migration on rural society is the weakening of the community sense and community values, not only among those who go out but also among those who remain behind, because the final exit from rural areas takes many generations to be effected. They frequently go back to their villages. They send money to their families who are generally left behind. And so on. The net effect is to establish a continuing contact of the member continuing to stay in the village with the outside world, which leads to a slow but steady erosion of the stability of the rural society.

A closely allied problem is that of spatial scatter of human conglomerations and the irrational and iniquitous relationship amongst them. These settlements may be divided into three types: villages, small towns and cities. The village-city relationship is exploitative. The primary products are taken from villages to cities, where they are processed and the profits are garnered by the latter. Cheap machine-made goods are dumped on villages, destroying the handicrafts, which alone enable the people to fight unemployment and under-employment to some extent. All the talent and enterprise of villages, sooner or later, migrate to the cities. Cities in turn burst at the seams with increasing slums of extreme poverty and deprivation. As regards small and medium towns (i.e. those with a population below 20,000), they have been growing marginally, even those with a population from 20,000 to 99,000 registered an increase of 153.5 per cent during 1961-91 against the country's overall increase of 175.4 per cent.[2] A meaningful and mutually beneficial relationship among three units is urgently called for. Various ways in which that can be done have already been spelt out. The central idea in most of these measures is to promote small towns, which are favourably situated for fanning out services to rural areas and for collection of their products for efficient marketing as "growth centres". They would in turn be effectively linked to cities. While large scale industry would be promoted in cities, these growth centres will become centres for medium and small-scale industry. Some states are in a fairly advanced stage of preparation for carrying out 'growth centres' or 'economic zones' while others are experimenting with pilot projects. This idea is likely to gain further momentum in the years to come.

Some occupational mobility on the basis of economic incentives is visible in varying degrees, in spite of caste. The caste, however, still continues to be the dominant force in ordering the social and economic life of rural India. While the lower castes are becoming increasingly impatient with their status, they do not challenge the system as such and are only anxious to move up the hierarchical ladder of caste, which is resisted by the upper castes, who combine their command of the levers of social status with that of political and economic power. In turn, castes struggling to move up are anxious to avoid the polluting touch of those below them, especially of those immediately next to them in the hierarchy. This comes out very vividly in the micro-study of the Raigar (Chamar) community in the village Takor (Rajasthan), conducted by the Indian Institute of Management, Ahmedabad and graphically narrated by Ravi Mathai. The position of the under-dog in the social and economic life of the village is fixed. His equality of opportunity, requiring perfect mobility is "illusory" and his "freedom", as Mathai puts it. "is the freedom to starve".

State intervention to secure mobility through distributive justice, ironically goes to strengthen the very feudal system, which denies it. This is how it happens. The big farmer owns lot of land and through this he occupies a commanding position in the economic life of the village. He lends money to the villagers and if they fail to pay the agreed instalment or interest in time their small patch of land may be attached, products from their craft skill may be annexed and they may be forced to do free labour on subsistence wages. Their voting power may be channeled to their creditor against his certifying their "Weaker Section" status. Every government help requires a certificate and every certificate has its price and is the main instrument, combined with the prevailing indebtedness, for channeling government aid to the better off classes. Mathai writes:

> "But in the traditional hierarchical system in which he lives, his opportunities are limited by his capacity to obtain certificates verifying his destitution. These certificates he will have to obtain through the goodwill of the system that has a vested interest in his destitution."

In such a situation, where local leadership has complete strangle-hold on the masses, political leadership at the top has a strong tendency to increasingly depend upon local barons; and the bureaucracy, for its very survival, has to collude with them for defeating the aims of distributive justice while "achieving" the quantitative targets of schemes of helping the "weaker sections" which is politically expedient. The danger of this triple collusion to defeat the ends of democracy, while swearing by it, is well brought out by Matthai in the following words:

> "If democracy is an internationally respectable front for our traditional hierarchical system, and if the economic activities within the democratic framework feed into, sustain and create growth in the parallel structure by transforming inputs for democratic distributive justice into patronage aimed at retaining a feudal relationship, this process is not without its benefits. But this does raise the question as to whether political power becomes increasingly dependent on the economic activities of the extra-legal systems and the vice versa. The feudalism of rural India has its compensations, but in areas of greater human density and concentration, urban and metropolitan, the traditional forms of behavioural control gives way and the control exercised through the legal structures of our democracy are wholly inadequate to cope with political indiscipline, undemocratic behaviour and the growing spheres of illicit activities which in these circumstances are regarded as "fair game". "Number two money" or "number two goods" are very widely understood and used phrases in "the parallel system."

In these circumstances, the only remedy is to develop and strengthen self-reliance of the people, through an appropriate programme of an action-oriented, life-centred and problem-centred education so that people understand the forces that enmesh them and know how to meet them through individual and group action. That will reduce power of local barons and the need of the political leadership to depend upon intermediaries and thereby break the unholy alliance of democratic leaders and the feudal lords. The leaders will have to seek their election without the intervention of intermediaries. The honest bureaucrat will be saved from a very difficult situation and the dishonest ones will be duly alerted.

The Ahmedabad group has also made beginnings of such an educational programme and achieved modest success – all that could be expected within the short time at its disposal. Our target-oriented planners will have to learn that durable results, which education seeks to achieve, require time. Professor Nurul Hasan, former Union Education Minister, related similar stories about the situation in Uttar Pradesh villages: 'the sweeper does not want to sweep, the plough man does not want to plough and so on. He, however, would have no objection to carrying on his earlier vocation provided the technology was so altered as to dissociate it from the caste and social stigma'.

The traditional sector is our only safeguard against large scale unemployment and under-employment and any dislocation of it would be disastrous to rural economy. It has, therefore, to become a top priority, for any planner dealing with rural development, to up-grade its technologies, without destroying its decentralized character, and increase credit support and marketing and sales facilities. With that will come increasing mobility and the dissociation of profession from caste.

The Preferred Future

It has been rightly said, that where there is no knowledge of the past there can be no vision of the future. While the future has to evolve from the past and the present, to save ourselves from the impending catastrophe to which the main thrust of our development would lead us requires massive interventions. We must, therefore, design the future with utmost care. In this task, our Constitution and national consensus that has emerged as a result of the professions of various governments since independence and our experience of development should provide valuable guidance. So also will our insights about the likely impact of world forces on our society. For, we are living in a closely knit world with mutually interacting units. The process of social and economic integration has been further boosted by globalization, which has overtaken the World since early nineties.

In order to delineate the future, a preliminary statement we prepared in the light of the available guidelines indicated above and sent to over thirty development planners, thinkers, political leaders, educationists and senior administrators. Critical areas were identified on which their views, in particular, were sought. Some of these eminent persons sent written replies. Others were personally contacted and the issues discussed. The preliminary statement was modified and expanded in the light of these responses. The discussion in this section draws heavily on these responses.

The Central Aim

The central goal of future development ought to be to preserve and promote dignity of the individual and to move towards a non-exploitative and a "caring society", where individuals are bound together by ties of friendship and mutual concern. There was unanimous agreement on this score among the respondents. The question, that emerges, is whether it would be a feasible proposition in a highly competitive and atomized world of today and of the likely future. The main features of the preferred goals are:

(1) There is a growing realization in the world that inevitable denouement of present trends of cut-throat competition and confrontation unleashed by forces of globalization will lead to complete annihilation of mankind. While forces of sanity have not yet been able to devise mechanisms through which their voice could be effectively heard at decision-making points, it is significant that forces of destruction have yet not dared reach a point of no-return.

(2) The predominance of good over evil in man, would enable the world to continue to survive under adverse circumstances. Conditions can be created to enable man's goodness to be vivified and made effective in terms of social and political action as was demonstrated in recent times on a country-wide scale in India by Gandhiji during the freedom struggle and elsewhere,

on a smaller scale, by men like Martin Luther King and his civil disobedience movement in the USA. In both cases large masses of human beings rose above their petty selves to suffer for the causes they held dear. All the great religions of the world play an important part in moulding the conscious and sub-conscious self of billions of human beings, preach goodness, sacrifice and service. These ideals have been translated in varying degrees and forms into social institutions in various parts of the world. It is these ideals that have guided the various declarations of the United Nations. One can cynically dismiss this as hypocrisy but one can also look at them as the ideals that humanity is striving to reach in spite of its repeated failure due to man's greed and selfishness.

(3) In India, in particular, respect for goodness, service and sacrifice is almost universal in mass consciousness. Great men and women have again and again enabled people to reflect this inner psyche in the form of social and political action. It is only in India perhaps that Vinoba Bhave could collect thousands of acres of land for distribution to the landless and that too in a land hungry country. The Indian Constitution, the Plan documents and the professions of political parties reflect modern reaffirmation of these ancient values sorely needed today.

(4) Even if we were sure that the world is rushing headlong towards death and destruction, common sense would still demand that we would continue till the last moment to plan for a life worth living.

This question also provokes the counter-question as to whether the atomized world of today will survive or go up in flames sooner than most of us are willing to believe. At any rate, the former is a goal worth striving for provided we work out its implications and are prepared to accept as well as work for them. We should, however, be as realistic as anybody can be in this world of cataclysmic change. These implications may be studied under four broad heads: economic, political, cultural and educational.

Economic Order

The basic goal of the economic system should be employment for all; without it there can be no equality of opportunity and no dignity for the individual. A non productive individual is rejected as a useless burden on society. Nor can we be economically efficient if we fail to utilize our major resource namely the manpower. We must be efficient and produce more if we are to survive.

It will, however, neither be feasible nor even relevant in a country with a large section of the labour force being self-employed to aim at "employment for all" in the Western sense of wage employment. The goal should be: "work for all those who are willing and able to work". This should ensure in return that basic needs of the individual are met. So important is this right that where society cannot provide useful work, it must pay for even useless work, honestly performed and duly certified by the community, as a better alternative to the employment dole, which encourages laziness. The necessary social structures required for the realization of this goal would have to be devised.

Equally important with production is the question of equitable distribution. This is especially important in a country where roughly one fourth of the population lives below the poverty line. This calls for a decentralized economy, where large industries are kept to the minimum essential and most production is through cottage, small and medium industries. As decentralization has to be combined with efficiency, a major R & D effort will have to be mounted to evolve appropriate technologies and discover and develop decentralized sources of energy. It will have to be supported by an efficient extension system for the transfer of technology to millions of families and individuals, spread through the length and breadth of the country. It will also call for cooperative organization and management training. The subsidizing of cottage and small-scale industries is questioned on the ground that they are unable to compete with large scale industry and to subsidize them is to encourage inefficient production units. It is often forgotten that large-scale industry is heavily subsidized by the state in the form of infrastructure facilities it provides to it. As a matter of fact, small industry has many advantages of space, management and (in the case of cottage industries) utilization of small units of labour, which would otherwise be wasted, as well as in terms of the happiness of and lack of tension among workers.

This is, however, not to belittle the importance of large-scale industry, which will still be fairly great. Its maximum possible operations, however, should be formed out to ancillaries – through legislation where necessary – over which the mother plant exercises the required quality control to increase its spread effect and employment potential. That this is economically feasible and advantageous has been amply demonstrated by the example of the United States of America, where outsourcing has become the most accepted from of production.

As a matter of fact, there has to be an integrated policy in regard to large, medium-sized, small scale and cottage industries and the decision in regard to every activity and operation must be to allot it to the scale which suits it.

In the field of agriculture, we should, first of all, have the support of a vigorous family planning and population control programme, if our efforts to feed the population are to succeed. Secondly, we must create a climate of contentment by ending the present iniquitous distribution of land, which is the root cause of all injustices in the countryside. A vigorous land reform programme, with all the legal loopholes in present legislation plugged, must be mounted. Land ceiling, land distribution, consolidation of holdings – all these will need serious attention. Radical redistribution of land has taken place in Kerala and West Bengal. The R & D effort will have to be concentrated largely on the problems of small and marginal farmers, dry farming etc. It will need to be supported by a vastly expanded extension services. Special emphasis will have to be given to develop and utilize to utmost advantage resources of recycled human and animal waste and green manure to enrich the soil and develop resources of renewable energy for agricultural purposes. Mechanization will come in but very discriminatingly – only in operations, where it does not displace labour or where there is a net increase of labour employed. The employment in agriculture will need to be made fuller by the further development of subsidiary industries including those dependent on the products of activities allied to agriculture like dairying, piggery, poultry etc. The whole system will need to be given administrative, credit and marketing support. Preservation and storage of farm produce will require attention.

While the above measures will improve the viability of the small and marginal farmers, who constitute the vast majority of farmers, two issues have emerged in development of agriculture in connection with the need to increase production and productivity in agriculture and to provide opportunities for rural youth somewhat comparable to the opportunities available in urban areas to check avoidable and socially costly migration to urban areas. These are: when and how far to mechanize agriculture and the degree of reliance on chemical fertilizers, which are becoming prohibitively costly. In the light of the prevailing situation – when agriculture is, and is likely to remain in the foreseeable future, as the only occupation available for the vast majority of the people – mechanization has to be introduced very selectively, viz., where it does not displace labour and leads to a net addition to employment. Where there is assured water supply and mechanization makes multi-cropping possible; it leads to increased labour demand as well as demand for small machines and machine tools and thus leads to the welcome diversification of the rural economy, thereby increasing and improving employment opportunities, as it happened in the Punjab. In such cases, mechanization is to be welcomed, otherwise it would need to be avoided. That does not, however, preclude the need for improvement of agricultural implements, which must be steadily improved. Thus mechanization will have to be decided upon in the light of the local situation. The acid test is that at least existing employment opportunities do not shrink. Another issue relates to the shortage of commercial energy. This will call for the development of alternative sources of energy, especially those that can produce energy on a decentralized basis in view of the scattered nature of farming.

As regards chemical fertilizers, their cost has become so heavy as to make modern agriculture unprofitable or only marginally profitable. If they are to be used on a mass scale, state must heavily subsidize them. This is, however, not possible in a country of India's size and agricultural predominance. While, therefore, chemical fertilizers may have to be supplied at remunerative prices in selected areas and to selected categories where they can be most profitably used in the interest of production, the emphasis in the majority of the areas will need to be on development of our indigenous resources of manures through the recycling of human, animal and vegetable waste and use of green manure. These resources are considerable and at the doorsteps of our people. Educational institutions can play an important part in their development.

It is necessary to evolve ways and means whereby crops can be fully safeguarded from damage done be rodents, locusts and other agents.

Lastly, in the new economic order, a consumption ethics will need to be evolved so that goods needed by masses and providing them their basic minimum needs, get the highest priority. The disparities in income will need to be radically reduced, an atmosphere of austerity created and ostentatious living avoided. There can be enough for everybody's needs if the greed of the few is kept in check.

Such an economic order will have implications for the organization of space and the establishment of mutually supportive relationships between cities, small towns and villages as is already being propagated under the concept of "growth centres" described earlier.

Political Order

Decentralized, widely dispersed and yet efficient, economic activity is only possible under a decentralized political system with full involvement of the people. 'Participatory democracy' alone can ensure economic and social justice. Exercise of political power by the people at local levels is also essential for realizing their own dignity and self-respect and for having the feeling that they are masters of their own destiny. Education and training for decentralized decision marking will be required.

The Constitution of India and Plan documents have emphasized, implicitly and explicitly, the necessity of preventing concentration of political and economic power and of building up democracy from below as well as local and micro-planning to ensure maximum local involvement. In this context the most relevant development, India launched is the massive programme of transferring power to the Panchayati Raj institutions (*local bodies*). Radical reforms are bound to be slow in taking roots. They are delayed by subtle pressures of the vested interests embodied in the status quo as well as by slow development of capacity in the new incumbents to exercise power with wisdom and restraint. The introduction of elections at all levels has so far tended to disrupt the cohesion – essential for effective economic and political decentralization of local communities. Massive efforts will be required to make these bodies capable of influencing decisions in social, political and economic fields so as to bring the new order into being. Some hopeful signs have, however, already emerged:

(1) With the introduction of adult franchise, the centre of power has shifted to the rural areas. It has, however, remained the preserve of rural elite who have strengthened themselves further by aligning with urban elite as well as by the traditional support of the local bureaucracy. The landed gentry captured important positions not only in Panchayats but also in State legislatures and Parliament. That position is beginning to be challenged now by younger generation and weaker sections. It is reported that younger people are increasingly emerging in the Panchayat elections, though Panchayats are by and large still dominated by upper classes because of naked use of economic strangle-hold and violence, which subverts the voice of numbers. A massive educational effort is required to ensure that change over to the new reality is smooth in the enlightened self-interest of the elite themselves. In state legislatures and the Parliament, however, the numbers are beginning to count more and more, reflected in the composition and general atmosphere in these bodies, which is now more down-right earthy and "crude", lacking the traditional sophistication of the middle and upper classes. No Parliamentary seat, for example, can be won by any one without expressing deep concern – genuine or otherwise – for weaker sections and the masses.

(2) With the introduction of elections at all levels there was a tendency among all India political parties to spread their influence down the line leading thereby to political centralization to the detriment of grass-root level institutions. It, however, soon became clear that perceptions at different levels would differ. Even when the Indian National Congress was in power both at the

centre and in states, – in the long period following independence – state leaders frequently differed with the Central leaders, as was amply evident in the meetings of the National Development Council. Even at local level – as was reported from Gujarat, for example – Panchayat leaders are frequently looked upon as powerful rivals, because they directly control votes, rather than being mere camp-followers of the higher level leadership of the party.

(3) The steady spread of education in rural areas, in general, and among weaker sections, in particular, as well as other measures being adopted to lift weaker sections, socially and economically are bound to strengthen them and, in course of time, to enable them to claim and get their rightful share in political and economic power, even though their present handicaps prevent them from taking full advantage of the governmental programmes designed for their benefit.

Each political party should have, what may be called a 'performance – audit cell'. This cell should, from time to time and constituency to constituency, asses the performance of its members and ensure that promises made to the people on election eve are fulfilled. As it is, such an assessment is left to the so called 'social audit' which comes at the end of the term, which can not retrieve the loss suffered by the people in the interim period.

The Cultural Dimension

An inevitable requirement for the growth of any nation is the establishment of its distinct identity. It is only thus that it can contribute to world development and cultural regeneration. Culture may be broadly divided into two parts: values which have continued to guide a society over centuries of its existences and which are not out-dated as shown by rigorous, critical analysis; and the accumulated experience in various fields – art, architecture, music, administration etc. The former is necessary to determine goals and the direction of our growth. The latter is a rich heritage, which should be taken full advantage of. For, we can have it at practically no cost.

At present, we seem to deny ourselves the benefit of both. We tend to become rudderless and in the matter of knowledge we very often become carbon copies of the West, thereby doing injustice to the West as well as to ourselves. The Preferred Future should be based on full awareness of and pride in our own identity, which we should try to discover and promote. Some of the most important ingredients of our culture, which the world badly needs today, are tolerance, synthesis, respect for the individual, balance between the material and the spiritual, spirit of service and sacrifice etc.

India is rich by virtue of its diversity. There is, however, a unity underlying this diversity. A type of cultural division which divides and hurts Indian society are the cultural divisions between urban and rural areas, between the elite and the masses, between the high and the lower castes and between the traditionalists and those who claim to be modern. In these cases cultural differences are not indicative of the variety of life but the "superiority" of one/section over the other. This kind of division between man and man can have no place in an egalitarian society and such divisions can only sow the seeds of discord and tension. These divisions, to be removed, will require, firstly, provision of minimum needs for all and the progressive reduction of economic disparities; secondly, the establishment of participatory democracy; thirdly, the organization of space and the establishment of mutually beneficial relationship and inter-communication among villages, small towns and cities; and finally, support of an appropriate system of education.

The Educational Support

To bring future order into being and to sustain it, the support of an appropriate system of education will be the most crucial. Education will need to provide not only trained manpower for handling various jobs required by this decentralized but highly efficient society, based on widespread and intensive use of science and technology, but will also have to create the necessary climate for development by developing attitudes and sense of values required by the future society. The leadership qualities of initiative, resourcefulness, enterprise and social commitment will need to be identified and further developed in a large number of people so that there is a sizeable number of leaders at various levels of a decentralized society. Under the impact of science and technology, such a society will be subject to rapid changes and the citizens will need to develop a scientific temper and a capacity for adapting themselves to change. Education provided will have to be life-centred and problem-oriented in content and methodology. Educational projects will be life's actual problems and the aim will be to develop in students the capacity to solve them. Knowledge of disciplines will be given in response to the requirements of problem solving. Another aspect of the approach will be to create, through educational projects, as much of their own finance as possible to accelerate the pace of education as well as to train people in self-reliance bit by bit so that they can sustain and develop an effective basis for economic and political power at various levels of a decentralized society. We have the rudiments of such an educational system in *Nayee Talim* – the richest gift of the Father of the Nation – which will need to be perfected through intensive experimentation.

A very important step in education, which will have far-reaching implications, will be to link universities very closely with the rural development. That would be in the interest both of higher education and of rural development. With this objective in view location, course content and transactional technology will need to be re-examined with a view to modernizing them. Apart from the formal system, a comprehensive programme of non-formal education, with an immediate linkage with life's struggles and problems will be required to be organized. The support of an appropriately designed system of education will ensure the necessary Research and Development (R & D) input, which the development process requires.

Strategies of Development

The obvious question that arises is: How do we go from the present to the preferred future? The answer to this question will determine whether our preferred future is merely utopian or something realizable and worth striving for. Feasible development assumes that direction of growth has been decided upon or is likely to be decided upon by the competent authority, which has the necessary competence, power and will to pursue policies and programmes designed to achieve the desired levels of development; and that there are ways and means to strengthen the will and capacity of the competent authority to achieve the goal.

We have the necessary national consensus – it is important in a democracy – on broad goals and the means of achieving them. We agree on an egalitarian, non-exploitative society as well as on decentralization of economic and political power as a means of achieving it. The Panchayati Raj institutions and the Cooperatives are the principal institutions through which decentralization of political and economic power can be attained. We have designed various devices to provide help to the poor and the weak such as reservation of seats in educational institutions and of jobs under government, extension machinery for transfer of technology to them, expansion of credit facilities etc. We have enacted legislation, introduced land reforms, abolished bonded labour, fixed the minimum agricultural wage, declared untouchability as unlawful, given to women equal rights in parental property etc. We have devised administrative measures: setting up decentralized units of administration, adopting "area development" and "target group" approaches etc. We have also given the right to seek information to people to ensure transparency. We have the legislative and administrative framework, which certifies that national consensus as embodied in the Constitution is being maintained in the post-independence period. There is not a single political party whose declared policy is different. And, yet it is universally admitted that as a result of developments during the last five decades, the gap between the rich and the poor has widened. Why?

This is a clear indication that government, in spite of its intentions, does not have the will and/or the capacity to implement its intentions. An uncharitable view could be that various measures were only a smoke-screen to delude the masses that development was in their interest. A deeper analysis would, however, reveal that actions of a democratic government are the resultant of various pressures and to expect that a government will be able to effectively espouse the cause of the poor, without the poor and the weak having developed their own strength, is unrealistic. Therefore, the key strategy for growth with justice is to develop strength of the weak and banish the poverty of the poor. Another truth is that nobody can understand better your interests than you yourself and that nobody but you will safeguard them.

Therefore, the key task of rural development – development of the vast majority, the poor, the lowly and the oppressed – is to put the destiny in their own hands. That was the main thrust of the strategy of development advocated by the Father of the Nation.

We, however, seem to be ending up in a vicious circle: the poor need help because they are poor and yet nobody will help them so long as they are poor. Even at best when government wants to help them there are serious limitations to what it can do. No government can create a people's movement, a movement from the grassroots. There should be an urge for self-help, without which no development in the interests of the poor can take place. Most people do not generally have amongst them leaders, with knowledge and dedication, who can create such a movement. Only voluntary organizations and individuals can provide such a leadership. Such individuals and organizations, however, do not come up on demand or command. All that government can do is to encourage them when and where they are found. Local politicians and the bureaucracy, who are generally in league with the local vested interests, defeat even this policy. Yet the Welfare State cannot wait on account of moral and political expediency. Government has to act, but a government-sponsored movement turns out to be a lame and halting movement – a movement without a soul, a movement without momentum.

The strategy for development has, therefore, to be chalked out in the framework of inherent difficulties and limitations mentioned above. The basic elements of the strategy would seem to be:

(1) Education system must primarily aim at enabling students to increase production and character building. Life in educational institutions should be based on simplicity, austerity, cooperation and self-government, of course, guided by teachers. Methods used should promote scientific temper: power of detailed observation, spirit of enquiry, capacity to generalize from observed facts as well as to test these generalizations by observation and analysis of more

facts; and build up initiative, resourcefulness, team spirit and qualities of leadership. Educational projects should be selected from the problems of the natural, social and economic environment. The germs of such a system are there in the *Nayee Taleem* (New Education) System given to the country by Gandhiji and these should be nurtured through carefully conducted experiments in which some of our best brains should be involved. There should be a method by which these experiments are periodically evaluated and whatever has successfully passed the stage of experimentation should be introduced into the general system. The government alone can take up such a responsibility. Voluntary workers and organizations can give invaluable support by conducting pilot projects and making their results known through proper evaluation.

(2) Every step should be taken to build cohesiveness of the community. Its strength, vis-à-vis the wider world, will depend not only upon the quality of individuals but also on its capacity to stand together.

Without strong local communities, self-governing and self-sufficient in regard to their basic needs, it would be impossible to build democracy from the grassroots or to have a strong decentralized economic order. For the following reasons also, development of the local communities has to be the basic strategy for rural development:

- Barring a few well-to-do families, the large majority in the villages are poor and weak. The strength of the weak lies in their unity;
- Because of a common destiny forged by living in close physical proximity, it should be much easier to work out common goals for the village elite and village masses than for the weak in the village and the strong in the town.
- Because of the vastly dispersed nature of inequalities, it is extremely difficult for an outside agency to render adequate help to the weak against the strong and perhaps the only way is to awaken the sense of responsibility among the strong for the weak and to

design administrative and social structures which would steadily strengthen the weak without bringing them into direct confrontation with the strong;

- The delivery system of a welfare state is steadily expanding, but without an adequate receiving mechanism; most services do not yield optimum benefits, especially to the intended beneficiaries;
- It is impossible to utilize technical services on an individual basis; and
- Without evoking the maximum possible and ever growing capacity for self-help in people, it would be well – nigh impossible for a developing country like India to provide social services to the vast mass of people on any adequate scale. Self-reliance can best be generated within the framework of a close-knit community capable of joint planning and action.

Self-governing local communities were India's strength and ensured its stability through centuries till the British, through the influx of cheap machine-made goods, destroyed their handicrafts and their economic self-sufficiency. The new judicial system destroyed the power and authority of the *Panchayats* to administer justice. So did the police undermine the capacity and the will to stand together against internal disorder and external attack.

The process of undermining the self-sufficient character of local communities continued after Independence. Expanding the network of roads and consequent influx of exploiting traders from urban areas accelerated the pace. Lack of sufficient employment in villages led to migration of the more enterprising among the community to towns, leading to impoverishment of the community. With increasing mobility of its manpower, came the further weakening of its social cohesion. The introduction of elections has also divided the community. Our discussions at Mohendergarh, revealed that half the time was spent in electioneering and the other half in rewarding one's friends and settling scores with opponents. The old norms of behaviour and the restraints built into the old balance between the classes, which had emerged from enlightened self-interest, have been seriously disturbed and the cooperatives as well as Panchayats have in many places become agencies of exploitation. The new paraphernalia of banks, agricultural extension etc. has further wetted the appetite of the better off classes in the community.

In this context, if a community has to be revived and made vibrant as a major basic agency of social, economic and political development of rural areas, a major intervention by the political authority, voluntary organizations and education system will be called for. In this effort, the first task will be to identify, utilize and strengthen the small surviving community-spirit and organization. It is a measure of the vitality of the community-organization that despite vicious onslaught of the forces of modernization, community spirit still prevails in many places – especially those distant from the towns. During their enquiries undertaken in connection with the scheme to introduce an environment-based education, the National Council of Educational Research and Training found that the local community was still a force in South India and the North East. It was, however, fast disappearing in Northern India. Therefore, author was pleasantly surprised when he was told by the Haryana Director of Public Instruction (Schools), that community was still a force in some of the districts of Haryana. He gave the following instances.

One thing, which indicates community's capacity to lay down its own norms and enforce strict compliance by its members, is the way they treat their girls. Every girl of the village is regarded as a sister. Nobody can tease her with impunity. Nobody can take bath at the village well with an under-wear. He has to put on a dhoti (long cloth). Women go for toilet in one direction and men have to take another direction (they all go for the toilet in the open). When a marriage party from village A goes to village B, a list is prepared of all the girls of village A, who are married in village B and sweets are sent to them as "sisters" of the bridegroom. Once a thief was bragging to a neighbour that he has succeeded in stealing quite a lot of Jewellery from a neighbouring village. The next day one of the "daughters of the village" came crying that her father-in-law's house had been broken into and her jewellery also had been stolen and that the thief was reported to have run away in the direction of her father's village. The neighbour, recollecting the thief's bragging the night before, called him and questioned him. As it turned out, he was the thief who had stolen the jewellery of his own "sister". So as the tradition was that a thief would not commit theft in his own village he immediately set out to make amends and brought all the jewellery he had stolen and laid it before his 'sister', asking her to identify and take back only her *own* jewellery and not that of her in-laws, which she scrupulously did. Again, when women of the lower castes work in the houses of upper castes, they are treated with a measure of respect and addressed as sister, aunt etc.

Another instance quoted was that of a *Rajput* village of ex-servicemen. One of them beat a *Harijan* teacher for having beaten his son. It became a caste question. The Deputy Commissioner, went to the village to investigate the matter. The erring person promised before the whole community that he would never do it again. On the teacher still insisting upon an effective guarantee, one of the community members got up and vowed that if it happened again, he would cut his own finger. As the vow of a Rajput means what it says, it settled the matter.

The community spirit, to the extent that it survives, is a valuable asset and the new institutional structures must build upon and strengthen it and not disrupt it. From this point of view, the system of elections at the village level needs serious re-examination. The traditional concept of decision by consensus may prove fruitful, as has been stressed by serious thinkers like Vinoba Bhave. Some other steps, which could help in this direction are:

- The weaker sections must be given weightage in representation on local bodies. It is by sitting together and discovering that there are areas of common interest, that the various sections of the community can come closer.
- The strength of the various cohesive interest groups, especially of the weaker sections, must be built up through cooperatively organized productive activities used as projects of education. This would add to the knowledge of the beneficiaries and build up the necessary attitudes, apart from improving their economic position. This should be done without bringing the various groups into confrontation with each other. Rather, where interests conflict, the conflict

should be resolved through discussion, making use of the machinery of the *Panchayat*, the community leaders, voluntary organizations etc. As the weak become strong, they will have a much better chance of being equal partners in developmental work. In this way, slowly and steadily, new balances and new equations will emerge. It will be unrealistic to hope that the passage to the new balances will be smooth. Tensions will mount and methods will have to be devised to resolve them. A very alert bureaucracy, especially at the district level, should ensure that local officers do not join hands with local elite to oppress the weak. Law and order must be maintained to contain local tensions, when they mount, in spite of everything, within manageable limits so that they do not leave behind scars difficult to heal.

- The sense of common destiny and common interests will also develop through collective performance of common tasks, the area of which should be continually enlarged. The formulation of village plans should provide an occasion for understanding and working for a common destiny.
- The building up of the community will prepare the receiving mechanism to optimize the impact of various services provided by the State through the delivery system.
- Again, the underdog and those interested in him must identify, create and develop their own lobby at various levels of the political hierarchy. They must build up their own strength and seek their own allies. Whereas the vested interests hold a position of strength at present, the future is with the weak. Because of their large numbers, their potential strength is bound to be recognized and attract friends. And there are some genuine friends of the poor at all strategic points. These must be identified and their help mobilized by the leaders of the poor.
- As regards change-agents, the Welfare State has to mount a programme of helping the poor and build up their strength. It will be "a movement without a soul"

> but it will provide the framework within which individuals and organizations have a chance of making their contribution. It should be a definite policy of government to encourage such individuals and organizations as a matter of top-most priority.

Conclusion

The development of rural areas has a three-fold significance: numbers involved, power of the vote in the democratic set-up and the danger of the eruption of a volcanic situation created by extreme poverty and misery, social ostracism and political neglect of this vast mass of humanity. If the forces, hitherto operative in the situation, are allowed to have a free play, a point of no return will soon be reached and the world will be torn asunder. In response to the challenge of the situation, awareness is dim and the action half-hearted. In India, constructive basis of the struggle for freedom led to the highlighting of the problems and developing many insights in regard to their solutions. These were embodied in the Constitution and have been guiding the pronouncements of various political parties and the programmes and policies of the various Five Year Plans.

Considerable investment has been made in rural development. An impressive array of legislation has been passed to protect the interests of weaker sections. Many attempts have been made to adapt administration to the needs of the situation in which the interests of the backward sections have to be safeguarded. Yet the whole exercise seems to have fallen short with the result that net effect of our planned development over the last sixty years has been the widening of gap between the rich and the poor. A massive intervention is called for if the existing trends are to be altered effectively. This should be mainly on two fronts: (a) a movement in the direction of helping the poor and the depressed needs to be accelerated and effectiveness the various steps taken so far needs to be examined so that deficiencies are remedied; and (b) beneficiaries must be organized and strengthened primarily through character-building, developing their productive competence and improving education for self-reliance. Of the two, second is even more important than the first and is the missing link, which has largely prevented the poor from taking advantage even of the measures undertaken for their benefit.

The main features of educational reorientation have to be: cooperatively organized productive activities as the main centres of interest; promotion of community cohesion through community participation in a progressively enlarging area of common interests; building up the strength of different cohesive interest groups, constituting the community, without bringing one group into confrontation with the other, so as to make cooperation on more or less equal terms possible; forging linkages between educational institutions and development agencies; and evolving creative methods of teaching to build up individuals with initiative, resourcefulness, engendering the scientific spirit, capacity for team work, social commitment and qualities of leadership. Such an educational system – including both the formal and the non-formal – will throw up leaders who will galvanize local communities to have a strong commitment for development and self-upliftment and make effective decentralization of economic and political power a reality. The basic task is to strengthen the poor at the bottom, and development with distributive justice will follow. The basic premise is that nobody can help the poor except the poor himself. External agencies can act only as catalysts. The best agencies are dedicated individuals and voluntary organizations; whom full but discriminatory encouragement should be given as a part of state policy so that grain can be separated from the chaff.

REFERENCES

1. *Census of India 2001.*
2. *Ibid.*

Chapter 3

Educational Imperatives
Processes, Programmes and Structures

School Education and Non-formal Education

Deprivation is part of the rural life in most parts of the globe. Growing up in rural areas is most likely to mean facing poverty, illiteracy and hunger. About 850 million people in the world are undernourished, 860 million illiterate; and 130 million out-of-school. About 70 per cent of the world's poor live in rural areas.[1] Food scarcity, low access and attainment levels and gender inequality are some of the critical issues concerning education in rural areas. It is estimated that around one-third of the world's poor live in India. There are more poor in India than in entire Sub-Saharan Africa. Although official estimates of the Government of India indicate that every fourth Indian is poor[2], according to the estimates of the internationally recognized poverty level of dollar a day, 44 per cent of the people in the country are poor, and 86 per cent of the people earn less than $2 a day.

Indian poverty is predominantly rural, where landless labourers and casual workers comprise the worst off economic group. Scheduled Castes and Scheduled Tribes, women and matriarchal families, old people and girls face more deprivation than others. The vast majority of rural poor in the country are engaged in farming, fishery and livestock, either as wage labourers or marginal farmers. First, almost 42 per cent of the rural poor fall into the most economically disadvantaged group of agricultural labour. Furthermore, more than half of this group consists of Scheduled Castes and Scheduled Tribes (SCs and STs). Overall, SCs and STs constitute about 25 per cent of the rural population but account for more than 42 per cent of the poor. This imbalance has prompted a series of affirmative interventions in favour of SCs and STs.

A better understanding of the diverse needs and specificities of rural people is needed to ensure sustainable development, particularly the achievement of Millennium Development Goals (MDGs). People-centred approach needs to be adopted to provide education for rural people. While the country has committed to provide education for all by 2010 and to meet learning needs of young adults through equitable access to appropriate learning and life skills programmes, much needs to be seen in terms of implementation of these programmes. Elimination of gender disparity and improvement of quality and relevance of education in rural areas are two other critical issues, which need to be addressed on priority basis to ensure sustainable development.

Recognizing the importance of education in rural areas and adopting appropriate policies and operational strategies are necessary steps towards empowering the rural mass. The country has made tremendous progress in education during the last six decades; much still needs to be done in terms of reducing geographical and social disparities in access to educational opportunities. Several strategies have been adopted for effective delivery of educational services in the countryside which, among others, include expanding network of schools in rural areas, promoting gender and social equity, providing nutritional support to young children, aligning school curricula, at least partially, to local needs and culture, ensuring participation in planning and management of education through decentralized planning and management, etc. However, strategies like linking food security and access to learning, strengthening rural learning communities[3], making curricula relevant to rural people, etc. are some other alternative strategies that need to be effectively implemented in the Indian context. Promoting enabling skills of rural people to diversify their livelihood, such as literacy and numeracy, farming skills, skills for off-farm activities and micro-business management are important to reduce vulnerability and poverty.

Given the context, this chapter aims at discussing educational imperatives, particularly in rural areas. Attempt has also been made to briefly present related policies and programmes at various levels of education. The focus of the chapter, however, is to critically reflect on relevance and delivery of educational services in rural areas.

Methodological Imperative

The central objective of education is to develop an individual- "body, mind and spirit". The individual, however, does not grow in a vacuum. He develops in active interaction with his environment—natural, social, economic and political. Education has to relate to the environment, especially its dynamic aspects, which means development. There is a natural linkage between education and development, and the mutually reinforcement capabilities must be exploited in order to maximize returns from investments.

Problem-Centred and Life-Centred Education

Linking education with environment means centreing education on the problems of life around the individual. Education must be problem-centred; since these problems are related to life, education also becomes life-centred. To put it in another way, education should be life-centred and the problems of life must provide the 'Centres of Interest' around which knowledge and disciplines are built. Thereby, knowledge is verified as an instrument for solving our life problems. This is known as the technique of co-relation. Education system suggested by *Gandhiji* is based on the methodology of *Nayee Taleem* (New Education). *Nayee Taleem* emphasizes the co-relation technique and has the following advantages:

- The problems provide the criteria of selection of relevant knowledge. With the explosion of knowledge, the earlier objective of education, viz., to provide maximum knowledge, has had to change to the development of the capacity of search for relevant knowledge when needed. For, if filling in the maximum possible knowledge was to remain as the educational objective, an individual will be in danger of exploding along with the "explosion of knowledge".
- As education given in a concrete manner in the context of real life problems knowledge, gained strongly fixes itself in the mind. It is immediately appropriated and does not need a painful memorizing effort, as in traditional methods

of learning, where all the time effort has to be made to keep information, gained in the abstract way, from slipping out of the mind.

- As it has been gained in relation to problems which are always recurring, knowledge continues to come back to the mind with a pleasant sense of rediscovery. In addition, a continuous revision is also taking place. Retention of knowledge ceases to be an effort and a burden.
- Knowledge gained in a concrete way and problems solved therewith, promote self-confidence and develops decision-making capacity.
- Such a method, where knowledge is gained by asking the 'why and wherefore' of life's problems, promotes a spirit of enquiry, which is at the heart of the scientific temper, in relation to problems of daily living and thereby leads to its rationalization and all-round improvement. It also leads to the habit of detailed observation because one is trying to critically understand every bit of the environment and the development of the capacity for "induction" and "deduction", and by continuous to and fro movement between 'scientific principles' and 'concrete situations'. These are the other ingredients of the scientific mind. Such a capacity built in the people would set in motion a process of all-round rationalization and improvement of their lives.

A number of problems, however, are encountered in linking education with local environment using the technique of correlation. As education in different areas has to be provided through local environment, it becomes very difficult to secure uniformity of standards, recognized all over the country, which is necessary for ensuring mobility of students from one part of the country to another. This difficulty, however, can be overcome by defining standards in terms of disciplines, which are the same, irrespective of the environment medium through which their knowledge is imparted. It is true that cent per cent similarity will not be possible but a rough equivalence on a nationwide basis can be worked out. Even now, we have different methods of direct teaching and concrete knowledge of disciplines. There are also a number of different types of schools affiliated to different boards – Indian School Certificate, Central Board, Delhi Board and State Boards. A rough equivalence is being worked out for purposes of admission to institutions of higher education, employment, etc. When basic education was introduced many State Governments had worked out the content of disciplines for various classes correlated to diverse activities.

The question, which is naturally and often asked is why basic education did not succeed in spite of being the national development priority after Independence. The discussion that follows attempts to provide answers to this question. The main reason was the failure to take adequate measures on all the three fronts — technical, administrative and public awareness. On the technical front, training of teachers and the preparation of guides left much to be desired, both qualitatively and quantitatively. The research support was, on the whole, negligible. There was hardly any reorientation of the officers occupying strategic positions in Inspectorates and Directorates who, with their fixed ideas and inadequate knowledge of the new reforms, were unsympathetic and even hostile. Hardly any attempt was made to educate the general public in regard to the meaning and significance of the proposed educational reform. Its implementation was confined to rural areas because to *Gandhiji* they were the real India. The priority given to it led to general suspicion that the reform was intended to keep rural areas subservient.

The other question is: what are the stages of education at which environment, problem and life-centered education can be provided? While there is little experience of the application of this methodology at secondary and higher stages of education, the principle is theoretically, of universal application; since education has to train people for life the central objective should be to develop the capacity of individuals to seek relevant knowledge at the appropriate time to solve problems. The concept of environment will, however, differ. While at the elementary stage the environment would be local, its scope will broaden progressively at later stages. For, with the development of mind and of education, wider and wider areas can be used for understanding and interaction. The problems will need to be seen in a national and international perspective. Similarly, in building loyalties growth through ever-widening concentric circles is necessary and possible.

The methodology should be easier to adopt at higher stages of education than at lower stages. For, the capacity to search for information by oneself increases and it is possible to work out a larger and more sophisticated and intricate problem-knowledge relationship than is possible at earlier stages, when a child is largely dependant on the teacher. In a way, it becomes an advantage. It acts as a spur to search information by oneself. The teacher can act more as a guide than as an instructor. The comparatively smaller number of pupils at this stage makes individual approach easier. Well-stocked libraries and well equipped laboratories are the main requisites.

The preference given to seminars and discussions in advanced universities of the world is indicative of the rationale and relevance of the above approach to higher stages of education. A discussion or a seminar requires among other things a project or thematic approach. Greater and greater emphasis is being given to projects. The emphasis on inter-disciplinary approach also favours this method. The project/theme provides a focus around which knowledge from various disciplines can be naturally woven. The advanced level of the mind of students at the higher stages of education also makes it possible to have long alternating spans of project work and theoretical knowledge much more easily and naturally than small bits of knowledge related to small bits of activities. In a large module of work, a type of activity is likely to be repeated a number of times. Therefore, a single explanation of the underlying principle will suffice. The chunk of background knowledge that may have to be given through direct teaching will also not appear so large as it will when given while explaining the principle underlying a single activity. Here, the knowledge imparted directly per activity, every time it is repeated, will become K, 'n' 'K' denoting the quantum of knowledge imparted through direct teaching and 'n' the number of times an activity (or a related activity) is repeated in the module.

A further advantage will be that when a number of illustrations are used at a time to illustrate a principle, the first impression is much firmer and leads to greater and easier retention. Another thing that emerges and needs to be underlined is that, wherever necessary, direct teaching responds to the project approach, and also to vivify and explain problem arising therein. Another difficulty that was noticed in the experiment of correlated teaching was that with his/her traditional preoccupation with the quantum of knowledge, a teacher tended to drag in all sorts of information even when remotely connected with the problem in hand. This made correlation far-fetched and unnatural and tended to obscure the central objective of education, which was to focus attention on the problem and bring in only the knowledge relevant to its solution. Instead of becoming a criterion of selection of knowledge, a problem became a focus of aggregation of relevant and not so relevant knowledge bundled in a heap. This difficulty, however, can be overcome through practice which can demonstrate that even relevant knowledge can be fairly sizeable and where it is continually dinned into the ears of the teachers that the central objective of education is not any information but only relevant information required for the solution of the problem in life so as to develop among pupils problem-solving capability. The experience gained in basic education, in some places, gave reasonable hope for overcoming this difficulty in the course of time.

There was the apprehension that if direct teaching of disciplines is avoided and only knowledge naturally related to problems is given, the knowledge imparted will be insufficient. The correlation with the craft of spinning had been attempted and it was found that it easily meets the knowledge needs of secondary school students. The third difficulty that was that whereas a teacher was required to follow the sequence of life, textbooks that were available recorded the sequence of disciplines. For example, there may be cholera and the problem may be to clean the wells with the help of potassium permanganate. Students may never have heard of elements and compounds and it would be difficult for a teacher to promote among them sufficient comprehension of chemical composition of substance, called potassium permanganate. Two solutions are possible:

- Students in early classes would only be told of the properties and actions of the compound without being dragged into its chemical composition and the problem of elements and compounds and their chemical reactions, etc; and
- Even at an advanced stage, if by chance an occasion has not arisen earlier for giving them the knowledge about

elements and compounds, it could be given directly. This is not succumbing to the temptations of direct teaching. For we would be teaching this with the problem of cleaning of water in the wells with chemical action staring us in the face. Even this direct teaching will not disturb the central position of the problem in a limited way.

It is easy for a teacher to teach from a discipline-based textbook, it becomes extremely difficult for him/her to teach without a textbook and having to cull out related knowledge from many books. Producing problem-based textbooks to match problem-based curriculum could solve this difficulty. Teams of multi-disciplinary teachers under expert guidance could do this. It should be possible to have a book, say, on the science of a kitchen so that all problems relating to the kitchen are explained therein, in their natural sequence. It should be as easy for the teacher to teach science of the kitchen as physics and chemistry from the traditional textbooks. Problem-based textbooks would also help to remove another difficulty. A teacher of Physics may not find it very easy to transfer his/her knowledge of the book to understanding of the phenomena he is observing around himself – the sweeping of the floor, cooking of meals etc. He/She may not have sufficiently observed the phenomena of daily life to be able to see the science behind them. His own knowledge may also not have been sufficiently absorbed to enable him to transfer it to an understanding of the phenomena other than those mentioned in the book. The problem-based textbooks should break the barrier between book knowledge and life. These textbooks, however, should not be used by students but rather serve as guidebooks for teachers. They should enable even a teacher of mediocre ability to teach through the correlation method; thus, criticism that ordinary teachers could not teach through it would no longer be valid.

Activity-Centred Education

Another imperative of development is that education should be activity-centred. As the objective of education is to build the integrated personality of the student, intelligently and scientifically conducted physical activity, in which the whole personality is automatically involved, is a much better medium of education than just the book or theoretical instruction. The condition, however, is that the physical activity must not be mechanically conducted but scientifically — asking the 'why and wherefore' of every process involved. This is the only way of understanding science behind activities, which is a pre-requisite to develop capacity to improve them. Activities should be pre-planned, intelligently and scientifically executed, carefully evaluated and future planning thereof corrected in light of the feedback. Thereby, we can start building managerial attitudes and management capabilities — our greatest weakness and the most urgent need of development — in the children through elementary activities in which they can be engaged.

At higher stages, activities become more complex and ramification of the thought behind them extends beyond the immediate palpable present. The modules of thought and the modules of action tend to become larger and alternate instead of being more or less simultaneous as at the earlier stage. The activity, however, still provides the integrating focus for knowledge and education.

At all higher stages, activity or a series of related activities may become so complex as to be beyond the capacity of a single individual to comprehend and execute. His place has to be taken by a group, each one of whose members comprehends (specializes in) each part. But even then the need for integration continues undiminished – as a matter of fact, increases, lest things may fall apart and the partial truth may pass off as the whole truth.

Hence the urgency with which the deficiency of the modern age of specialization has been felt and the cry has gone up for adopting inter-disciplinary and an integrated approach. Integration, however, requires an integrating focus, which can be provided only by a Project, Theme or Activity.

In education, at earlier stages, a unit has to be a simple physical activity, comprehensible by and capable of being performed by an individual student or a group of students. At later stages, activities become much more complex and needs to be broken up into different modules or specializations which, however, must keep the overall product design in view and frequently interact so that the entire activity providing the integrating focus gets enriched and provides an enriching educational experience to students.

The above methodology would correct two major defects of present day education:

(*i*) its highly theoretical character and lack of practical ability in students, and

(*ii*) narrow specialization, which leads to the application of partial approaches to problems requiring an integrated approach.

Some movement towards these goals is visible at least in advanced countries and some successes have also been achieved; but more experimentation would be necessary before this method can be adopted in our colleges and universities, where the trend is just in the opposite direction; viz. specialization and compartmentalization.

Production-Centred Education

Educationally, production is as good an activity as any other for acting as the medium of education and focus for integration of knowledge. It, however, becomes the most effective instrument of getting knowledge in a poor country with poverty as the central fact of life, because of its capability to provide the strongest motivation. In *Nayee Taleem* while students meaningfully interacted with the total environment — economic, social and natural — pride of place was given to the rural craft as the principal centre of correlation and the main instrument of self-reliance.

Creating a Scientific Temper

As the aim of education is to develop a dynamic personality, scientific temper — observing everything or being alert about everything in the environment, enquiring the "why and wherefore" of everything in order to understand it and improve it etc.— being basic to such a character can not but be most germane to the education process. Scientific temper is usually confused with scientific knowledge and immediately the spectre of having to provide thousands of well-equipped laboratories and millions of rupees required, therefore, seems to arise. We come back to the earth sobered and put the promotion of a scientific temper in the people at large in a low key. The fact of the matter, however, is that only a few may aspire to heights of scientific spirit to: (a) set in motion the rationalization process over the entire spectrum of national life; (b) to stimulate creativity and inventiveness in millions of people and reap the cumulative benefit — which would be tremendous — thereof; and (c) to give the initial push and help to identify our top talent in science. This task is as much educational as developmental. The key to this problem is to use the correlated method of teaching, which is otherwise also required as a sound method of education, as the cheapest means of achieving our objectives.

Teaching the Cooperative and Democratic Way of Life

The democratic way is linked with the highest and noblest goals of education since it allows the maximum possible freedom for individual growth. Similarly, cooperation is the only way in which interests of the weaker sections can be secured. Our basic institutions are the cooperatives and the Panchayats and hence training in effective citizenship, which is one of the prime aims of education, require training for effective participation in running these institutions.

For this, perhaps the most effective way is to organize a school as a community on cooperative lines, governing itself under the guidance of teachers. This makes school life most interesting, especially if a school is residential and students themselves do various chores, with activities being handled educationally and scientifically. These activities introduced at pre-school and elementary stages will build among students basic attitudes, which are today absent. In higher classes, the principles and structures of cooperation and democracy which can be taught and demonstrated. Life in *Nayee Taleem* institutions was organized on cooperation and self-government as the bases.

Development of Personality Traits and Leadership Qualities

The personality traits, which need to be inculcated for development, are: initiative, resourcefulness, team spirit, management attitudes and capability, capacity for leadership and social commitment. These qualities can be best developed through cooperatively organized activities providing the foci for integration of knowledge and problem-solving. Responsibility given, challenges thrown up and met in the living in dynamic situations are likely to build and develop the requisite capacities. This was aimed at and achieved in *Nayee Taleem* institutions.

Such a method of education will also develop the desire and capacity for community organization, which is a basic necessity for any effective strategy for rural development.

Major Issues and the Content Imperatives

Rural development has the following major issues which need to be reflected on in a pointed and functional manner and sufficiently detailed out to provide guidance to local activities in the syllabus and the textbooks:

- Energy;
- Ecological balance;
- Population explosion and the problems of health;
- Technology transfer and up-gradation of skills; and
- Building community cohesion and the cooperative way of life.

Energy

Students may be given an idea of the global nature of energy crisis, national perspective and our own energy needs and resources. This should then be linked to local situation, where carefully designed programmes would need to be launched for developing alternative sources of energy. Recycling of human, animal and vegetable waste efficiently — with trench latrines or septic tanks, compost pits, utilization of kitchen water for kitchen gardening, *gobar* (cow dung) gas plants etc. — ought to become a neat, clean and efficient way of energy creation and utilization. It will have the additional advantage of keeping surroundings clean, which would be a great service, which educational institutions can render to our villages. Scientific processes involved in conversion of waste matter into energy and its utilization should be taught to students in a graded fashion so that the whole thing becomes an educational activity.

Similarly, solar energy, as an inexhaustible source of energy ought to be a subject of study in our educational institutions. Students should be taught how sun's energy is already operating day in and day out in their surroundings, facilitating their activities such on drying clothes, purifying and disinfecting surroundings, etc. Simple gadgets that have already been designed for harnessing sun's energy should be made available to institutions so that students operate them, learn the science behind them and begin to think of ways to improve them. In mountains and near coasts small wind mills ought to be a subject of study in institutions. These new sources of energy properly tapped ought to be put into use for up-gradation of technology available to rural people for productive purposes. Students can also be told about planets which go round the sun and get light from it.

Ecological Balance

Students ought to be taught — again in a graded fashion — the way nature keeps its balance to keep life sustaining elements — water and air-pure. Distortions that man's ever-increasing need for energy and living space creates through deforestation, pollution of water and air through industrial waste, nuclear waste, etc. ought to be explained to students. The existing wasteful practices in their own rural surroundings ought to be studied and linked up with the macro situation at the national and global levels. Concrete activities of planting trees and nurturing them ought to be an essential activity and should be linked to the beautification of the campus. Trees grown will also provide shade and places for rest and discussion. The science of plants, and the way they can be planted ought to become a subject of study. The planting and nurturing of trees should be organized with the help of forest authorities for whom this could be a useful extension activity.

Population Explosion

One of the most serious problems the world faces — especially, developing countries like India — is the population explosion. Population education becomes one of the most important tasks for the education system. As in case of other problems, population problem also has macro and micro dimensions; interaction of the two has to be made clear to students. On the face of it, however, a study of the two dimensions does not lead to the same conclusion; and there is no problem perhaps in which the micro dimension is so crucial.

There is a limit to the burden of population that local resources can carry. The question of sub-division of land into uneconomic holdings will also need to be examined. People will have to be educated with regard to nutritional standards and their present insufficiency as indicated by infant mortality, incidence of disease, death rate, etc. Studies of local area would be necessary to appreciate serious impact of unchecked population growth on size of land holdings, unemployment situation, standard of living, the overcrowding of living space, etc. Population education, therefore, will have the additional advantage of assisting area-planning. It would entail the building up of a data base required for the purpose, which is today lacking and which educational institutions can help to build.

After local base and justification for family planning has been established, it could be reinforced by macro study of the world situation — of its resources and needs. In many other cases, it would perhaps be otherwise. One would begin with a study of overall macro situation, which is then reinforced by a study of the local situation. The approach needed is, however, in keeping with educational methodology advocated here, in which we move from the immediate to the remote, from the familiar to the unfamiliar, from the near to the distant, and from the concrete to the abstract.

Transfer of Technology

In a poor country the most important task is that of increasing production and productivity. This can only be done by studying production processes and the science behind them and to identify processes to improve them. Educational institutions, therefore, must include, in their curriculum, production activities and make them centres of interest around which knowledge of disciplines can be woven to throw light on problems arising in production and productivity. There are difficulties of entrusting this task entirely to engineers and technologists: firstly, they would consider small occupations and crafts in which millions of people are engaged as too insignificant to justify their involvement in solving their problems; and secondly, when an engineer touches a small machine, it inevitably ends up by becoming more complicated and bigger, which makes it irrelevant to the village situation in which it has to be operated. As modern science of assessment of technology emphasizes, the value of technology can be judged only by its impact on total socio-economic situation. Where large, underprivileged masses are involved, technology cannot be allowed to have unfettered play and technological evolution becomes a more sensible strategy than a technological revolution. An education system, centreing on existing productive activities, is the best way to ensure this evolutionary process. Millions and millions of intelligent minds, continuously thinking on problems of small crafts and agriculture, will provide the most relevant and effective tools required for technological improvement.

Building of Community Cohesion

A strong community organization existed in India. It ensured survival of the village in the face of an ever changing and unstable political situation. Centuries of experience of the need for and advantage of interdependence led to strong village organizations, which have persisted till today. Modern forces, however have tended to destroy this cohesion. Easy transport has led to free flow of cheap machine-made goods and rendered economic interdependence of members of the village community impracticable. Political forces have tended to divide the village and led to new alignments, which have seriously disturbed existing relationships. The increasing pressure on land and the consequent movement of an increasing number of people migrating to urban areas in search of employment has also adversely affected the sense of a common destiny among the people living in a village. And yet new needs have arisen which make community cohesion indispensable. Dispersed as population is, it is practically impossible for the state to ensure social justice without involving local people and arousing their sense of responsibility.

Social services cannot be delivered effectively to individuals. They need a discriminating organization at the local level to ensure that utmost advantage accrues therefrom and the services reach the intended beneficiaries. Technology has entered the Indian villages — especially agriculture — in a big way. Technological services cannot reach individuals; they require an organization at the village level. Instances include pest control, post-harvesting technology which can be delivered by community organization. Another aspect of the same situation is that provisions like health and education cannot be organized and funded entirely by the government; the Constitutional commitment notwithstanding. A considerable amount of self-help is needed, which is only possible by an organized community. Organized community requires: appreciation of value of a cooperative way of life and attitudes, which would make such an organization of life feasible. The political developments in the country also require well-organized local communities. Decentralization of power without a cooperative organization and education only leads to exploitation of the weaker sections of society by local elites, who manage to build their links with the elites in urban areas and on upper rungs of the hierarchical ladder — economic, political and administrative. To provide training to future citizens for assuming responsibility, much of the institutional life should be organized on cooperative community lines. The building up of the school community, intimately interacting with and reinforcing community life around, has to be, therefore, an essential part of education.

Interaction between school and the rural community would ensure that information regarding various schemes initiated by the government for the uplift of latter reaches it so that it is able to take full advantage of these schemes. The National Employment Guarantee Act, 2005; Sampoorna Grameen Rozgar Yojna; Swarnajyanti Gram Swarojgar Yojana; Pradhan Mantri Gram Sadak Yojana are some of the schemes launched to alleviate the poverty of rural population, particularly those segments which are socially and economically disadvantaged Rural population must know about them and derive benefits from them.

Linking School Education to Rural Development

Pre-school Education

The earliest formal documentation of ECCE as an organized initiative in India dates back to the later half of the nineteenth century. The early pioneers of the ECCE movement included Gijubhai Badheka and Tarabai Modak, who among others, established under the influence of Madame Montessori, pre-school education centres in Gujarat. In 1946 Madame Montessori met Mahatma Gandhi, who asked her to 'indianize' her method to make preschool education available to a large majority of children. That was the beginning of 'pre basic' education in rural parts of the country, largely through voluntary effort. The first government initiative was the setting up of a Central Social Welfare board in 1953, which started a grant-in-aid scheme for voluntary agencies. Over the later part of half century, however, the concept of early childhood care and education, integrating health, nutrition and education had taken primacy. India has in this context, been able to put together a fairly supportive policy framework and has launched some major initiatives for children for this stage of development. Prominent among these are some centrally supported schemes such as the Reproductive Child Health Scheme, (RCH) of the Department of Health and Family Welfare, the Integrated Child Development Services (ICDS) of Department of Women and Child Development (DWCD) recently rechristened as Ministry of Women and Child Development (MWCD) and preschool education provisions in conjunction with some primary education programmes. As a result, there has been noticeable progress over the last fifty years in provision for children, be it the ICDS or the primary education service deliveries network across the country.

Early Childhood Care and Education (ECCE) found its due place in the policy framework in India way back in 1986 when an exclusive chapter of the National Policy on Education was devoted to it. ECCE was defined, in the Policy document, as an integrated and holistic concept of care and education of children between 0-6 years particularly for disadvantaged groups. This provision was seen as a foundation for life and a support service for girls and working mothers. ECCE was further conceptualized as early stimulation for children under 3 years and a more organized centre, based ECCE programme (preschool education) for 3-6 year olds. The policy emphasized the joyful nature of ECCE and stressed the need to discourage any formal instruction of 3R's at this stage of education. ECCE programmes for children have assumed various nomenclatures and definitions, depending on the priority a particular programme serves. There are ECE/preschool education programmes which are focused only on preschool education for 3-6 year olds (for example nurseries, kindergartens, preparatory schools, pre primary classes etc.). These do not have any health or nutrition component; they are often part of primary schools and generally in the non-governmental or private sector. The other category is of the more holistic programme of ECCE or Early Childhood Development (ECD) which address all round development of the child and adopts a life cycle approach, as in the ICDS, which targets in addition to the child, pregnant and lactating mothers and adolescent girls.

As a sequel to the adoption of the National Policy for Children, Government of India initiated the Integrated Child Development Services Scheme (ICDS), on pilot basis in 1975. In the last three decades, however, the scheme has emerged as a major national strategy, promoting a holistic strategy for early childhood development. Beginning with 33 Projects in 1975, ICDS has now expanded to 6113 sanctioned projects in all 35 States/Union Territories. Each Project covers a Block, which is the smallest administrative unit. Of these, 5635 are currently operational. They had 7,44,887 Anganwadi Centres as on 30th September 2005. Though the programme covers mainly rural and tribal population, it is also operational in urban areas through 523 ICDS projects, which cater to the population living in slums and underdeveloped areas. As stated elsewhere, the share of urban population in the country is approximately 27.78 per cent. Thus, only about 13 per cent of all ICDS projects are located in urban areas providing services to the urban poor.

In the Indian context, especially in rural areas and urban slums, the three main objectives of pre-school education are: ensuring health and sanitation, providing nutrition and initiating formation of healthy habits and attitudes in their simplest and most elementary form. As regards health, personal cleanliness of the child, in cooperation with his parents, is an important responsibility of the school. If the parents become sufficiently enlightened burden of the teacher is considerably reduced. The task becomes manageable. Moreover, when children are at home, clean habits formed at school can be reinforced by parents. There is thus a natural and close tie up between pre-school education and adult education. This tie up is today not sufficiently close and needs to be firmly established.

The Health Department can assist in training of teachers to provide them with knowledge of healthy habits required of children of that age group. Local health workers can also train teachers in health checkup and in identifying and treating simple ailments while referring more serious cases to the nearby Primary Health Care Centre and Rural Dispensary. Apart from participation in regular training courses, health workers need to visit schools frequently to give on-the-spot guidance and help to teachers.

Nutrition is an area where Departments and local social community workers can collaborate. The Departments of: Food and Agriculture, Health, Education and Science and Technology are the concerned departments. The Health Department can lay down nutritional standards for children of this age group (3-6). The Food and Agriculture Department, in conjunction with *Vigyan Mandirs* of the Department of Science and Technology can identify locally grown products that can be grown to meet nutritional standards. It should be the duty of social workers to collect these materials from the community at harvest time. A teacher should be a part of the collecting team. Social workers and willing parents can also assist in cooking of meals for children. Bringing in social workers and setting up of parent-teacher associations, where they don't exist, would be very helpful.

Formation of habits is another very important element of education at this stage: habits of orderly sitting and moving in groups, habit of going to bathroom, habit of storing one's play things in proper order, etc. This objective should be constantly kept in mind by a teacher and every opportunity must be used to develop these habits and reinforce them continuously. Stories are a powerful tool through which imagination of children can be stirred and satisfied. Story telling should be an important activity for education at this stage.

There is at present too much emphasis on learning alphabets and counting of numbers. It has been found that children who start reading and writing at a later stage are able to make more rapid progress and consequently there is hardly any difference between those who start their literacy and numeracy at the pre-school stage and those who start reading and writing at the primary stage training.

Sarva Shiksha Abhiyan (SSA) acknowledges the importance of ECCE, particularly as a programme to support girls' education. ECCE prefers children, of the ages of 6 years, for entry into primary schools. A controversy has arisen regarding the entry age for the ECCE – whether it should be 3½ years or 4 years. Anganwadis running under the ICDS (Integrated Child Development Services) have been in many cases linked to ECCE.

ECCE centres are being established in primary schools, their timings are synchronized with the timings of these schools. Resource persons are being trained for these centres and additional financial provisions are being made to promote the ECCE.

Elementary Education

The Constitution of India makes a commitment to provide free and compulsory education for all children up to the age of fourteen. The National Policy on Education (NPE) in 1986, and its revised version in 1992, detail the policy measures and broad interventions for providing basic education for all. The international developments in the 1990s for EFA [viz., the World Declaration on Education for All at Jomtien, 1990; and the Dakar Framework for Action, 2000] together with several positive developments within India brought the need for recognizing basic education as a fundamental right of every citizen. In 2002, with the 93rd Constitutional Amendment, 8 years of elementary schooling became the fundamental right of every child The Government of India also adopted the National Charter for Children (NCC) in 2003 and reiterated its commitment to provide free and compulsory education to all children of the age of six to fourteen years (Article 21.A). The NCC, 2003 also states: "It is a fundamental duty of a parent or guardian to provide opportunities for education to his child or ward between the age of six and fourteen years (Article 51A)".

Accordingly, the central government, in partnership with state governments, has initiated a number of programmes during the last one and half decades to achieve the EFA goals. Building on the lessons learnt from the implementation of these programmes, the Government of India launched, in the mission mode, the *Sarva Shiksha Abhiyan (SSA)* (i.e. the programme for universal elementary education) in the year 2000. In the SSA, effective management of teachers and resources at local level, particularly at the sub-district levels is recognized as extremely critical. Therefore, decentralization of planning and management of elementary education as a strategy has been given greater emphasis in the Tenth Plan.

From early 1990s, several programmes have been implemented to promote elementary education. The important large-scale basic education development programmes include: the District Primary Education Programme (DPEP); *Shiksha Karmi* Project (SKP); *Mahila Samakhya* (MS); Alternative and Innovative Education and Education Guarantee Scheme (AIE & EGS); Mid-day Meal Scheme (MDM); Teacher Education Programme (TEP); Integrated Child Development Services Scheme (ICDS); Uttar Pradesh Basic Education Programme (UPBEP); Bihar Education Project (BEP) and the *Lok Jumbish* (LJ); and the *Sarva Shiksha Abhiyan* (SSA). The SSA is an "umbrella programme" which subsumes all on-going projects, programmes and schemes.

In the Tenth Plan (2002-07), elementary education has been given the highest priority within the education sector. The SSA forms the major Education for All (EFA) programme in the Plan. Decentralization of planning, supervision and management of education through local bodies at the district, block and village levels is one of the major strategies in the Tenth Plan to achieve the goal of EFA. Besides, as part of a follow-up, a National Plan of Action for EFA (NPAEFA) was developed in 2003, which further details out the strategies and interventions for achieving the goals of EFA.

Education for All (EFA) is being implemented by India and several other countries. The following goals were adopted for the programme in 2000 AD at an international meeting of 164 countries.

- Expanding and improving early childhood care especially for vulnerable sections of society.
- By 2015, all girls should have access to free and compulsory education of good quality.
- All young people and adults to be provided opportunities for learning and getting training in life-skills.
- Achieving 50 per cent improvement in adult literacy, especially for women, by 2015.
- Eliminating gender disparities in education.
- Improving all aspects of quality education.

The progress of this programme is reviewed annually by UNESCO. Education Ministers and Heads of States participate in the review meetings.

The SSA, an umbrella programme for universal elementary education, aims at providing useful and quality elementary education for all children of the 6-14 age group by 2010. Through the SSA, the country, for the first time, is attempting to translate its commitments into a programme of UEE, which provides for greater democratic participation and community involvement; decentralized planning and management with a specific focus on local requirements and the needs of the disadvantaged regions, social groups, girls and children in difficult circumstances. The programme calls for community ownership of schools and interventions through effective decentralization. This is facilitated by involvement of women's groups, Village Education Committee (VEC) members and the members of *Panchayati Raj* Institutions.

The SSA covers the entire country and addresses the needs of nearly 192 million children in 1.1 million habitations. The specific objectives of the SSA include: (i) all children to be in school, EGS Centre/alternate school/back-to-school camp by 2003; (ii) all children complete five years of primary schooling by 2007; (iii) all children complete eight years of schooling by 2010; (iv) providing elementary education of satisfactory quality with emphasis on education for life; (v) bridging all gender and social gaps at primary stage by 2007, and at elementary education level by 2010; and (vi) universal retention by 2010.

In the post-independence period, the primary and upper primary schooling facilities have been expanded to cover small and un-served habitations in remote rural areas. Since 1950-51, the number of primary and upper primary schools have increased substantially, more than doubling the number of primary schools by 2001-02, and the number of upper primary schools increasing more than fifteen times over the same period. The percentage of habitations and rural population served by primary and upper primary schools/sections within a distance of 1 and 3 km respectively has also been increasing. Eighty-eight per cent of habitations in 2002 had a primary school/section within or at a walking distance of 1 km, and 78% had an upper primary school facility within or at a walking distance of 3 km.[4] The ratio of upper primary schools to primary schools has improved to 1: 2.7 in 2002.

In addition, there are a large number of Alternative and Innovative Education (AIE) centres, Education Guarantee Scheme (EGS) centres and unrecognized schools which impart both primary as well as upper primary education, the former for children who, because of their circumstances, cannot enter full time schooling. Under the EGS/AIE, 6.64 million children have been covered as on March 2004 (MHRD, Annual Report 2003-04). Under the SSA, arrangements have been made to open 80,000 new schools, appoint 0.45 million teachers during the last two years. Under the programme, physical infrastructure has been improved through the provision of more than 1,00,000 additional classrooms, around 60,000 school buildings, 1,00,000 toilets, and drinking water facilities in 75,000 schools. In spite of the substantial expansion of elementary education, disparities among and within states prevail. There are also gender and social disparities in access to elementary education. Even after this expansion of elementary education facilities, some rural habitations do not have schooling facilities. Most of these unserved habitations are sparsely populated.

Enrolment at primary level (grades I-V) was 122.13 million[5] (964.94 million boys and 57.19 million girls) in 2002-03. At the upper primary level (grades VI-VIII), enrolment was 46.94 million (26.3 million boys and 20.61 million girls) in 2002-03. At the primary and upper primary levels, enrolment has increased at an average annual rate of 3.56% and 4.74% respectively between 2000-01 and 2002-03. During the same period, enrolment at the elementary level has increased at an average annual rate of 3.91%.

The high dropout rates at the primary and upper primary levels continue to plague the system. However, in recent years, the dropout rates seem to be decreasing steadily. The dropout rate at primary level has decreased from 40.07% (39.7% for boys and 41.9% for girls) in 2001-02 to 35.06% (36.0% for boys and 33.32% for girls) in 2002-03[6]. At the upper primary level, the dropout rate has marginally decreased to 52.79% (52.28% for boys and 53.45% for girls) in 2002-03 from 53.7% (50.3% for boys and 57.7% for girls) in 2001-02. In spite of the policy of no detention up to Grade V, a large number of children continue to repeat grades; gender differential in their repetition rate is almost negligible. Specific measures to reduce gender gap include:

- Under the SSA residential 'bridge course' (of classes 1-7 levels) was organized for girls of 10-14 years of age in

Lucknow (UP), an idea of a 'school on boat' was floated in East Godawri district (AP) for the children (5-15 years' age) for fishermen living in different areas. Spatial data was collected with the help of Geographic Information Technologies (GIS) for proper positioning of schools in habitation without schools.

- Numerous minorities – concentrated areas have been identified in different states, and EGS (Education Guarantee Scheme) centre have been opened.
- This flagship programme of SSA, made several provisions for girls' education. Some of these are supply of free text-books, increasing the number of women teachers, setting up of alternative facility for education with EGS, community mobilization for increasing involvement of girls and retaining them in schools, holding special camps for supply of teaching-learning equipment.
- As in the case of girls' education, there have been specific interventions to expand the network of institutions for SC's and ST's.
- The programme, of Inclusive Education (IE) is an important element of the SSA. This programmes caters to the requirements of special needs children. There is an additional financial provision per child for all children of this category. Several states have undertaken innovative programmes to enable children with Special Needs (CWSN) to prepare them for regular schools. Teacher-training projects have been implemented to orient teachers to IE.
- Computer Aided Learning (CAL) is a significant part of the SSA. Under this scheme schools are equipped with computers; software centered is developed and teachers are trained.

Elementary school is in some respects the most important educational institution. The whole nation is exposed to the influence of the elementary school. The opportunity is now available for inculcating certain basic values, attitudes and habits in every child in a controlled environment at the most impressionable period of the child's life. When properly organized, a primary school should be able to make the first serious attempt to introduce equality of opportunity.

The main objectives of elementary education — apart from introducing the pupils to basic literacy and numeracy — should be to broaden and strengthen the habits, sought to be formed at the pre-school stage. Elementary school occupies a strategic position in local community and, therefore, can be an important instrument of socio-economic extension. A teacher is even today the most educated person in a village and still commands considerable influence with the local community. There is no agency other than the school, which can reach every family in the village. The objectives of the school — according to the needs of the times, discussed earlier – require that the subjects in school relate to the problems of the village. Hence the contact between the school and the village community can be very intimate. The following paragraphs indicate the possible linkages, which can be forged between the school and the other departments.

Health

Education and health are perhaps the most natural allies. The development of the body is an important educational objective. The Health Department cannot discharge its responsibilities unless nine-tenths of its work is taken care of by the people themselves, leaving only one-tenth to be performed by health experts through a referral system. People can be taught to do that through education.

School curriculum should, therefore, contain a general understanding of the body and how it functions, rules of health and such effective systems of exercises as yoga, etc. A student must be given an idea of a balanced diet and how it could be prepared by using local materials that were being grown or could be grown in the village. Common diseases and their home remedies also ought to be a subject of study. Training in first aid and elementary nursing should be provided to every child. A teacher should be trained to conduct health check of pupils and refer cases where required to Primary Health Centre. Students can play an important part in not only keeping themselves healthy but also help in cleaning of wells, streets and drains with help of villagers, teaching them the advantage of cleanliness. They can also act as alert and well informed citizens and work as the interpreters of the doctor's instructions at their homes. The Health Department can help by supplying materials like potassium permanganate for cleaning wells and by training of teachers. The material put out by awareness of the education of the people could also be useful for inclusion in school textbooks.

In order to improve the nutritional status of students of primary stage, and more so in drought-affected areas, mid-day meal scheme (MDM) was launched in August 1995. The scheme envisages a provision of a cooked mid-day meal with minimum of 300 calories and 8-12 grammes of protein for all children in classes I-V. The scheme covers 12 crore children in government, local body and government-aided schools. The programme is implemented in a decentralized manner. Local agencies such as village panchayats, village education committees, school managing committees, parent-teacher associations etc. are involved in planning and monitoring the scheme. Women cooks are engaged for cooking of meals. Though it is the world's largest-programme, the country has yet to achieve complete nation-wide coverage.

Agriculture

A large number of children, particularly in rural areas, do not continue beyond Class VIII, and most of them enter life either as farmers/farm labour or as rural artisans — the majority, of course, engaging in agriculture. They must be given knowledge of modern practices of agriculture before they leave school. They should also be made conscious of fast depleting environmental resources as well as of method to stop this depletion and make up for the damage already done. This can be done either on school farm wherever available or on the farm of a progressive farmer. The knowledge of agriculture, however, must be given in the local context, which alone would be relevant to them. This should create in the students' sufficient curiosity about improvements in agriculture, elementary knowledge of new agricultural practices and receptivity to new ideas. When they enter life, they will be the most promising foci on which agricultural extension agents could concentrate and from whom they could get maximum cooperation. The knowledge would, of course, be what can be given to children of that age and within the constraints of the time available.

Knowledge of subsidiary crafts should also be given so that pupils can later deal with underemployment in agriculture sector. Each pupil should be given sufficient skill at least in one craft, to enable him to earn his livelihood. Agriculture Department and the Department of Rural Industries can assist by training teachers, supplying inputs to the school farm and workshop and providing material, which could be used for textbook purposes.

Although there is some difference of opinion about when training in skills should be imparted – given the fact that large number of children discontinue education or will do so for many more years to come – specific skill training needs to the given at elementary stage. Children dropping out of the system can, with appropriate knowledge and skills, bring about improvements in farming practices of the families that are engaged in and introduce in the community production activities which are not usually engaged in, such as pisci-culture, bee and poultry farming, preservation and marketing of perishable farm produce etc.

Another important objective should be to-upgrade productivity of existing occupations. Intelligent use of improved seeds and fertilizers in farming, use of improved dyes and designs in village crafts are illustrations of the measures that can affect productivity of occupations. Management of water resources, including rain water harvesting should be an important area for imparting knowledge and skills.

The third important area which requires inputs of knowledge and skills in rural areas, particularly in the case of school dropouts and school leavers is the organization and delivery of services. As economic capacity of rural households increases, there will be increasing demand for services of different kind – child and family welfare, health and sanitation, early childcare and education, credit marketing facilities, governance of community affairs, maintenance and repair of equipment and appliances etc. These services are at present being provided by under qualified and untrained personnel.

Cooperation

A base can be prepared for the programmes of Cooperative Department by introducing cooperative activities in schools, so that the cooperative attitudes and habits are formed and an appreciation promoted for cooperative living. An elementary knowledge of cooperative structures should also be given. In these tasks, the Registrar of Cooperatives and his local level representatives could help.

Education and Employment

The school, as already discussed, can be a powerful agent of extending the message of developmental. Teachers and senior students can help in non-formal education. Education can make a four-fold contribution to the improvement of employment and reduction in the incidence of underemployment in rural areas. It can promote skills, which could enable students to enter a vocation, in regard to which sufficient skill should be developed during the elementary stage. It can teach subsidiary industries to farmers to enable them to supplement their income from agriculture. It can start the process of building up managerial capability — both attitudes and skills — so important in preparing people for self-employment and for increasing the productivity in every venture. It can develop finger skills, which could form the basis for more complicated technical skills to be learnt later on. Elementary schools can also be effectively linked with other sectors of development to mutual advantage.

Secondary Education

Secondary education has remained a weak link in the education chain. Its importance, although recognized for the preparation of middle level manpower, for teacher preparation for elementary schools and of entrants to higher stages of education, secondary education has not led to meaningful action in defining its objectives and reforming of its structures and practices. The restructuring of the secondary stage by the Secondary Education Commission, 1953 was given up without allowing it to take roots. The 1966 recommendations of the Education Commission – 10+2 pattern and vocationalization of education – took almost two decades for being initiated. Their implementation has remained haphazard. The large majority of government schools remain ill equipped and the benefits of government interventions – establishing and equipping of laboratories, smart schools etc. – have gone largely to well endowed schools. Curriculum, teaching practices and evaluation systems remain geared to the requirements of university stage. Meanwhile, two types of secondary schools have been allowed to exist; those patronized by the affluent and upwardly mobile segments and those which draw their clientele from the less affluent segments. That the disparity that this dual system leads to – in terms of opportunities for gainful employment and economic and social mobility is not fully recognized; nor are the implications for social cohesion and political stability.

The POA 1992 recognized the increased demand for secondary education and backed the NPE 1986 by calling for *a planned expansion of secondary education facilities* all over the country. It emphasized the need for higher participation of girls, SCs/STs; transformation and reorganization of boards of secondary education and vesting them with autonomy so that they have the capacity to improve the quality of secondary education and equipping secondary level institutions with computers so that children develop necessary computer skills to be effective in ongoing developments in technological world.

The secondary and higher secondary education in India has been consistently expanding since independence. Data from the Sixth All India Educational Survey of the National Council for Educational Research and Training (NCERT), New Delhi and the Ministry of HRD, Government of India show that expansion of this level of education is higher in rural areas than in urban areas. In 1950-51, total number of secondary/higher secondary schools in the country was 7,416, out of which 38.79 per cent in rural areas. In 2003-04, the number of institutions at secondary/ higher secondary education (i.e. high/higher secondary schools, and pre-degree/junior colleges) increased to 1,45,962, an increase of more than 17 times the number of institutions in 1950-51. The average annual growth rate of these institutions during 1950-51 to 2003-04 was 5.8 per cent. In 1950-51, the ratio of upper primary to secondary/higher secondary schools was 1.83, which marginally improved to 1.79 in 2003-04. The improvement in the ratio indicates more schooling facilities at secondary level of education. However, it may be kept in mind that, the number of secondary/higher secondary schools in the base year (1950-51) was too small compared to that of the upper primary schools.

In 1950-51, total enrolment at secondary/higher secondary stage was 1.5 million, out of which 13.9 per cent (0.21 million) were girls. In 2003-04, total enrolment at this level of education increased to 35 million, out of which 14.4 million (41.1 per cent) were girls. Total enrolment of boys and girls increased by 16 and 72 times respectively during 1950-51 and 2003-04. The enrolment at secondary stage of education has increased at an average annual growth rate of 6.0 per cent during the period 1950-51 and 2000-01. Growth of girls' enrolment at this stage of education is relatively much faster (8.28 per cent) during this period mainly because of the lower base. During the 1950s and 1960s, boys' enrolment at secondary/higher secondary level increased at faster rate compared to that of the girls. However, in the 1980s and 1990s, growth rate of girls' enrolment was much higher compared to that of the boys. This indicates improvements in the participation rate of girls in secondary education, and also in the gender parity index. Even after so much progress in secondary education in India, gender and social disparity in participation rates continue to be a major concern.

In 1960-61, the Gross Enrolment Ratio (GER) at secondary/higher secondary level was only 10.6 per cent, which increased to 30 per cent in 1993-94, the latest year for which data are available. According to 52nd Round (NSSO, 1998), the Gross Attendance Ratio at secondary (Grades IX-X) and higher secondary (Grades XI-XII) levels was 51 per cent and 32 per cent, respectively. The Net Attendance Rate was much lower being 26 per cent and 15 per cent respectively in classes IX-X and XI-XII.

The number of teachers in secondary/higher secondary schools has increased from 0.13 million in 1950-51 to 2.02 million in 2003-04. The share of female teachers which was 15.74 per cent in 1950-51 has increased to 32.77 per cent in 2003-04. Between 1950-51 and 2003-04, the increase in total number of teachers in secondary/higher secondary schools was around 16 times, and it was around 12 times for males and about 39 times for females. The average annual growth rate of teachers at secondary/higher secondary level of education was 5.4 per cent (4.7 per cent for males and 7.1 for females). The teacher-pupil ratio at this stage was 1:21 in 1950-51, which increased to 33:1 in 2003-04. The number of female teachers per hundred male teachers has increased from 19 to 62 during to 2003-04.

The Central Government's intervention in secondary education is at two levels; (i) through apex national level bodies like National Council of Educational Research and Training (NCERT), Central Board of Secondary Education (CBSE), National Institute of Open Schooling (NIOS), Navodaya Vidyalaya Samiti (NVS), Kendriya Vidyalaya Sangthan (KVS), and Central Tibetan School Administration (CTSA); and (ii) through Centrally Sponsored Schemes such as (a) Boarding and Hostel Facilities to Girl Students of Secondary and Higher Secondary Schools, (b) Integrated Education for Disabled Children, (c) Information and Communication Technology in Schools, and (d) Quality Improvement in Schools.

Over the years, several interventions have been made by the Central Government for development of secondary education, particularly in rural and backward areas. The main intervention was for increasing access to secondary education ('Access with Equity' scheme) which has two components; (a) strengthening of boarding and hostel facilities for girls; and (b) setting up of schools in educationally backward blocks through provision of a one-time Central grant to state governments, NGOs and registered societies.

The Government of India sanctions a grant on a cent per cent basis to NGOs to run hostels for 100 girls per hostel. A recurring grant of Rs.10,000/- per annum per girl boarder and non-recurring grant per girl boarder @ Rs.3,000/-is provided to the registered societies and NGOs running boarding and hostel facilities for girls pursuing education at Secondary and Senior Secondary stages in rural, desert and hilly areas, particularly those predominantly habited by scheduled castes, scheduled tribes and educationally backward minorities. The scheme is NGO driven and about 100 NGOs/Societies are presently being assisted under the scheme.

The IEDC Scheme, launched in 1974 was revised in 1992 in the light of the provisions of the National Policy on Education, 1986 and the Programme of Action, 1992. The present scheme intends to provide educational opportunities for the disabled children in common schools setting, to facilitate their retention in school and to integrate the places in special schools once they acquire communication and daily living skills at a functional level. The scheme is being implemented through the Education Departments of State Governments and UT Administrations as well as through non-governmental organizations. 100%

assistance is being provided under various components for education of children suffering from mild to moderate disabilities in common schools. The present scheme is largely NGO driven. Over 250 NGOs were implementing the scheme during 2005-06.

The scheme of Information Computer Technology (ICT) in schools is intended to establish an enabling environment to promote usage of ICT, especially in higher secondary and secondary government schools in rural areas. Critical factors of such an enabling environment include: widespread availability of access devices, connectivity to Internet and promotion of ICT literacy, to ensure availability of quality content on-line and access devices (in the private sector and by SIETs), enrichment of existing curriculum and pedagogy by employing ICT tools for teaching and learning, enable students to acquire skills needed for the Digital world for higher studies and gainful employment, provide an effective learning environment for children through ICT tools, promote critical thinking and analytical skills by developing self-learning (for transforming the classroom environment from teacher-centric to student-centric learning), and promote the use of ICT tools in distance education including the employment of audio-visual medium and satellite-based devices. The scheme has four major components: partnership with the State Governments and Union Territories Administrations for providing computer-aided education to secondary and senior secondary government and government aided Schools, establishment of SMART schools, which shall be Technology Demonstrators; universalisation of Computer Literacy through the network of KVS and NVS to neighbouring schools; and activities of the SIETs.

The Centrally Sponsored Scheme of Quality Improvement Inputs is an amalgamation of the Ninth Plan schemes of Improvement in Science Education, Mathematics Olympiads, Environment Orientation, Promotion of Yoga and Population Education and has a new component of Educational Libraries. Under the scheme, state governments and registered societies are given grants for specified activities under each of the erstwhile programmes.

Adolescence Education Programme (AEP), as a centrally sponsored scheme, is being implemented as a key intervention for empowering adolescents to deal with risky situations, preventing new HIV infections, reducing vulnerability to infection and influencing positive behaviour development. The AEP covers: (a) all secondary and senior secondary schools, rural, urban and transitional areas across the country; (b) all students of secondary and senior secondary stages in government, local body and government-aided schools; (c) learners in educational guarantee schemes, alternative innovative schemes, across the country; and (d) all out of school children and adolescents being catered to by the adult literacy programmes; and students of open schooling/open university systems. Two main components of the scheme are: (a) life skills focusing on co-curricular activities in schools and (b) curricular integration in school curriculum, curricula and study materials for out of schools target audiences and teacher education courses and materials. Almost all institutions engaged in school education, teacher education, and adult literacy programmes, and innovative education schemes at national, state and district levels are involved in the implementation of this programme.

There is a need to reform secondary education in order to make it relevant. The secondary stage, comprising lower secondary (classes IX and X) and the higher/senior secondary (classes XI and XII) levels, should be located under a common roof as far as possible and their objectives should be made explicit. Lower secondary stage should further the process of general education. The medium of education should still be the local environment, but it should be seen in a progressively wider perspective and in relationship with the outside world. The correlated knowledge and science behind the environmental phenomena and processes will be deeper and more sophisticated. Similarly, productive craft, including agriculture, should be studied more as a vocation — comprehending its productive, marketing and organizational aspects. This would reduce mismatch between demand and supply. Technical, economic and social aspects should be studied in much greater depth than hitherto. While the aim of the productive activity will still be to promote skills and attitudes, sufficient competence should be developed by the end of class X to enable a child to take a vocation and make a good start. For example, a student will no longer confine himself/herself to the simple craft of spinning or weaving but also include in his/her study the art of designing, dyeing and printing and will learn all the problems involved in buying of raw materials and marketing of finished goods, credits and other assistance available from financial institutions and cooperative organizations through which the government mostly channels loans and other assistance. Similarly, in regard to agriculture, all modern agricultural practices and science behind them ought to be taught at the secondary stage. A student should learn the economics of all the commercial operations in which a farmer is engaged. The problems of storage, marketing, credit, etc. will also be part of the course.

The National Open School system operating under the autonomous organization National Institute of Open Schooling (NIOS) since 1989, is the largest open schooling system. The system operates in India and abroad. It works under the overall supervision of the Ministry of HRD of the Government of India. It reaches those who are unreached by normal schooling system and also physically, mentally and visually challenged children.

Open Basic Education Programme (OBE) as part of NIOS, is being implemented in three parts: upto class III, class V and Class VIII through Zila Saksharta Samiti, State Open Schools and other agencies with participation of the community.

The curriculum of secondary and senior secondary stages has been prepared keeping in view the National Curriculum Framework. Self instructional material has also been prepared in different languages. The NIOS takes care of the differently abled adolescents under the project 'Adolescent Education Open Schooling System'.

NIOS offers a variety of vocational education courses in agriculture, technology, health, business and commerce, home science, computer science, teacher training etc. Short-term six months education courses are also developed to cater to the needs of rural youth. The duration of courses varies from six months to two years and their number is more than one hundred. Steps are being taken for collaboration between industry and NIOS.

Given this approach, two distinct features of the secondary school will emerge:

- As different students will choose different crafts, a school will become the hub of economic activities and cater to various technical, economic and organizational problems of its catchments area. If extension agencies concentrate their effort on it, a school can become the most effective extension and demonstration centre for the area. Students and the teachers can be the voluntary agents of the extension agencies. The liaison between school and extension agencies will become considerably closer and more meaningful if, space permitting, their local offices is also located on the school campus.

- Further, while the productive activities will occupy a central place and provide the most important centre of interest, other activities reflecting the health and social problems of rural community will not be neglected.

As the "catchment area" of a high school has to be much wider than a village or a group of nearby villages, such a school can best be run as a residential school, particularly in remote and difficult rural areas. If the school is run on principles of self-help and self-reliance, and local life style in regard to buildings, etc. is followed, the cost need not be very high – especially when measured in terms of the social returns to secondary schooling.

The higher/senior secondary stage, while continuing general activities as a part of routine, should concentrate on preparing pupils for vocations, selected after a careful survey of the labour market, with particular focus on available and emerging employment opportunities in the rural economy. All aspects of a vocation — technical, commercial and organizational — need to be taught in depth and in conjunction with requirement of the labour market, as far as possible. The Self-employment aspect must, however, be kept in view. Various personality traits developed during the earlier stages will come in handy. The knowledge of the government schemes to promote self-employment would be of immense help, which need to be imparted at this stage of schooling. Such an approach, however, implies considerable infrastructure requirements to create an enabling environment of schooling at the higher secondary stage. The advantage of locating high school and higher secondary school on the same campus will be that both can share the facilities provided.

The crucial recommendation of the 'Education Commission' 1966 viz. vocationalization of education, particularly at the plus 2 stage has not been implemented with the vigour that it required; nor were the resources needed for introduction of employment related vocational courses – financial and of expertise fully provided. Like the multipurpose schools doubts have been expressed on the utility and desirability of "terminal" vocational courses. It would seem that implementation has been affected by the perceptions of these who seek for their wards, entry into institutions of higher learning.

The addition of a year to secondary stage – from three to four years – has not necessarily led to its development as an independent identity, with distinct objectives and serving the interests of a clientele with diverse purposes. The stage remains largely university preparatory – that is why its objectives are determined largely by what universities and other institutions of higher learning expect of its entrants.

Rural secondary schools seem particularly at a disadvantage. Poor infrastructure, inadequate financial resources do not allow them even to fulfill the objective of preparing students for entry into higher education. The quality of instruction in rural schools and of attainment level of students remain low. At the same time, perception of rewards, that general education seems to ensure "compels" students and parents to stick to education which is irrelevant to rural needs; lack of clarity and of resources do not allow rural secondary education to aim at enhancing productivity of occupations and or diversification of rural economy.

Secondary school — including both lower and higher secondary classes — will need to and should be able to perform the following extension functions:

- Continuing education to those who have entered life after some education, especially after class VII as farmers, artisans, etc. through correspondence courses in conjunction with a centralized agency. Short-term contact programme can be organized for each group, so that their vocational problems can be taken up at their convenience. The extension functions of the schools must be performed in close cooperation with the extension agencies. The occupational improvement extension service should include the organizational and commercial aspects besides the technical.

- Field visits by staff to up-grade skills, solve problems on the spot, and themselves learn at first hand the problems of the field. Those problems that they cannot solve themselves, they can pass on to the appropriate laboratories and agencies between whom and the field workers (villagers) they can act as intermediaries. Thereby, they will also up-grade their own knowledge and technical competence, which will make them more effective teachers.
- The school can also act as a cultural centre, using the local cultural agencies for purposes of education and social reform as well as for entertainment.
- Teachers and senior students can also be trained in local surveys and village planning.

Budget 2007-08 of the Ministry of Finance and the Ministry of Human Resource Development break several new grounds. The education cess is to be increased from 2 per cent to 3 per cent. This would mobilize more resources for the SSA as well as for other educational programmes. School education budget has been hiked by about 35%. In order to help post class-VIII dropouts, the government has announced 10,000 merit-cum-means scholarships every year for students of class IX to XII.

More than 1000 Kendriya Vidyalayas (KVs) are proposed to be opened during the 11th five year plan (2007-2012).. Some of these vidyalayas will be set up in minority dominated areas having less than 1 per cent female literacy.

Some other programmes introduced for achieving better coverage as well as quantitative and qualitative improvement include:

- District Primary Education Programme: this programme has three objectives – reduce drop-out rate to less than 10%, bring down disparity between gender and social groups to less than 5% and improve the level of learning achievement. To achieve these targets village committee have been set up to supervise the pilot projects. Other steps include organizing mobile libraries, book festivals, workshop for developing supplementary material;

improving evaluation tools and arranging remedial teaching for slow-learners.

- Strengthening of teacher education: State governments are required to make plans to ensure maximum and best operationalisation of the primary and secondary schools run by them. These plans are to be coordinated at the national levels with the support of the National Council for Teacher Education (NCTE), National Institute of Educational Planning and Administration (NIEPA) now as a National University of Educational Planning and Administration (Deemed to be University), National Council for Educational Research and Training (NCERT), universities etc.

National Council for Teacher Education (NCTE) was set-up in 1995 in order to ensure planned and coordinated development of teacher-education throughout the country and for regulation of and maintenance of proper standards for teacher-education NCTE is responsible for reogranising teacher-education institutions, laying norms for teachers – education courses, encouraging innovations, defining qualification for appointment of teachers and laying down measures to check commercialization of teacher-education. NCTE functions through its regional committees (RCs).

National Bal Bhavan (NBB) is an autonomous institution fully funded by the Department of Elementary Education and Literacy. It was established in 1956 at the initiative of the then Prime Minister Jawahar Lal Nehru, with the objective of enhancing education in the age group 5-16. It has various activities in its vast campas in the spheres of physical education, creative arts, science education, literacy activities, performing arts, photography, home management, publication, museum techniques etc. The emphasis is on talent-exploration and giving them opportunity to express themselves.

There are 73 Bal Bhavans in states, which are affiliated to the National Bal Bhavan. National Bal Bhavan organizes activities at the local, state, national and international levels to provide learning experience to children. Training of teachers at the National Training Resource Centre (NTRC), with the aim of promoting all round development of children, is a unique programme of the Bhawan. The Bhavan has implemented a

National Bal Shree Award Scheme under which exceptionally creative children participate in the Bal Shree Camp. The participants are given awards for their exceptional achievements in various fields.

REFERENCES

1. FAO and IIEP (2005), *Education for Rural People to Achieve EFA and the MDGs*, UNESCO, Paris.
2. The proportion of overall population below the poverty line is more likely to be of the order of 30 per cent than the officially claimed 26.1 per cent in 1999–2000. Even the official statistics indicate that two out of three children are moderately or severely malnourished. Saxena, N.C. and Farrington John, 2003), *Trends and Prospects of Poverty Reduction in Rural India: Context and Options*, Working Paper 198, Overseas Development Institute, London.
3. Community Learning Centre (CLC) is found to be important source of education in rural areas. The integrated approach of CLC activities is a crucial aspect of their relevance to rural people. Learning subjects offered through CLCs may include: basic education and literacy; agriculture and other skills for income generation; re-skilling to adjust to changed economic needs; environmental education; population and gender issues, health; peace and civic rights; culture; and science and technology. Gasperini, Lavinia and Atchoarena, David (2005), *Education for Rural People to Achieve EFA and MDGs*, paper jointly prepared by FAO, Rome and IIEP, Paris.
4. Seventh All India Educational Survey, 2002 excludes Assam, Bihar, Orissa and Nagaland, as data have not been received from these states.
5. Provisional, Abstract of Selected Educational Statistics 2002-03, MHRD, GOI.
6. Provisional. Selected Educational Statistics, various years, MHRD, GOI.

Chapter 4
Higher Education

University Education

Access to higher education in India continues to be very low, more so for the socio-economically disadvantaged sections of the population. Unfortunately, country has no comprehensive data-base to help assess the response of higher education to the impact of globalization during the last one-and-a-half decades. The degree – awarding institutions of higher learning in India may be grouped into six broad categories: Central Universities, State Universities, Deemed to be Universities, Private Universities, Institutions of National Importance, and Institutions established under Acts of State Legislatures as on March 31, 2006 India had 20 Central Universities, 217 State Universities, 102 Deemed to be Universities, 10 Private Universities, 13 Institutions of National Importance and 5 Institutions established under the State Legislative Acts (UGC, 2006). It is evident from available data that within a span of four years since March 2002, the number of Central Universities has increased by 11%, State Universities by 22% and the Deemed to be universities by 96%. Further, for the first time 10 Private Universities have come into being during this period.

After independence, the number of colleges and universities has registered a significant increase. Between 1950-51 and 2004-05, while the number of universities increased from 28 to 348, the number of colleges went up from 578 to 17,625. During this period, enrolment in higher education institutions registered a steep hike starting from around 0.174 million to 10.48 million. The number of teachers manning the system went up from about 24,000 in 1950-51 to 472,000 in 2004-05. It is evident from this data that, during this period, universities and colleges grew on an average annual growth rate of 4.94% and 6.66% respectively. The decadal growth in the number of universities and institutions was much higher between 1950s and 1960s, primarily because of the relatively very small number of such institutions which existed at the beginning of the planned expansion of higher education after independence. During 1970s and 1980s, the growth of institutions of higher learning was relatively slow; it picked up from 1990 onwards. This has happened because of the increased demand for higher education and participation of the private sector, particularly in technical and professional education.

The rapid expansion, however, hides the stark inequality in access to higher education across states and union territories. In 2003-04 while higher education institutions were nearly absent in Dadra and Nagar Haveli and Lakshadweep; 14 states and UTs had much higher level of access to higher education compared to the national average (12.17) in terms of the number of institutions available per lakh of population in the age group of 18-23. While Pondicherry had around 27 higher education institutions per lakh population of the age group 18-23, West Bengal had the lowest level of access, with only around 5 such institutions per lakh of population. The number of higher education institutions available for one lakh population (18-23 age group) was around 7 or less in 5 states and union territories namely, West Bengal, Tripura, Jharkhand, Daman & Diu and Uttar Pradesh; and ranged between 8 and 9 in 4 states and UTs, i.e. Uttarakhand,, Andaman & Nicobar Islands, Sikkim and Delhi. There were about 19 states where the number of institutions of higher learning per lakh of population ranged between 10 to 19. There were four states and one union territory, namely Manipur, Karnataka, Goa, Mizoram and Pondicherry wherein the number of institutions available per lakh of population (18-23 age group) varied from 22 to 27.

Access to engineering and technical colleges is relatively very high in Andhra Pradesh (2.59 institutions per lakh of population in the age group 18-23) followed by Goa (2.34), Karnataka (1.86), Kerala (1.81), Chandigarh (1.59), Maharashtra (1.56), Sikkim (1.41) and Tamil Nadu (1.27).[1] These states and union territories also have high concentration of medical colleges per lakh of population. It would be pertinent to point out that such an indicator, i.e. the number of higher education institutions per lakh of population in the age group 18-23, is a crude one which does not reflect the level of access to higher and professional education, which is largely determined by household demand and capacity to pay as also the learning ability of individual students. This indicator, however, provides a fair understanding of the spatial distribution and availability of opportunities for higher education in the country.

In India, about 742 million (72.2%) live in rural areas (Census of India 2001). More than 58% of country's population depends on agriculture, a sector producing only 22% of GDP. In the rural areas nearly 51% of the people live below the poverty line; yet the rural areas contribute, through agriculture and allied activities 39.5 percent of the national income. The rural population has far less access to higher education. It would seem a fact that in spite of university fees in India being among the lowest in the world, the highly subsidized education, is availed of largely by the middle and upper classes of society. The prime social responsibility of university community towards the development of the rural areas is so clear that any denial of it by profession or action would seem to be gross injustice and would constitute the most vulnerable point in our social and political system.

The university faculty, except a microscopic minority, and authorities, have little time and less interest in things outside their assigned tasks. Some think that involvement of universities in rural development would be wasteful, using high-level inputs for low-level outputs. People outside universities are doubtful about the capacity of the universities, as they are constituted today, to do anything worthwhile in rural areas. Perceptions of what universities should engage in remain largely unaltered.

Yet it would be tragic if seats of higher learning, which train our leaders for top and middle levels in almost all walks of life, were allowed to continue to remain ignorant of and indifferent to the problems of over 72% of the population, whose hard labour heavily subsidises their sustenance. They are ignorant, having been denied even the opportunity of understanding rural people, which physical proximity provides; universities are all bottled up in urban areas. The present state of affairs has led to gap between the elite and the masses, which is at the root of many of our troubles, not only in India but in other developing countries as well. Universities, indifferent to character building and cut off from the rhythm of national life and its moorings — its value system, the problem of the masses, their mode of thinking and feeling — are training a leadership which does not understand fully the implications of our richest resource — the human resources, distorts our priorities, accelerates the pace of exploitation and social injustice, and is consequently responsible for political and social unrest and instability. Knowledge and intelligence without character and commitment to people has a negative effect on the national good. Such leaders discover the loopholes and weaknesses of society and their intelligence enables them to exploit the people more effectively — as a matter of fact, in proportion to their intelligence. The social good they are able to achieve is in inverse proportion to their ability. To the extent that some university academics are still good and socially useful is in spite of the system, not because of it. To have a leadership steadfastly loyal to the masses, which a democracy requires, education of prospective leaders must take place in close relationship with people, so that they can feel their problems "in the blood and all along the heart".

Further, by keeping aloof from people, universities are unwittingly denying themselves the possibilities of virgin soil, where they can undertake original and worthwhile research and win international recognition, apart from meeting urgent national needs. Hence, if educational planning has to have any meaning, it should assign the top-most priority to establishing firm links of understanding and commitment between universities and rural communities.

The situation in universities, as elsewhere, however, varies and the first task of future planning is to study the present status to gauge the strength of obstacles; even more importantly, to identify favourable forces and devise appropriate strategies to strengthen them. To do this, four studies were launched:

- A questionnaire was administered, to three batches of 83 principals of colleges (Arts, Science and Commerce), from all over the country, who had come for training at the National Institute of Educational Planning and Administration, New Delhi between November 20, 1981 and February 25, 1982. Apart from ascertaining present position, the questionnaire put forth tentative views about future planning to which reactions of the Principals were invited. The tentative framework for action was explained to the participants before they were asked to answer the questionnaire.

- The second study sought information from 136 universities and institutions of national importance — 22 agricultural, 7 technical, 3 medical and 91 general universities and 13 others – about the courses that they had started in rural development, their physical involvement in rural development and their participation in local planning.
- For the third study, a letter was addressed to 435 polytechnics and engineering colleges asking them as to what steps they were taking in assessing of human and material resources of the nearby rural areas as well as planning for their development and utilization through upgrading of human skills, devising of appropriate technology, etc; and, secondly, what more they could do and under what conditions.
- The responses were, thereafter analyzed and the question of the linkages of universities with community was discussed with some Vice-Chancellors, thinkers, planners and administrators.

A digest of the findings of these studies is presented in the paragraphs that follow. Advantage was also taken of a number of seminars that had been held on specific and related themes such as the Pune Seminar in February, 1982 on Education for Rural Development, the IIT, Delhi seminar on Select Dimensions of Rural Energy Systems (1981); the New Delhi Seminar on the Role of Private Industry in Rural Development, etc.

Over-all Constraints and Required Strategies

While there are problems specific and peculiar to each of the categories of universities — general (arts, science and commerce), technical, agricultural and medical — there are certain overall constraints of the university system and certain overall strategies that are required to overcome them. We discuss them briefly.

Location

The first problem relates to the location of universities. Most universities — even the agricultural universities — are located in urban areas. They hardly have any worthwhile contact with rural areas. While the agricultural universities have at least their research stations and a vast extension machinery to establish contact with the field, it is a point for consideration if identification of needs - especially of small and marginal farmers - would not have been more effective and the movement from lab to land should not have been appropriately preceded by a land to lab movement. This might have made the return response from lab to land more relevant, effective and rewarding. While our agricultural universities have made a substantial contribution to increase in our agricultural production, it is doubtful whether our strategies have been conceived keeping in view the total socio-economic conditions of vast mass of small and marginal farmers to whom, for example, our inputs remain too costly to be relevant and who are being progressively forced to sell their land to swell the pool of landless labourers working on big farms to which alone the new technology is relevant. Very few of the ideas born in laboratory become part of our agricultural practices. In urban industry also the hiatus is there – only a few of the laboratory inventions are accepted — but there is also the problem of bridging the gap — mental and physical. The problem in both cases is one of building over-bridges. In case of agriculture, physical proximity is extremely important because problems are not only technical but integrally related to total socio-economic situation.

What is true of agricultural universities is even truer of general universities. They do not have — nor can they afford — expensive extension machinery of the type that agricultural universities have for spreading their ideas. At present, their contacts with rural areas are few and far between. The position of technical and medical universities and colleges is more or less similar.

The implications of institutions of higher learning remaining largely aloof from the environment is serious for scientists, and technologists and other university faculty since they do not seem so far to be intimately involved in development effort in the country. Some important areas have remained neglected. This would not have been so had scientists concentrated their attention and effort on our own environment. A greater effort is needed to understand tropical and soil biology to improve cropping pattern. Agriculture as an efficient converter of solar energy needs our concentrated attention. So does the exploitation of water resources. And so on. This has also resulted in the unwitting denial to ourselves of the rich store of technology relevant to our people and conserved in rural areas. We could have had it at no cost. For example, it was for the OXFAM team to discover in its report on Andhra cyclone that roofing that was used traditionally was very good for withstanding cyclones. The tanning process unknown to modern science has been known to Indian villagers since long past. They complete the process in three hours. It is an important piece of knowledge which needs to be transformed into technology developed to construct cyclone-proof structures in coastal areas. But to get an insight into our technological heritage one must go to and talk to villagers who use these technologies without the knowledge base. It leads to spread of careless and inappropriate technology, which does much harm to natural and social environment. Appropriate technology requires a thorough understanding of social structure and the eco-system. Moreover, not living amidst them, problems have no opportunity to be dealt with by scientists, technologists and social scientists, with the intensity required to invent and innovate. Being removed from rural environment institutions of higher learning do not develop any commitment or sense of responsibility to the people there and their problems. The top most priority in research is the manner in which minimum needs of the community can be met and the manner in which social and technical services to the community can be most effectively and economically delivered. Such research obviously requires above all, an intimate contact with the community and its needs, and some form of physical proximity.

Keeping the above situation in view, it is felt that most universities and colleges should be moved to rural areas. Such a step will have several advantages:

- By putting seats of modern knowledge, acquainted as they are with international knowledge, right in the midst of our problem, it would be possible to link knowledge and problems in more effective ways helping in the evolution of the most up-to-date and yet relevant technology.

- By making problems the concern of universities in such a way will make it impossible for the latter to ignore them as they seem to be doing at present.
- With close interaction between science and technology on the one hand and society on the other, correct priorities for our R & D efforts will emerge in unmistakable terms.
- A close linkage between science and technology and the social environment, in which they have to be oprationalized, will provide an excellent opportunity for the growth of the science of Technology Assessment and the training of cadres.
- It will provide a living laboratory — both technological and social — for students and teachers and help in detailed identification of problems and resources, both human and material.
- Face to face with the problems they are more likely to discover solutions and test them in the total situation around them. It will link modernity, through universities, and traditional culture, of which rural areas are always the best repositories. The presence of the universities and colleges will strengthen planning mechanism at the grassroots — so essential for decentralized and micro planning and so urgently called for in the development of rural areas. Development agencies can also be located on the campuses to promote close interaction between them and universities. It will reduce the gap between the elite, nurtured in universities and masses and throw up leaders in various walks of life who will have the intellectual understanding of rural India and an emotional link with it. It will reduce student unrest by taking students away from concentrated dens of politicians, by bringing them in close touch with the grim realities of life, by giving them something really worthwhile to do, by forcing the pace of educational change, which, such a close confrontation with reality will ensure, by providing them cheap and healthy recreation, and by giving them

cheap and functional hostel facilities. Residential life, if properly organized, can provide excellent training in self-help and simple corporate living. If built with local materials and local labour, the cost of buildings can be reduced. The sale of existing buildings in urban areas should fetch fabulous sums, which will facilitate physical shifting of higher education to rural areas.

The measures advocated, however, are likely to be opposed as being unrealistic as centres of economic and political power are in urban areas. It is unrealistic to expect academic authorities to willingly move to rural areas. Today universities are very closely linked to political power structure; removing them away from the centres of political power will have a salutary effect on the intended autonomy of universities by weakening the unholy alliance between politician and some academicians. It should be welcomed by all well-meaning people inside and outside the government. Motivation of teaching community to serve in the rural areas could be strengthened through an appropriate national wage policy, through which we direct manpower where it is needed.

Education and health facilities are so poor in rural-areas that most academicians would hesitate to work in rural areas. However, if universities move to rural areas, they will turn out to be rewarding, particularly for education of their wards. As regards health facilities, they are bound to follow the conglomerates that universities represent. Rural areas, being repositories of our cultural tradition, can provide enough scope for recreation. Electronic media, like the radio and television, have already reached rural areas. A concentration of the academic community on the campus, which is, not the case in urban areas, where the teachers and students are spread out, should provide a rich cultural and social life.

Due to distance and communication difficulties, it will be difficult for universities to maintain free flow of information, which is necessary for a university to remain up-to-date. Given the recent developments with large-scale electrification of villages, growth of information technology, rapid development of roads and rail transport, this difficulty can be easily addressed. Journals could reach universities with ease. So could up-to-date and sophisticated equipment, which could be operated by universities. Universities can keep themselves effectively connected through Internet and telecommunication facilities. It should, however, be stated that just moving universities to rural areas may not achieve anything worthwhile. They will be and will remain mere exotic importations and showpieces. Many changes in curriculum, methods of teaching and evaluation, etc. will need to be effected before universities can become agencies of development and social transformation. Fortunately, there is a fair amount of agreement on these changes in the university system and these will be helped and not hindered by rural location of the universities.

The third set of alternative suggestions with regard to location of universities provides an intermediate step. While universities could continue to be in urban areas, their affiliated colleges could be located both in urban and rural areas. Some of these colleges could house research centres. These centres would be located right in the rural areas and would be periodically visited by some of the best faculty of the university. They would also house research scholars. Colleges in the rural areas would act as extension agents, transferring ideas and technologies to community and providing feedback to research centres and the university. Although this seems to be a worth while suggestion, some method must be devised to ensure that sufficient interest is generated in rural problems and recognition is given to work on these problems so that best faculty do actually visit and guide these centres. This will, however, still be a partial remedy; at best, an intermediate step. For, it will mobilize and utilize only a part of universities expertise and that also not always the most proficient.

It follows from the above discussions that, as far as possible, all new universities should be located at district headquarters so that they can be intimately involved with the District Development Authority — for which purpose its important role in the district development team should be clearly defined – and yet be sufficiently close to the problems of the country-side for social action and research. That would not prevent some of outstanding faculty from participating in State and Central Planning teams. As a matter of fact, their knowledge of micro situation should enable them to supply the missing link in such teams. There should be a phased programme of shifting universities from capital and metropolitan cities to district headquarters. Pending their being finally shifted to district towns, each university should have a number of research centres preferably located in rural colleges, which should be periodically visited by eminent professors. Each college should have its own extension net work in the community. Each department must identify priority problems; on which Ph. D. students can work.

Integration of Theory and Practice

The second problem is one of integrating of activities and theoretical instruction. For involvement in development implies participation in activities. In order to evoke motivation of students and faculty, as well as to optimize the educational benefit of this participation, it is essential that they should be an integral part of the curriculum; and theory and action clarify and reinforce each other. A problem-centred, rather than a discipline-centred approach, already dealt with in an earlier section, can best achieve this. Again, while evaluating a student, credit should be given for his participation in activities. So should this count in the workload assigned to a teacher. Some experiments in this regard are going on. Considerable work, however, needs to be done in this direction on a priority basis before this can become a common practice in all universities. This change would revolutionize teaching-learning process and the university and society relationship.

Coordination

The third problem is one of coordination of a university with government, non-government, and voluntary agencies. This is absolutely essential for effective assistance to development. The experience of institutions, which have attempted to work in rural areas, shows that cooperation of voluntary organizations is very helpful in identification of the needs of rural communities, which have to be the basis for any plan of action for their improvement. Government agencies can provide resources-financial and organizational. As a matter of fact, the Deputy Commissioner at the district level and the Block Development Officer at the block level can be significant coordinators at their respective levels. Universities and colleges — represented by their vice-chancellors and principals respectively and appropriately assisted by their staff – can provide the expertise as well as an army of intelligent and dedicated workers. The role of universities and colleges should be well understood and recognized at the highest level of the Government hierarchy and communicated all down the line. An involvement in development team will also facilitate cooperation from field level functionaries of government. This coordination and cooperation between universities and government agencies will, however, not be easy in view of the different cultures prevailing in academic institutions and government offices, and will require patience and understanding on both sides as well as a steady support for this policy of coordination and cooperation. The planning for physical proximity of district offices and university campus will facilitate growth of appropriate conventions.

Clear Reiteration of the University's Responsibility

The fourth problem relates to a clear definition of the objectives of higher education, where inculcation of commitment to and a sense of social responsibility towards rural areas figures prominently. Seminars and symposia on the linkage between universities and rural development would be helpful.

Improving General Atmosphere

Lastly, there is the basic constraint to any constructive effort by the universities viz. The atmosphere prevailing in universities today, which calls for clean administration and a sense of fair play. This presumes the prevalence of required atmosphere in the political and social life of the country as a whole and political non-interference in affairs of universities. It is a very difficult question with very large ramifications and, therefore, can be stated in general terms at this stage. Involvement of universities in rural development and the scope it will give to idealism of students and some of the faculty will start a healthy process, which may help in breaking the vicious circle: because the general atmosphere is bad, so no constructive activity can be taken up, and because no constructive activity is taken up, general atmosphere can not be improved.

Overall Programmes: Some Significant Beginnings

Before we come to the present situation, and possible further action in different categories of institutions, it is proposed to deal with some overall programmes: the NSS, adult and continuing education, and the involvement of universities in development.

National Service

The scheme which is a part of the programmes of the Ministry of Youth Affairs and Sports, was introduced in 1969 in 37 universities. To start with, it had an enrolment of 40,000 students, whereas in 2006-07 it had 2.6 million students in its ambit. The scheme is now working in 198 universities and also in some (+2) Senior Secondary institutions. The volunteers of NSS participate in the Republic Day Parade also. The scheme aims at personality development of students through community work. According to the Ministry's statistics, from its inception to 2006-07, 2.8 crore students have participated in the NSS activity. The following five focal points have been identified for NSS with:

a) National Integration and Social Harmony
b) Literacy,
c) Gender Justice,
d) Village Adoption, and
e) Life Skills Education.

The National Service Scheme (NSS) is operational in most institutions of higher education. It represents the most widely spread link between universities and rural development. It is a movement linking almost all universities and institutions of higher learning and, therefore, provides a unique forum for inter-disciplinary and inter-university interaction. Although performance has varied in different institutions, depending upon local leadership, the results achieved have been sufficient to indicate its vast potential for assisting rural development. As a matter of fact, all development, both of an individual and the community is important. It is, therefore necessary to strengthen the movement to realize its full potential for assisting development. To fully motivate students and their parents, to incorporate in the movement the entire academic community, to legitimize use for it of institutional resources for education and development of the community, and to maximize utilization of learning opportunities provided by involvement in development, it is necessary to make the NSS a part of the curriculum. Through activities under the NSS, every effort should be made to link every subject with "practical problems and socially useful work" (Fifth Plan p.201). Considerable thinking on these lines has been done and some spadework has also been done[2], which can form an excellent starting point for further intensive work. Such a measure will call for considerable reorientation of university curricula as well as the of NS Programme. The directions include the following:

- NSS will become compulsory, and become an integral part of every subject.
- It will require continuous contact with field and will therefore be an all-the-year-round activity. A nearby village (or slum) can be selected. This does not and need not rule out short specific purpose camps. To the extent that these camps are not related to the curriculum they need not be compulsory.
- To the extent the NSS becomes a part of the curriculum, expenditure on it would be spread over the entire student community and not on only the exchequer as at present. Such a diffusion of the expenditure could make it possible to have universal and compulsory NSS.
- While the NSS Coordinator will need to continue as a catalyst, and help various departments and student bodies to contact relevant government departments and voluntary agencies, whose help would be needed in organizing student activities, major burden for each batch of students will have to be borne by the department.
- While some activities will need to be organized departmentally, a number of projects, requiring a multi-disciplinary and inter-departmental effort will also be necessary and require an appropriate organization at the university or college level.
- Linkage with the curricula will also call for a much closer organizational linkage at the Central and State levels. At the Central level, the University Grants Commission would become the most appropriate body to handle the scheme.
- Camps, with a specific and clearly defined objective should, because of financial constraints, continue to be held on voluntary basis, for their educational value even though

they may not be directly related to the curriculum. Their management, however, needs considerable improvement. For, a badly planned camp is educationally poor and financially extravagant. By organizing these camps on maximum self-reliance basis — as, for example, in basic education institutions — their cost can be cut down and their educational potency increased. Well-managed activities should also yield considerable tangible and intangible benefits. To the extent possible, these benefits should be computed, and in evaluating camp expenditure, the idea of net cost should be introduced, which would show the expenditure on these camps in proper perspective. If NSS activities are properly coordinated with their activities, some of the expenditure could be debited to departments for which conventions will need to be developed. This will not only reduce the burden on the NSS budget thereby enabling larger expansion of the programme, but also firmly establish the usefulness of these camps. Large scale expansion of the NSS should also provide to various departments an ever-growing force of disciplined students and teachers, who can also act as the eyes and ears of the senior officers and thereby enable them to keep a strict watch on their field level representatives so that their narrow vested interests do not sabotage the coordination policy. This will, however, require a culture of coordination and a policy decision at the top, communicated by all the departments down the line to their field level agencies.

- Programmes of national priority need to be identified and camps organized around them so as to vivify serious challenges. This would awaken the maximum response as well as heighten the sense of achievement of the participants. The cost-benefit considerations will also dictate the choice of such projects which require large scale input of semi-skilled and un-skilled but disciplined labour like afforestation programmes etc.
- Efficiently organized and managed and efficient techniques of fair assessment could, also justify the issue of special certificates and special preference in jobs on the basis thereof.

- NSS is a programme of economic development and social change. Social processes are a complex phenomenon and strategies to engineer them need careful study and planning. To assist this activity and to make possible cross-fertilization of experience required to hasten the learning process, it would be useful to document in detail the success stories and make them widely available.

Continuing Education, Adult Education and Extension Work

For making higher education socially relevant, the UGC initiated in 1970 the programme of continuing education in 21 universities. With the launching of the National Adult Education Programme in 1978, adult education was started in 68 universities and 705 colleges. The UGC has also been trying to add to the two generally practised functions of teaching and research the third legitimate and urgently needed function of extension, thereby, testing the relevance of its teaching and research programme to community needs, as well as to effect correction, indicated by feedback provided by extension activities in the community. The aim is to set guidelines for restructuring of courses and identify socially relevant problems needing research. While specific thrust of each of these programmes is different, they have considerable areas of overlap and have the common aim of establishing the university-community links, thereby affirming the responsibility of the university for assisting the community to solve its problems with the help of the academic community and the physical resources at its command. The Guidelines issued by the UGC in 1982 brought together continuing education, adult education, extension work and allied activities like population education, nutrition education, planning forums, etc. under a single department designated as the Department/Centre of Continuing Education and Extension Work.

A department is given an equal recognition and academic status with the other departments of the university, with which it is conceived as actively interacting. While the Department could initiate and manage some courses/activities by itself, it is expected to work largely in close cooperation with the other departments. In such cases, while the Department discharges its coordinating functions, academic content of the programmes is expected to be provided by other departments. The Department is also expected to draw upon resources outside the university, represented by government and voluntary agencies. Academic input in such cases has to be provided by university departments. Similarly, colleges, especially professional colleges like those of engineering, medicine, agriculture, Home Science, etc., are to be fully involved in this work.

The objectives of the programmes are to meet the varied needs of different sections of the adopted community. A nearby community/area is expected to be adopted by each university or college. To meet these needs the university can start, where necessary, need-based courses at the required level. Such intimate involvement of students and the faculty in community problems should lead to enrichment of the curriculum and help in restructuring of courses. Another objective is to give to students field experience and thereby sensitize them to the problems of people and to social realities. Students and faculty would also pick up nationally significant problems for research.

The method and approach recommended for adoption in this work will be unconventional, innovative and problem-centred and consequently multi-disciplinary. The programmes to be taken up are broadly of four categories: creating and feeding interest in contemporary affairs and issues; provision of literacy and numeracy and post-literacy and supplementary education; providing training to impart professional and technical skills; and establishing linkages between curriculum and problem-oriented action. The specific programme undertaken at any particular time will, however, be determined by the identified felt needs of the community and the resources that a Department can muster from within and outside the university.

The special target groups indicated are especially those in rural and slum areas; Scheduled Castes and Scheduled Tribes; dropouts; unemployed and out-of-school youth; the handicapped; workers in organized and un-organized sectors; teachers of primary and secondary classes; and university students from under-privileged sections from rural areas and slums. University/college can also identify other groups needing special assistance.

The programme is of tremendous significance. It requires continuous and vigorous efforts for increasing awareness of university community. It needs motivational support through recognition and encouragement, and, above all, technical support for proper organization of activities and their linkages with the curriculum. Only then will it be possible to overcome the usual conservatism of university academics and their lethargy and vested interest in maintenance of the status quo.

The Department of Adult and Continuing Education, under the UGC, has been trying to:

(*a*) arrange programmes for those who had the benefit of 'university education' and who wish to update their knowledge;

(*b*) Training persons who did not receive university education by organizing short-term courses for them; and

(*c*) Reaching groups living in different geographical regions.

University Involvement in Eco-development

A very significant step was taken in the Sixth Five Year Plan to enlarge areas of interest and responsibility for universities by involving them in eco-development in a big way. India being predominantly a land of the young, the Planning Commission recommended a three-pronged strategy to involve the youth in eco-development: creating awareness of the problem through action programmes like the eco-development camps, designed to assist in restoring eco-systems and in establishing marine and inland national parks, geese sanctuaries and biosphere reserves-activities, "involving both brain and brawn" and recognized not as mere social service but as "instruments of learning" for which academic credit should be awarded; channelising efforts of university researchers for problems of converting the environmental resources into wealth with a view to improving the life of the people; making university researchers work not only on frontiers of knowledge but also on frontiers of problems; and finally, taking up coordinated action research projects in a similar agro-ecological regions.

In pursuit of these recommendations and intense interaction with universities, the Planning Commission decided to support in the Sixth Plan three coordinated action research projects in the Himalayan, Western Ghats and Gangetic regions. All universities in each belt were involved. The belt was divided into different parts; the coordination responsibility for each part was entrusted to the Vice-Chancellor of one of the universities. There was coordination at the university level — between different departments, between faculty and students and between universities and other governmental and non-governmental agencies. Then there was coordination at the cluster level — universities and other governmental and non-governmental agencies working in each part of a project —say, the Northeastern part of the Himalayan Project. There was also coordination at the project level, suitably situated at one of the cooperating universities. There was finally a coordinating body under the auspices of the Planning Commission and consisting of all Vice-Chancellors involved in various projects.

Student involvement was of crucial importance and was on the following lines:

- Integration of eco-development in the curriculum;
- Assignment of Research Projects;
- Participation in Field Projects; and
- Organization of Eco-Development Camps.

Participation in fieldwork, however, was on a voluntary basis in the beginning, being confined to those really interested in the programme. The scope was widened as interest in fieldwork grew. The importance of involvement of students and faculty could be gauged from the fact that their number in three Projects reached over one million — a tremendously important force for action and research projects at the field level.

The importance and future possibilities of this project were summed up by the Planning Minister in his inaugural address to the March, 1982 meeting:

"If these three action research projects strike root during this Plan period, we can consider expanding such programmes during the VII Plan Period. This will mark the beginning of a new movement in our country where learning by doing becomes an instrument of bringing institutions of higher learning and the community at large together in a shared endeavour to conserve and enrich our basic environmental assets."

Such projects, apart from the support that universities would procure for eco-development, would have considerable significance for re-orientation of an 'ivory tower' and knowledge based education towards a problem and activity-centred education, following a multi-disciplinary approach. Universities would get intimately involved in eco-improvement, inculcating social awareness, commitment and accountability.

Some other useful schemes pursued at higher education stage are:

- ***Yoga Centre:*** UGC has approved 64 universities for establishing yoga canters. They are to coordinate with eminent yoga institutions for promoting yoga-learning.
- ***Special Studies on Social Thinkers and Leaders:*** Under this programme, 25 such centres have been set up in the 10th Five Year Plan. Among them 8 centres are on Gandhian Studies, 7 for Buddhist Studies, 6 for Ambedkar Studies and 4 for Aurobindo Studies.
- ***Promotion of Women and Family Studies:*** Under this scheme, assistance is given to universities to undertake research, develop curricula, organize training and extension work of gender equity, girls' education, population education, human rights, prevention of exploitation and other likewise issues. There are women studies centres in 34 universities.
- ***Facilities for Disabled Persons:*** Two schemes are being Implemented under this programme: (*a*) Teachers' Preparation in Special Education; and (*b*) Higher Education for Persons with Special Needs. The UGC has identified 10 universities/colleges for scheme (a) and 19 for scheme (b).
- ***Promotion of Socially Relevant Education:*** The object of this scheme is to ensure that graduates who pass out have knowledge, skills, and aptitude for gainful self-employment. Colleges which opt for this scheme identify, on their own, three 'Need Based Courses' of inter-disciplinary nature.
- ***Improvement of Quality:*** To achieve excellence in higher education, the UGC has devised the following additional measures: (a) strengthening of physical and academic infrastructure in teaching and research; (b) Achieving excellence in training so as to face the challenge of globalization with entry of foreign universities in India;

(c) travel grants to college teachers and vice-chancellors to travel abroad to attend international conferences, area study projects in economic, political and cultural affairs; bilateral cultural exchange between India and other countries; (d) free flow of student from other nations to India and vice-versa; and (e) research and emeritus fellowships to provide facilities to national and foreign scholars of developing countries and to experienced teachers and thus add to the store-house of knowledge and opportunities for creation of new knowledge. It has been observed that the knowledge gained at these international and national meetings is not put to maximum use. It should be ensured that the said store house of knowledge is availed of by as many individuals and institutions as possible.

- ***Indian Council of Social Science Research (ICSSR):*** the Indian Council of Philosophical Research (ICPR) and Indian Council of Historical Research (ICHR) promote creative research in their respective areas by awarding fellowships of different levels. The fellows must present a couple of papers, based on their findings, before a selected group of scholars chosen by ICSSR/ICPR/ICHR. Such a step will have two advantages:
  - o It would help the ICSSR/ICPR/ICHR to see the quality of the work done by a fellow; and
  - o Disseminate the findings among scholars, through whom the findings may travel further.
- ***Indira Gandhi National Open University (IGNOU):*** IGNOU was established in 1985 to enhance access to higher education. The University provides facilities for general education; programmes for disadvantaged groups, minority sections, physically challenged etc. It has 1.2 million students on rolls and offers more than 70 programmes. The University has adopted use of multi-media strategy consisting of print media, radio, T.V., video-conferencing and face-to-face counseling at study centres. It has a net work of 46 regional and over 700 study centres. IGNOU has been vested with the twin responsibility of acting as an Open University and offering need-based education, training and extension programmes and acting

as a nodal agency to determine and maintain standards in distance education. It has 24 hours a day TV channel – Gyan Darshan – and 40 F.M. channels – Gyan Vani. IGNOU targets to extend the coverage of the open learning system to backward regions, remote inaccessible areas of the northeast and low female literacy blocks in some of the eastern states.

Restructuring of Courses and Reorientation of Methodology

Running through above programmes are questions of restructuring courses, making them socially relevant and integrating theory with practice through adoption of a problem-centred, rather than a discipline-centred approach. This trend is of such social and pedagogic importance that it needs to be separated from individual programmes and strengthened for its inherent worth.

The significance and implications of this reform may be summed up as follows:

- Knowledge is a digest of life and in order to remain up-to-date and alive, it must perpetually renew itself by a continuous contact with life.
- The first specimen of real-life is the immediate natural and social environment, where knowledge must be tested, modified or rejected. The importance of the immediate environment in the learning process is not sufficiently realized. If we cannot understand and interact with our immediate environment, our chances of understanding and interacting with a distant environment are remote.
- Interaction with life and the testing of knowledge in life situations means meaningful activity, trying to solve some problems.
- Life's problems, however, are multidimensional and require for solution help of many disciplines. In a life-centred education an inter-disciplinary approach becomes inevitable. The movement towards integrated education as a means of understanding and helping solve life's problems is considered a necessary complement to the trend towards atomized and highly specialized knowledge. This companionship of specialization or disintegration and

integration is essential for the discovery of truth, as is shown by growing importance of research in inter-face areas between various disciplines, each of which cannot be understood except by a multi-disciplinary approach.

- The learning process becomes a much more interesting process as links between books and life are established. Life provides the data, with which students and teachers can actively respond to what they are told by books, instead of learning them up by heart and accepting what is stated there blindly. Students also are no longer passive recipients of what their teachers tell them but become intelligent and active partners in the discovery of truth. Such an exercise is much more interesting than passive reception.

Relevant education, therefore, means an activity-centred and problem-centred education through which accumulated knowledge guides life and is in turn invigorated by life. It requires a multi-disciplinary and integrated approach. Such an approach is very essential for making education interesting and useful as a cooperative learning process between teachers and students and between academic community and the local community. Insights developed at the local level can be stretched out profitably to understanding of and interaction with the wider community.

The reform may, however, meet strong opposition from academic vested interests. While some would dare to question in principle the need to make higher education socially relevant and an instrument of social change, few have cared to work out its implications for content and. methodology of teaching. Instead, most have steadily sabotaged any serious effort made in that direction. In the Fifth Plan, the Planning Commission had recommended that every subject should be linked with "practical problems and socially useful work (p.201). The UGC set up three panels to see how this could be done. The academic community, however, opposed it. Most universities have not taken any steps to grapple with issues involved in making higher education socially relevant. Gangrade and Singh point out:

- The University Grants Commission recommended a policy of linking education with the needs and problems of the people making it socially relevant and practice oriented. At the first degree stage, it was recommended that one of the optional subjects should be of an applied nature.* As an illustration some of the course combinations recommended are given below:

In Science:

(*i*) Mathematics, Physics and Electronic/Applied Physics (Workshop Technology/Machine shop Practice/ Instrumentation).

(*ii*) Botany, Chemistry and Horticulture.

(*iii*) Biology, Chemistry and Fisheries.

In Social Sciences:

(*i*) Economics, Commerce and Agricultural Marketing.

(*ii*) Economics, Commerce and Farm Management

(*iii*) Political Science, Economics and Community Development.

The Commission also recommended inter-disciplinary teaching in adequately equipped departments. The favourable features in the situation were the UGC support for the reform; a group of involved people, who have thought of the reform in some detail. It should be our endeavour to recognize and strengthen these initiatives.

There is need to organize a public debate on the reform through a series of seminars, upon the strength of the detailed work already done, trends in advanced countries, difficulties of implementation and how they could be overcome. Detailed projects for experiments should be invited from universities and adequately financed and duly monitored and evaluated. Success stories, carefully evaluated and documented in detail, should be widely circulated. Some of the autonomous colleges, which have greater flexibility in curricular reform, may prove valuable pioneering squads in this reform of restructuring of courses.

Specific Categories: Present Position and Further Recommendations

The following conclusions have emerged from the study in respect of developments in regard to the present position as well as the lessons learned thereform:

General Universities

There is very little of systematic academic involvement of general universities in rural development. Some significant beginnings have, however, been made which have shown the possibility of establishing rural development as a major area of university – study from the point of view of complexity and sophistication as well as the multi-disciplinary approach that it requires. The experience of South Gujarat University, for example, has further established that students taking up courses in rural development will be in demand as they will be meeting specific manpower needs. Several specialized universities and institutions offering courses relating to rural development have come up in the country. To make these courses effective, a close linkage with employing agencies will, however, need to be established at every step. Gainful employment is the most important consumer expectation from education.

While it is important to include rural development in various subjects like Economics, Sociology, Cooperation, etc., there is need for a separate department which while, drawing upon the expertise available in various departments, can act as a catalyst and serve to bring the various aspects of rural development together into an integral whole. Apart from its academic aspect, there appears to be a need in the employment market for the product of such an integrated course. Where significant work is done in any university, development agencies are anxious to take advantage of the staff expertise in research, investigation and planning. Such an involvement in developmental work also enables a university to generate original teaching material. If resources are made available, many more universities would be keen to set up departments of rural development, which is the first necessary step for their involvement in community life. With that step it would be possible to put in position a number of people who think day and night as to how to make the programme a success, if only to justify their own existence.

Agricultural Universities

Agricultural universities have rendered a significant service to the cause of higher education by demonstrating, with signal success, the working of a model in which teaching, research and extension are integrally linked. It is a model which university education in search of establishing its roots in the soil will find useful and necessary. Another significant feature of agricultural universities, which has a lesson for general universities, is the close linkage between university and the development department - the Agricultural Department of the state government. The conventions that have developed may provide useful lessons when linkages between general universities and development departments are sought to be established.

Technical Institutions

In spite of the urban and globally oriented culture of the IITs, significant beginnings have been made at Delhi, Kharagpur and Mumbai, as well as in the Indian Institute of Science, Bangalore in defining, evolving and transferring appropriate technology to rural areas. Apart from the inherent value of their work, these institutions have provided an example, which other institutions of technology are most likely to follow. As suggested by the IIT, Kharagpur, interaction among institutes of higher learning – universities, agricultural and technical – would be very profitable and efforts should be made to promote it through seminars, workshops, etc. jointly organized by the AICTE, the ICAR and the UGC.

College (Arts, Science and Commerce)

A project was undertaken to study the involvement of college (Arts, Science and Commerce) in rural development. It was found that there was unanimous acceptance of social responsibility of the academic community to development of rural areas which highly subsidise their education. Involvement of colleges (and other institutions of higher learning) is also necessary for sound pedagogic reasons. The natural and social environment provides an excellent field laboratory for illustrating and testing theoretical principles taught in a classroom. Interaction with natural and social environment is also indispensable for promoting the necessary attitudes and skills. Such an involvement also gives opportunities for concentrating on problem identification and problem solving and the multi-disciplinary approach that it entails.

The particular activity or activities a college chooses depends upon the interest and quality of local leadership, resource availability and the type of cooperating agencies available in the area. The potentiality, however, of colleges' involvement is much greater than has been developed and utilized so far. They can make significant contribution towards building of rural infrastructure and environment such as roads, construction or deepening of ponds for drinking water, building of culverts, afforestation, etc.; and in promoting literacy, numeracy and basic scientific knowledge, technical know-how and occupational skills involved in agriculture and allied activities like animal husbandry, fishery, poultry, bee-keeping, rural and cottage industries, etc. While agriculture and technical colleges can really do many of these things effectively, science departments of general colleges can make their own contribution. For example, chemistry and botany students can give valuable information on insecticides and pesticides; those from zoology departments can help in piggery, poultry; fishery, etc. Similarly, while industrial training can be provided mainly by technical institutions, physics and chemistry departments can help in setting up science-based industries like electronics. Social sciences, economics and management departments can provide valuable inputs from the point of view of organization and management to improve the economic efficiency of rural people. They can help them to organize themselves in cooperatives both for purpose of buying raw materials and marketing finished goods. Students of law can help village panchayats to settle minor disputes. This would help the panchayats to decide cases in keeping with, the provisions of the law, reduce the burden on the courts and result in quicker decisions. Citizenship training, social cohesion and national solidarity through education knowledge of rights and obligations, communal harmony, national integration, our basic culture and system of values can be imparted through such an arrangement. Colleges also raise awareness level on health, family planning and childcare.

Colleges can assist in planning and development through drawing of village maps, carrying out socio-economic surveys; collection, presentation and interpretation of data; identification of needs, assessment of resources and relating the two in village plans and adoption of village, etc. They can help in plan implementation by explaining government schemes and their benefits and getting the people in touch with appropriate assistance agencies; providing healthy recreation to the villagers through appropriate use of local cultural agencies, thereby increasing the relevance of these agencies in the modernization of the rural areas; up-grading schools in their areas through the establishment of school-college complexes.

Keeping in view, however, constraints of time, capacity and priorities, the following criteria may be used to select activities in which colleges should be involved:

- Study of the local environment - district level and below - as a compulsory part of the curriculum.
- Picking up such programmes from development spectrum as legitimately belong to a group of students and teachers – e.g. surveys of land holdings, family incomes etc. by students of economics.
- Drawing up of area development plans by college as a whole in which the various disciplines participate in an inter-disciplinary exercise. The exercise should be an important input to the local development authorities at the district, block and village levels.
- Picking up such programmes as are obviously in the interest of all sections of the community or assist the weaker groups so long as they do not bring them into direct confrontation with the other groups such as programmes of literacy, sanitation and epidemic control, composting, etc. Confrontation would create difficulties, which would be beyond the capacity of the college to manage and which may threaten to destroy all its work in the community and even its own.

The organization of participation in developmental activities should be at two levels: sectional activities under departmental heads; coordinated inter-disciplinary activities under the Principal with the head of the Department of Economics as the Member-Secretary of the inter-departmental team assisting the Principal, who would also represent the college in the District and Block Development Planning Committees set up by the Government. The colleges (or universities) should be given a well-recognized place in development committees.

Involvement of colleges in rural development in any appreciable way would require a phased programme of decision-making and implementation. The following steps are suggested:

- Consideration and acceptance of the policy by the UGC in consultation with the Association of Indian Universities (AIU) and the Ministry of Rural Development.
- Introducing the change in a few selected autonomous colleges and providing them with the necessary technical and financial inputs. Where a college in a rural area has really a competent and dedicated faculty and sufficient physical resources, its deficiencies should be made up and it should be given an autonomous status and the first preference in selection for this experiment.
- Perfecting the policy and programme through periodic discussions of experience of the participating colleges under the auspices of the UGC, with the assistance of the Ministry of Rural Development.
- Introducing the programme on a large scale after training of the Principals by the National University of Educational Planning and Administration, New Delhi in conjunction with the National Institute of Rural Development, Hyderabad on the one hand and the necessary financial assistance on the other.

During the expansion stage, it would be useful to select one college in each district as a lead college; which should be specially assisted, technically and financially. Teachers from other colleges can also be drawn to help this college on the basis of an honorarium.

Engineering Colleges and Polytechnics

The findings of the study of the problems and strategies of the involvement of engineering colleges and polytechnics are summed up below:

- Science and technology constitute perhaps the most important component of the multi-pronged strategy required for rural development. While science has primarily to create a scientific temper – the spirit of enquiry, rationality etc. – and provide an understanding of principles underlying phenomena and processes, technology harnesses natural phenomena to man's use and improves processes, through evolution of better technologies. Science is a part of general education and has to permeate the whole system. Technical institutions, however, have to understand the existing technologies being used in daily life and to constantly attempt to improve them. To meet manpower demands of a developing economy, India has been setting up more and more technical institutions. Today we have 7 Indian Institutes of Technology (IITs), 6 Indian Institute of Management (IIMs), and one Indian Institute of Science, Bangalore, where attainment of the highest international standards is aimed at. Besides, a total of 1969 degree institutions and 2475 post-graduate institutions have been approved by AICTE, (India, 2006). Besides a large number of Industrial Training Institute and industrial schools, variously designated, to train semi-skilled workers for industry have been set up. The investment in land, building and equipment is enormous. These institutions have so far been harnessed to the needs of the urban industry. They have tremendous potential for the development of rural areas.

- Involvement in rural development provides a challenge and an opportunity for technical institutions themselves in view of the fact that rural areas at present are largely undeveloped and their development will throw up many new problems, which these institutions can help to solve. The development of rural areas also will tremendously increase employment market for institutional products. Involvement in rural development will give them an opportunity for diversification, growth and development. Technical institutions represent varying levels of capacity. While polytechnic may be able to transfer appropriate technology and may even be able to evolve some very simple technologies and design simple machines, they may have problems, which they should be able to refer to and get guidance from higher-level institutions, which should be suitably equipped for this referral service. Such referral centres at engineering colleges/IITs should be identified and information in their regard made available to the polytechnics (and even the ITIs). Besides, there should be fabrication centres where new designs can be fabricated on a modest scale before they are picked up by the commercial channels of production. Training in installation, servicing and maintenance of new machines will also be an important function for which centres would need to be developed, preferably in existing institutions.

While some technical institutions may have effectively responded to needs of rural development, the number doing any significant work in rural development is not likely to be large. In view of the fact that rural development is of high priority, institutions actually doing development work would presumably be anxious to take credit for it. This presumption is further borne out by the fact that the tone of those not doing rural development work has been apologetic and they have been anxious to explain their lack of activity due to lack of financial/additional faculty support. They have also been handicapped by the lack of a clear policy support and by a curriculum, which is centrally controlled.

It becomes also clear from the above that, given a clear policy support, whereby participation in rural development becomes a part of the curriculum, and additional faculty and financial support, many more technical institutions would be anxious to participate in rural development. While at present the scale of participation in rural development by technical institutions is negligible, some significant qualitative beginnings have been made. These would enable guidelines to be drawn for large-scale participation. Some of these, which have become already clear, are:

- Technological inputs, which technical institutions can provide, have to be identified, developed and transferred for acceptance and adoption by a rural community within the parameters of its total-socio-economic situation, which needs to be carefully studied. The process of development and transfer of appropriate technology is a social process. Therefore, technical institutions require working as parts of a development team and must develop an understanding of the total process of social transformation as well as of the role of each agency therein. The leader of the team can only be the Deputy Commissioner/Collector of the District to whom technical institution can give massive intellectual support. Technical institutions, however, have serious limitations in themselves coordinating their role as they do not have the necessary administrative authority to ensure the fulfillment of their assigned role by each participating agency. But it is essential that the crucial role that technical institutions can play is recognized and fully supported and encouraged. Coordination, however, has proved to be the most intractable task and needs for its success policy support from the highest level, conveyed effectively all down the line in each department.

- In view of the multi-faceted nature of the role, which technical institutions have to play in rural development, it is necessary to have a separate unit or cell in each institution to act as a catalyst, while drawing upon the specific competencies of various departments.
- To the extent that students are involved in this work, it should be a part of their curriculum and they should get academic credit for the effort that they make.
- Development of appropriate technology and its transfer and adoption requires a systematic approach and a close-knit cycle of identification of needs, their translation into technological problems, solution for each such problem, demonstration of the efficiency of proposed action provision of finance, installation and maintenance of machinery and communication results as necessary feedback. The RDD chain here is much more complicated than in the case of industry and also needs to be much more compact in view of the general helplessness and vulnerability of the clientele.
- Technical institutions can make a significant contribution by imparting and upgrading of human skills - both technical and organizational - to provide employment and supply the growing needs of the rural areas for technical manpower, thereby increasing production and productivity and helping the diversification of rural economy; making provision of technical services through the opening of service centres and mobile units for helping the installation, repair and maintenance of farm equipment and machinery; providing consultancy services to farmers and entrepreneurs of small and village industries, the establishment of which they can promote in many ways;

- Helping farmers and entrepreneurs to obtain loans;
- Preparing feasibility reports for projects on small scale and village industries; promoting the setting up of cooperatives etc; and
- Identifying appropriate technology and its transfer, acceptance and adoption.

These activities have been started in many institutions, especially those selected by the Ministry of Human Resource Development for assistance and are being carried out with varying degrees of efficiency. These activities need to be introduced in all polytechnics in rural areas so that they are dynamically related to their environment and their students get conditioned to the field where they will find increasing employment.

The basic strategy for utilizing technical institutions for rural development should be to assess the excess capacity, faculty and physical resources available with them, and to utilize it for rural development. These could be supplemented by providing additional facilities to make it a really effective unit for assisting rural development. The curriculum and methodology of teaching can be so reoriented as to use rural environment as a field laboratory so that problems of environment become illustrative of theories and principles taught in the classroom and campus laboratory. Articles picked up for workshop practice and design and development should be such as are relevant to the area — agricultural implements, local problems of irrigation, drainage, etc.

While students and faculty of all technical institutions need to be involved in rural development, promote in them an understanding of the needs of, and a commitment to, the mass of their countrymen, this involvement can be more meaningfully effected in the case of technical institutions located in rural areas, to which their products will largely look for their employment. To supply the needs of rural development, therefore, it should be a definite policy of the State to set up technical institutions at the district level. The programme of having one polytechnic in each district, which was very enthusiastically pursued by he States at one time, could be much more meaningfully pursued now, with increasing demands of rural development.

The number of engineering colleges and polytechnics, should, however, be determined by the overall demand for their products. To the extent possible, these institutions should be located at district level in pursuit of the general policy of taking educational institutions at the post-secondary stage away from the capital and metropolitan cities, as well as from the point of view of utilizing the potentially of these institutions to contribute towards rural development and the growth of small towns. Wherever, however, it is not possible, on overall considerations of manpower supply and demand, to have a polytechnic at a district headquarter, some other suitable institutions should be strengthened to give institutional support to rural development.

Apprenticeship scheme started under the 1961 Act provides opportunities for one-year practical training to graduate engineers' diploma holders and 10+2 vocational pass-outs in about 8000 industrial establishments. The purpose of the scheme is to enable for the needs of the industries. This scheme should be implemented much more enthusiastically its implementation present.

Conclusions

Linking universities with the problems of rural areas and rural people should be a priority task in planning of university education. The aim should be to create a leadership at various levels, attuned to the people. It should also create an academic community committed to the utilization of our resources in an original way to find indigenous solutions to various problems, thereby establishing their claim to originality and creativity and winning international recognition as well as enriching international knowledge in science and technology and in the social sciences.

This would involve several steps, which are as follows:

- Declaring a long-term policy of moving all universities, as far as possible, to district headquarters to give them physical proximity to problems and people of rural areas as a first step towards understanding them;
- Locating most new universities at district headquarters;
- Drawing up a phased programme of shifting existing

universities from capital and metropolitan cities to district headquarters;

- Assigning to universities and colleges a well-defined place in development teams at district and block-level, which does not rule out the possibility and even necessity of using university experts in State level and even Central level development teams, where they would supply the usually missing link in such bodies-men with field and micro-level planning and implementation experience;
- Opening of colleges in typical rural areas and locating research and extension centres therein, closely linked with the university research centres and visited by university professors and research scholars, thereby identifying problems, finding solutions, taking full advantage of indigenous technologies, developed over the centuries and embodied in village practices, and creating original teaching materials;
- Changing curricula to make them problem-centred instead of discipline centred as at present, and giving problems of the rural areas a fair representation therein; and
- Adopting a multi-disciplinary approach and inter-institutional/agency cooperation in teaching, and developing suitable structures thereof.

Although existing involvement of post-secondary institutions in rural development apart from agricultural universities is very small, the following favourable beginnings need to be recognized and consciously strengthened:

- There is a growing awareness among university faculty and authorities of their responsibility towards rural development and the academic advantage of involvement therein. This awareness needs to be strengthened and universalized through seminars/ workshop, jointly organised by the UGC, the ICAR, the ICMR, the AICTE and the Ministries concerned, especially those of Human Resource Development and Rural Development. For rural development is a multi-faceted integrated process, in which professional and vocational institutions of agriculture, engineering and technology, and medicine as well as general universities and colleges have distinct contribution to make and yet each has to keep the integrated process of social transformation in view; and they all have to work in coordination and cooperation, along with other development agencies — governmental and voluntary.

- The success stories should be carefully evaluated and documented in detail and made widely available. They should provide excellent material for dissemination.
- Some attempts have been made to link curriculum with problems at the ground level and field activities. The scope and area of this experimentation should be widened and institutions carefully selected and given freedom to restructure courses. Vigorous interaction among these institutions should be promoted till the results of their experiments are mature for large-scale introduction into the system, for which a phased programme of training of key personnel should be organized.

Some of the most significant programmes include the establishment of Departments of Adult Education, Continuing Education and Extension Work in the general universities; involvement of universities in eco-development; definition, evolution and transfer of appropriate technology by technical and agricultural universities/institutions; and development of models of teaching, research and extension worked out by agricultural universities.

REFERENCES

1. *Selected Educational Statistics, 2003-04.*
2. UGC letter No. F.22-1/75 (ER) dated 4-11-1975.

* UGC letter No. F.22-1/75 (ER) dated 4-11-1975.

Chapter 5

Non-Formal Education and Rural Development

Non-formal education may be defined as an organized exercise in micro planning and implementation to meet educational needs of diverse cohesive interest groups constituting a community of space or a community of interest. In the latter case, it is not the compact spatial unit that gives members, who may be widely scattered, their group identify but their shared interest. Here, economies of scale can be exploited, while in the former case, the situation calls for on-the-spot methods devised to meet needs of each micro unit. In the context of rural development. We are largely concerned with spatial communities.

Modern life is changing fast and urgently calls for educational inputs to enable people, especially the weaker sections, to adapt themselves to change, to enable them to grasp the opportunities that change provides and to safeguard themselves against the dangers that accompany it. The educational task becomes, therefore, stupendous and cannot be met by the very limited formal education system. Nor is its character, with its rigid structures and standardized fare and method, suited to varying needs of different groups constituting the clientele; and they require educational inputs immediately transferable into concrete advantages in their lives. That is why facilities of education, even to the limited extent they are available, are not utilized fully, as is shown by the heavy dropout rate, which has continued un-arrested for many decades.

Objectives

While the programme for each target group will have to be tailor-made, it will in the context of rural development, need to have certain general characteristics, dictated by prevailing constraints. In view of the central fact of rural poverty, a meaningful programme of non-formal education, which will click, must first of all contribute to economic betterment. As Gandhiji put it, India is so poor that even God to be recognized must come in the form of a rice bowl. Economic betterment requires upgrading of skills, cooperative organization and managerial capability. These are the educational inputs required to be added to financial and physical inputs provided by the government. Upgrading of skills may mean improved output from existing skills (enabling movement) to a more lucrative profession requiring finer but allied skills, such as when a carpenter is trained for furniture making. The managerial capability would be required to tie up, more efficiently and cheaply, with procurement of raw material, production and sales. Initiative and resourcefulness also need to be developed to enable people to identify and exploit their environmental resources more fully and efficiently. An individual entrepreneur in rural areas needs to be strengthened by enlisting him in a cooperative organization so that he can bargain with outside forces on more equal terms and government assistance can be channeled to him more easily. This requires inculcation of attitudes of cooperation and teamwork and imparting of knowledge of the cooperative laws. Members must develop a sense of shared responsibility and goals.

Education must build up a cohesive community. Strong and self-sufficient village communities had been India's strength through the centuries, even in the midst of political and military upheavals. Many forces have combined to destroy this entity. The spread of transport facilities and influx of cheap machine-made goods from urban areas and outflow of products to urban markets have destroyed its economic self-sufficiency and the inter-dependence of various groups. Elections have divided villages as never before. Unemployment in rural areas and other forces have led to large scale migration to urban areas and labour mobility, which has weakened family and community ties. Modern forces, like education, have weakened old institutions like caste and destabilized relationships. And yet, community concept is by no means an anachronism to be forgotten and cast aside. As a matter of fact, revitalization of village community is an urgent necessity for socio-economic development.

It is uneconomical, inefficient and almost impossible to deliver technical and social services to rural areas on an individual basis. A well-organized community can provide the necessary receiving mechanism. For example, post-harvest technology is only possible on a cooperative, sharing basis. Facilities for credit, storage, marketing, etc. can be given only on a cooperative community basis. Target groups for governmental help again cannot be identified without the help of the community as a whole. Villages are still so scattered that they have still to depend primarily on their own cohesive strength to fight anti-social elements, within and without. Democratic decentralization is only possible if there is a sense of belonging and loyalty to the community. The delays in deciding cases now as they were before, are equally frustrating. The need is to entrust panchayats with functions to settle local disputes. Again, while there are divisions and tensions in rural areas; there are more serious clashes of interest between a rural community and the world outside. Whether it is against an exploiting middleman, or a city dweller encroaching on agricultural land, etc. the village community needs to stand together to safeguard its legitimate interests. Village level planning is regarded as the only way to ensure that local resources are fully and most efficiently utilized for local benefit. The family approach has been decided upon as the only way of helping weaker sections. No outsider can do what a conscientious and organized *Panchayat* can. The building of a strong sense of common purpose and common destiny in the local rural communities is essential for socio-economic development – even survival.

Another equally urgent task is to give the community and the individual an understanding of the developmental process and his/her role therein in a global, national and local perspective so that available options are clearly understood and choice is made with discrimination. When local tensions are shown in the national and international perspective, they can be viewed with greater balance and equanimity. Strategies chosen would also be more effective, for, if the same strategies are adopted at the local level and the wider national and international levels, they clarify and reinforce each other.

The most critical choice before humanity is between violence and non-violence, between love and hatred, between cooperation and confrontation, between war and peaceful negotiation as a means of removing existing injustices. The choice is at the local level as well as at the national and international levels. The nuclear threat has made it crystal clear that the path of violence or confrontation can only lead to universal destruction. Hence, no nation dare say that it will resort to war to maintain peace, and peace, it cannot deny, is the basic requirement for development and growth.

Another thing which is equally clear is that in this highly close-knit and interdependent world, where same laws and criteria of right and wrong need to be applied, one cannot fight for international justice while tolerating injustices at home. And, therefore, foundations of a just international order have to be laid in just dispensation and the creation of a harmonious and fair social, economic and political order at the local level.

The third lesson of the international situation is that building strength and self-reliance of individual nations is the first step towards achieving a just New Economic Order. It is however, not sufficiently realized that self-reliance to the maximum possible extent is equally important at each level. National and regional self-reliance can only be the end result of self-reliant individuals and self-reliant local communities, each speaking from a position of equality, while negotiating the terms and areas of cooperation.

A prime objective of non-formal education would be the creation of a scientific temper among people at large so as to enable them to examine critically the life around them, their social, occupational, political environment, and participate with increasing amount of initiative in making it rational. They can in this way become agents of and partners in ordered change, which is development, rather than be the victims of ad hoc change, which they do not understand, let alone control. In unordered change, it is the weak that suffer and cannot cope with. As change is the law of life, the choice before us is ordered change or chaotic change — change that is envisioned and prepared for or change the onslaught of which is not visualized and, therefore unprepared for. Any meaningful non-formal education programme should give to people at large an understanding of local problems in their local perspective — the problems of education, energy, population, employment, etc., and to develop in them the capability of solving them, thereby contributing their mite towards the solution of these problems on the global scale.

Suggested Criteria

Keeping in view its aims and objectives criteria of a suitable non-formal education programme would be:

- Its strict relevance to life's problems — the people concerned are so desperately caught in life's struggle that they can not afford to be distracted from it;
- Its high degree of efficiency, for whatever is taught must be immediately translatable into life's concrete advantages: knowledge, as a long gestation programme, is a luxury the masses can not afford, nor are they interested in it; and
- Its low cost-simply because resources required in usual format of education are just not available. The apparent contradiction between low cost and high degree of efficiency can only be resolved through maximum possible measure of self-support.

Present Position: A Critical Analysis

Keeping the over-all objectives in view and applying the acid test of its reality and genuineness, one can not help come to the depressing conclusion that, taken as a whole, adult education programme has been a dismal failure and with their uncanny sense of realism, state administrators and planners have invariably applied cut, when necessary, first of all, to programme of adult education. A critical examination of adult education programme, as it has developed over the years, reveals the following:

Heavy almost sole preoccupation with literacy: Literacy is used the entire world over as a measure of a country's educational level and general progress. As no country wants to be labeled backward, every country has been understandably trying to raise its literacy level particularly its politicians and administrators. The emphasis has been on physical targets and "concrete" achievements. The result has been that literacy, a convenient indicator, has been mistaken as the genuine and felt need of the clientele and a tool for human engineering. Adult education has to come in where its importance can carry conviction with the people enough to make them put forth a sustained effort required to make literacy functional. Otherwise, while there is a superficial respect for learning, which leads people even to enroll in literacy classes, they soon drop out. They neither find it interesting nor useful. The frothy enthusiasm of being able to sign one's name which one's fore-father were not able to do, is soon lost when hard pressed adult is not able to fit it as a sustained activity in his scheme of priorities. The only people who are enthusiastic about adult education are the officers conducting the programme. They appear to be its sole beneficiaries-except, of course, the "policy makers" – who must make an up-to-date, "forward-looking" statement that reads well. Literacy, which is a very important tool of communicating worth-while and relevant ideas and hence an essential part of adult education, becomes the greatest hurdle to it, being given at the wrong time, when an adult has not been prepared to appreciate it and before any useful ideas pertaining to the felt needs have been developed. Literacy has been the chief casualty in our campaigns to promote it.

Lack of a sense of direction and consistent approach: There has been no steady progress towards conceptual clarity, resulting from in-depth analysis of experience. There has been a see-saw movement in favour of and away from literacy. Adult education became social education, with a comprehensive content, as reflected in the Saxena Committee Report (1948), in the late forties and early fifties; in relation against the frothy enthusiasm and the wild expectation of the literacy campaigns of the late thirties, when the first experience of limited freedom inspired political leaders and voluntary organizations to launch literacy campaigns all over the country in the hope of awakening masses so that they could see and utilize the opportunities that freedom, which they saw coming, would open out to them. UNESCO's Fundamental Educational

Concept and the UNESCO-Government of India seminar on adult education in 1950 at Mysore reinforced this comprehensive concept of adult education. The community development movement also lent support to this view. The First Plan gave a forceful expression to the concept of a full-blooded programme of adult education. The concept, however, was very difficult to implement and very often the programme degenerated into the easy programme of mere recreation. Soon protagonists of literacy again had the upper hand. It began to be felt that the movement was losing its focus and a swing back to literacy became the order of the day, to which the Third Five-Year Plan gave utterance, especially in the light of the results of the 1961 Census, which showed that literacy percentage had increased only from 17 in 1951 to 24 in 1961. By the Fourth Plan, even the name of Social Education disappeared and was replaced by "Adult Education" with focus on adult literacy. Literacy became fashionable under UNESCO's name plate of Functional Literacy and some attempts were made to link up literacy with specific development programmes like that of the High Yielding Variety Programme in certain districts under the name of Farmers Functional Literacy Project. But due to failure of the literacy campaigns in our own town, country, and in the world outside, nobody dared identify adult education programme with literacy when enunciating the policy statement on adult education. Both in the Fifth Plan (1978-83) and the Sixth Plan (1980-85), the comprehensive concept of Adult/Social Education returned to the fore. The underscoring of literacy, however, continued. There is a very welcome emphasis in the Sixth Plan on technology, to be used "as a major instrument for the spread of literacy".* The field worker, however, had no illusions. Adult education was clearly identified with literacy consistently, in spite of change of nameplates.

Absence of effective implementation machinery: While there has often been a general agreement that adult education programme to be successful needs to be comprehensive and needs to meet basic needs of an adult as an individual and as a citizen, no effective machinery has been built to implement the idea. Too many agencies have been sought to be drawn in without a coordinating core agency to act as a catalyst and with a vision of the total integrated learning process of the group, to which various agencies can be brought in to make their specific contribution at specific points.

Theoretically, adult education is a programme to which every development agency ought to be anxious to contribute and be capable of contributing. For, adults are the clients to whom they are all anxious to sell their ideas as preliminary to their cooperation in their various programmes. And, each agency is doing some sort of extension work. They are however, not working in a coordinated manner and reinforcing each other's capabilities. Coordination has been the weakest link in the administrative chain. For example, while each department brings out substantial functionally relevant literature which could become excellent raw material for neo-literate literature, it is doubtful whether sufficient advantage is taken of this store-house by those who write books for neo-literates or for post-literacy classes. Again, while there are instructions to local officers to cooperate with adult education officers and vice versa, that cooperation in neither regular nor enthusiastic.

Centrally framed and directed programmes: There is insufficient identification of a cohesive group, area or community interests. Nor is there an effective strategy for effectively serving them and harmonizing them with a view to develop cohesive interest groups woven into a harmonious and vigorous community. Not being group, area or community specific, programmes are generalized activities and do not interest groups for whom they are meant. Nor is the potentiality of adult education to serve the needs of area development developed and exploited. The essential elements of adult education – worthwhile knowledge and experience, with the development departments, and literacy or the means of conserving it for reference at the appropriate time, with the Education Departments — lie scattered about without coming together and fusing into a coordinated programme, understood and wanted by the adult community. Thus natural allies in a programme of adult education — the Education Departments and the other development Departments — remain isolated and alienated from one another.

Lessons from Successful Experiments

While the programme of adult education as a whole has not got on to the rails – and does not seem to have found its direction – certain experiments conducted on a limited scale have succeeded. They need to be studied so that their vital elements can be absorbed into an effective strategy for a national programme. Some of these are as follows:

- ***Literacy Programmes:*** where they can be linked up with immediate specific economic gain or an equally intensely felt need - have been highly successful. This has happened in the night schools run by the Jamia Millia, where in half the usual time adults are able to get a fourth class pass certificate required for getting a job or confirmation therein. Similarly, the Central Social Welfare Board has catered to adult women, anxious to settle in a career, and, through an intensive condensed course, enabled them to get educational qualification required for a job.
- At ***Mysore Vidyapeeth:*** sons of farmers were brought for a short period and given experience of improved farming practices, with literacy thrown in as a part of programme of comprehensive daily living. The motivation is provided by the gain in learning and improved agricultural practices. (In urban areas the counterpart is the polyvalent centres, providing training in improved skills).
- ***Gram Shiksha Mohim:*** where hypnotic effect of a mass campaign was used to get over the initial hurdle, of illiteracy succeeded by a vigorous follow-up programme with cheap and relevant literature produced on a massive scale. Such an approach, however, depends for its success upon the quality of local leadership. In Maharashtra the movement collapsed with the removal of the founder of the movement, from the scene.
- ***National Literacy Mission (NLM):*** to increase the

level of literacy and eliminate residual illiteracy in the country, NLM authority was established in 1988. It was revamped in 1999. The scheme is meant mainly for the population in the age group 15-35, which is a major segment of workforce; persons outside this age-group are not excluded. Dropouts are also taken care of under this scheme. The objective of the Mission is to achieve functional literacy, which implies inculcation of following values in the beneficiaries:

- Respect for national integration;
- Conservation of environment;
- Women's equality;
- Observance of small-family norm;

and doing all that which makes adult a potent instrument of change and empowerment of society.

- ***Mahila Samakhya (MS):*** It is an externally assisted programme with a specific focus on gender. The Programme, started in five states in 1989, aims at promoting women's education as well as empowerment of women in rural areas. Under this programme 'women sanghas' are formed at the village-level. At the sangha meetings, women discuss various problems and issues, social customs which are oppressive, ask questions, voice their opinions fearlessly and analytically on different matters and suggest measures for improving them.

  The Sanghas are developing into federations, which coordinate the activities with the help of 'Sangha Yogins'.

  MS programme has generated demand for education for women. Under this scheme, gender sensitive pedagogical and learning material has been prepared, more investment has been made for vocational and skill development and women have been enabled to participate more effectively in village-level educational process.

  Evaluation studies have shown that the programme has been highly successful. Women's participation in the panchayat programme has increased, they are voicing for gender justice and demanding accountability for government system. Their recognition and visibility in the family and the community has increased. All these gains are important national gains.

- India has one of the most wide-spread and effective nation-wide network of **agricultural extension**, which could provide an important focus round which comprehensive programme of adult education could be built.
- **Primary health centres** dotting the countryside could also be similarly developed.
- Our **cultural agencies** have preserved a high level of mass consciousness of basic national values and are a very powerful tool available for socio-economic development and political education.
- ***Mass Media:*** Radio and Television — with community listening and T.V. sets provide important food for development of a comprehensive programme of adult education. The experience of Farm Forums, where listening groups of farmers were formed, was also useful. Immediately relevant programmes were broadcast to them, which they subsequently discussed. Relevant questions could be addressed to the broadcasting station concerned and answers obtained.
- Under Gandhiji's guidance some experiments were conducted in Sevagram by Shanta Naurulkar and in Noakhali by Gandhiji's Private Secretary, Pyarelal, where cooperative action round an economic activity — a grain bank, a milk cooperative, cooperative house-building, cooperative cocoanut oil production — was used as a means of building cohesion and self-reliance of the community. These experiments are some of the most significant experiments in adult education conducted anywhere in the world.

An Effective Strategy

Keeping in view the requirements of the situation and piecing together available experience, the following strategy is suggested:

- The basic requirement is a Community Organiser who understands the dynamics of community development and is committed to its service. He/she may be a social worker, preferably supported by a voluntary organisation. In his absence, it may be a local leader, a school teacher or anybody else, who satisfies the two basic conditions of knowledge and commitment. While any immediate circumstance may become the most convenient and effective entry point into the community for the organizer, he/she must quickly move on to a carefully identified productive activity, cooperatively organized, which would involve the largest section of the community, without antagonizing any segment. This would bring various segments of the community closer as common beneficiaries of a cooperative activity, and convince them of the value of cooperation and develop faith in the competence and bonafides of the organizer. Some funds would also become available for initiating the next activity for common benefit. During a cooperative activity, every attempt must be made to deepen the understanding of the cooperative principle and the cooperative organization through the technique of correlation.
- The next step would be to introduce literacy as a tool of communication of useful ideas, which can be kept in a convenient form for repeated reference at the right time. To reduce the gap between the learning of alphabet and being a recipients of useful knowledge, language used should be the local dialect which, seeing the spoken language in print, will have the additional advantage of arousing maximum interest and excitement.

The content, which would be most stimulating, would be the success stories of the community and further prescriptions for improvement — practical suggestions for improvement of the existing activities. As the content would be local specific, its clientele would be limited, it may not be or economically viable to print it. It may be possible to take help of local school children to write it down. China used school children to write out material for adults on a large scale. It may also be possible to Xerox the material.

With resources built up by and a communication tool designed by the above-mentioned steps, a community is well poised for further steps towards realization of their progressively enlarging area of felt needs; health, recreation, etc. With these three steps, a community, under the leadership of the Community Organizer, will be in a position to take advantage of outside help by bringing in other agencies at the appropriate time and for a specific purpose — credit from financial institutions, inputs from extension departments of Agriculture, Health, Cooperation, etc. Outside help will now come in a form where it strengthens community action and community self-reliance instead of weakening it.

The most difficult task, however, will be to replace the existing balance between various sections of the community — to the extent that it is still left — by a new balance on a more equalitarian basis. One way is to organize each section against the more affluent, leading to the well-known class war. To some extent, it has already started. This is because in the process of social transformation, it is the weaker sections that often suffer. The other option is one of persuasion; of education of each section in regard to the change that is inevitably coming; how that change could be brought about through organized effort and to the advantage of all. If in the new balance of forces some sections lose their present advantage, there were other potentialities in the situation, which could more than compensate them for that loss. Development means replacement of existing opportunities by new and better ones. For example, a law in regard to minimum wages may affect a landlord hard but development may open up opportunities for industrialization in which he may invest his money and enterprise and gain many times the advantage that he has lost. Education is essential for all sections of the population in the inevitability of change and how it could be brought about with maximum advantage to all, giving them a stake in social transformation in the right manner.

Another step would be to identify cohesive interest groups and organize their adult education, centering around their specific interests, their occupational improvement, etc. without bringing them into direct confrontation with other sections of the community. As a weaker section becomes economically stronger and gets better educated, emergence of a more equitable balance between them and those of higher caste would be only a matter of time. The process of education, mass media and cultural agencies, apart from suitable literature, would need to be brought in and tactfully used. In the production of this material, the software, closest link will need to be established between the produces and the local situation.

A number of institutions, which will need to be brought into meaningful coordination, through development of a suitable machinery at the District and the Block to help the village community build itself up, would include:

- Educational institutions, especially technical institutions, providing socio-economic extension for solving social, economic and technical problems;
- Financial institutions to provide credit;
- Voluntary organizations to help organize the community, to enable it to identify its needs and establish its contacts with agencies intended for helping it; and
- Law enforcement machinery.

The clearly identifiable groups, for which non-formal education is required, would be:

- Out-of-school children who have either not gone to school at all or have dropped out after insufficient schooling; they need to be given the equivalent of elementary level of education as a state responsibility under the Constitution.
- Those who have dropped out and entered life as farmers or artisans. Given the necessary educational assistance they could be developed as leaders in various fields of rural life — farming and other occupations, *Panchayats*, etc. They could also be good material for being developed as village functionaries or be trained for the many tasks that further mechanization of agriculture or rural industrialization would throw up. They are the young men who can be trained for diversification of rural economy and horizontal and vertical mobility of the labour force.
- The vast majority of rural adults, who are largely illiterate and who are engaged in a desperate struggle

with poverty. At the same time, they are the people, who have a full charge of the present and any improvement wrought to them has an immediate impact on life and development and because of their numbers, the impact, even of a small improvement is tremendous. They present the most intractable problem in developing countries.

In regard to the first group, the policy should be to recruit un-employed youths having, more or less, similar qualification of a primary school teacher to conduct classes to mainstream them. These instructors are generally dissatisfied, because of the low remuneration, and lack of job security. The second difficulty is the nature of the curriculum being developed and transacted in such classes, which has to be linked to the curriculum of the formal school. The inherent disadvantage of uninteresting and irrelevant curriculum, which led to, the dropping out of the large majority of children still continues in this case. The time is too short for satisfying the duality of objectives: functionality and linkage with formal schooling. The result is that these schools very often end up as inefficient units in a situation where a high degree of efficiency is required. The remedy of the situation is to reform the formal school system, making it relevant to life and interesting, so that the dropout rate is reduced considerably; those who will drop out, a linkage with the formal school can be established within the ambit of relevance.

As regards the second group, there is hardly any provision for them at the moment. Thus the potential of the most promising section of the rural labour force remains undeveloped. The strategy required calls for a two-pronged attack. Firstly, they should receive special attention of the extension services. Secondly, during off-season, they need to be brought together at a central place, either an educational institution or a research station, where, apart from improved agriculture, they are given an intensive training in corporate living and broad based general education, correlated to their own environment. Special emphasis should be given to creating an understanding of and competence to handle basic institutions in rural life, Cooperatives and Panchayats (and of development and social transformation) as well as giving them a broad perspective of the world. While the nodal department may be the Agriculture Department, other Departments must cooperate on a top priority basis, looking upon this programme as a rural leadership programme relevant to all departments. The Deputy Commissioner/Collector of the District, as the leader of the inter-departmental development team at that level, must lend his full support to this programme. The requirements and its strategy in regard to third group have already been dealt with at the beginning.

REFERENCES

* The Sixth Five-Year Plan (1980-85), Govt. of India. Planning Commission Govt. of India.

Chapter 6

Challenges of Implementation

Establishing appropriate linkages between education and, in mutual interest, rural development – as a matter of fact, with over-all development – will call for a radical over-haul of the education system and the existing interdepartmental relationships. Looking at our past record, the task may be difficult; but there is no option but to meet the challenge. The alternative is to let the situation drift, the consequences of which would be disastrous. We are spending over Rs. 1,00,000[1] crore annually on education. It is, however, less than four per cent of the GNP – less than six per cent recommended by the Education Commission, 1966. The momentum for more education is bound to grow and if its direction is not altered, much of the expenditure will go waste. The problem of educated unemployment would worsen. The number of people who would mishandle democratic tasks, that they would appropriate by virtue of their education, would also increase. The direction and priorities of development would to be distorted. The present ridiculous and mortifying situation – where everybody condemns the education system and yet the system goes on merrily – would continue. We have, therefore, no option but to stop the rot.

To develop an appropriate strategy to do so, it would first of all be necessary to analyse, in depth, the causes of our past inadequate performance in managing educational innovations. For this purpose the experience of four innovations, especially related to rural development, are sought to be analysed: basic education, basic and social education in the context of community development, Rural Institutes and National Adult Education Programme (NAEP).

Basic Education

Basic education was the most significant and revolutionary innovation in educational thought and practice in post – Independent India. It had been conceived by Father of the Nation as the "spear-head of a silent social revolution fraught with the most far-reaching consequences."[2] The University Education Commission (1949) stated:

> "At this fateful moment in our history, we have the extreme good fortune to have had presented to us a pattern and philosophy of education of such universal and fundamental worth that it may well serve as the type for bringing into being the new India which is the desire of many of us. We have no sympathy with hero worship, and feel that there should be no withholding of criticism of an educational plan because our great leader presented it. With some details of Gandhiji's programme of basic education, we may not agree. However, taking his concept as a whole it presents the seeds of a method for the fulfillment and refinement of human personality, the wisdom and excellence of which will become more apparent through the years, and will stand the test of time and of criticism. Years of time and vast effort will be required to ensure this movement against warped and mistaken expression, and to develop effective skills and methods; yet inherently, the concept is one of the world's great contributions to education.
>
> "The method outlined in its rudimentary form by Gandhiji is not just a way of meeting the educational needs of little children. He has stated the essential elements of a universal method of education, from the time a little child shares in its mother's work, through the whole process of growth of personality to the time when the mature man of disciplined mind and character works at the side of the master in the achievement of a great design. The essence of this philosophy is that education should combine practice in the everyday processes of living and working with more formal training. This is a fundamental concept, which is steadily gaining support and application in the educational world.
>
> "Gandhiji was not the first to have this vision. Aristotle, Francis Bacon, Milton and Louis Agassiz are among the

world's great men who specifically expressed similar conviction. But in one important respect he differed from most of the others. While their minds caught the vision of a new day, bookishness of their lives held some of them captive. Therein is Gandhiji's pre-eminence. No sooner a conviction matured in his mind, than he acted on it.

The 'Basic Education' Programme – to see rural higher education in good perspective – it is desirable to have a glimpse at the elementary and secondary education out of which it should emerge. As to the programme of Basic National Education for grades one to five, the revised syllabus published by Hindustani Talimi Sangh in 1947 may be taken as a representative statement. As we have seen this programme in practice in several parts of India, it seems to us in the main to be justifying the expectations of those who gave it form. A possible criticism of actual practice is overemphasis on the one process of producing fabric and cloth. This is highly valuable as a centre for correlation of learning, since clothing, like food and shelter, is a basic human need. Also it provides opportunity for children to experience skilful achievement, and to have first hand familiarity with an economic process from start to finish. However, in some cases, it seems that a more distributed interest and attention to varied processes of rural life would be desirable. Basic education should introduce children to all the chief issues and interests of living. It should not become a routine with spinning and weaving as its main expression.

"These first steps of the basic education programme have been clearly defined and, in some cases at least, given able and inspiring expression". (Report of the University Education Commission 1949, pp. 557-559).

John Dewey[3], the father of modern pedagogy, said that Gandhiji saw much further ahead than he did.

Gandhiji had perfected the concept, as was usual with him, through years of experimentation, which went as far back at the end of the last century of his stay in South Africa.[4]

The programme was launched in 1937 on a large scale, with his tremendous political prestige and planned with his usual meticulous care and eye for detail. The Vidya Mandir Scheme was under the Hindustani Talimi Sangh – which consisted of top political leaders, educationists and voluntary workers; most of them had direct experience of operating the programme under Gandhiji's direct leadership. The programme implementation was preceded by training of teachers and started in the best tradition of experimentation – of learning from experience. The programme was, however, rudely interrupted; when because of the policy of non-cooperation with Britain's war effort, the Congress Governments relinquished office. It was a tribute to the inherent worth of the scheme that the state of Jammu and Kashmir and Bihar Province continued to implement the scheme even after Congress Ministries had resigned. Many dedicated workers continued to work in spite of government apathy and even hostility at places. The final recognition came when Basic Education was included as the form of elementary education in the all-India plan of post-war Educational Development in India, popularly known as the Sergeant Report (1944).

Then came independence in 1947 and the problems of partition. When national reconstruction was taken up in the form of the First Five Year Plan, Basic Education was given priority and a phased programme of conversion of all elementary schools to basic pattern was drawn up. By that time, the idea of basic education had been given "inspiring expression"[5] at places. Many dedicated and capable leaders had been thrown up by the voluntary agencies that continued to work during war and thereafter with popular support that the programme had won, at times even in the teeth of government opposition,

The Central Government set up the National Institute of Basic Education in 1956 to give the programme academic and research support. Basic education expanded rapidly. With rapid expansion however, emerged many problems. Without correct handling these problems led to rapid deterioration of the programme and the edifice, built so hopefully and painstakingly, began to crumble. Still the programme continued as a national programme up to the end of the Third plan. The Education Commission (1964-66) gave it a 'decent' burial. The programme does not figure even as a fringe programme in the five-year plans. The National Policy on Education (1986), however, has extended its support to 'Institutions and Programmes of

Gandhian Basic Education'. The policy document, however, has not elaborated in detail the type of support that will be given to it.

What led the programme end on such a dismal note although it was launched under the most auspicious circumstances and had been nationally and internationally acclaimed? Why did what began with a bang end in a whimper? Sir Mirza Ismail, the Diwan of Mysore, accused Gandhiji of putting the clock back. The once enthusiastic champion of basic education, Dr. Zakir Hussain, who had given shape to Gandhiji's ideas of Basic Education, cried out in anguish, that Basic Education, being put into practice, was a fraud on the people.[6]

The fact of the matter is that it was not basic education that failed but we who failed basic education. We tried to implement a revolutionary educational reform as a democratic gimmick. The causes of the failure may be summed up as follows:

1. **End of the public debate:** Educational reform of such fundamental character, above all, requires basic understanding on the part of parents, teachers, administrators, politicians etc. For, each of them is vitally concerned and everyone feels that he understands the educational process, having been through it, and has a right to pronounce a judgement on educational problems and their solutions. Education, however, is a subtle science requiring sophisticated study; only those have a right to pronounce on it who have studied it in depth. No one conceded that the only remedy to meet the situation is to educate everyone about the new educational reform. Gandhiji carried on this process of education of the public through the columns of the Harijan. The programme having become a mass programme the need was to carry on that debate and offer clarifications at the state, district and community levels. Instead, the debate ceased even at the all-India level. One does not recall any public discussion of fundamental objectives of education and how basic education met them in a more effective way, especially in our socio-economic context, than the existing system of education. For example, one does not remember a single public rebuttal of Sir Mirza

Ismail's public statement by any man of consequence. Pronouncements, by public men, who either did not understand basic education or had half understood it, created doubts in public mind about the concept itself.

2. **Vested interest in ignorance and status quo of those in official positions:** The politicians never understood the reform in any depth. They passed on the word to their subordinates because it originated from Gandhiji. With Gandhiji's death, politician had lost the anchor and felt out of depth when considering the advice of his officials. Senior official's attitude has been that he knows everything worth knowing. He has no patience with 'new fangled' ideas especially those that dare to challenge and disturb his complacency and make impossible demands on his scarce time.

   The Secretariat, Directorate and Inspectorate of Education blissfully ignorant of the great reform did considerable damage by demoralizing teachers; reducing allocations and providing no guidance to teachers and field functionaries. One saw many an enthusiastic young men and women, trained in the new methodology, discouraged by inspectors who, instead of enquiring as to how the new methodology was working, what they had done in regard to craft work, building up of the school community, establishing relationship with the local community, difficulties they were facing in accomplishing new tasks etc. enquired only about the usual instructional arrangements. With inspector's report determining career of a teacher, one can understand the harm that had been done to the programme by such an attitude.

3. **Lack of an adequate research and development support:** Every educational programme requires continuous experimentation, especially in its early stages when the experience available is scanty; more so in case of a revolutionary programme like Basic Education which was different from the conventional ideology and practice. One single Institute of Basic Education set up in 1956 was insufficient for a country of India's size and in regard to a programme where

research was to be closely linked with practice in schools scattered in the far-flung villages. Problems relating to time, manner and extent of correlation remained largely unattended and teachers got practically no guidance. School-community relations, organization of craftwork and life in the school to create the necessary attitudes were some of the areas needing research and investigation. What craft should be selected in a particular area, how to get teachers, what to do with the product etc. were other questions that needed critical study. The village-teacher was left to his own resources. He could not be expected to be equal to the task. Textbooks had become irrelevant. Guidebooks were not available. The result was inefficient, insufficient, unnatural and far-fetched correlation. Craftwork was not educationally organized and educational opportunities it provides for promoting scientific temper and the desired social and individual attitudes were not exploited. A single craft was universally practised. Other crafts were ignored. The net result was a travesty of Basic Education. While the appearance remained, spirit was nowhere in evidence.

4. **Desire to catch the headlines:** So long as political patronage to the scheme remained, politicians of lesser breed and officials tried to get quick results. In U.P., for example, all schools became basic schools overnight. In Delhi an adventurous and ambitious Director of Education turned 150 schools over-night into basic schools. Very often the change effected was only the change of the nameplate. This happened more or less all over India. The few serious attempts at implementing the scheme were isolated and nobody studied their success stories in detail or tried to generalize from their experiences.
5. **Vested interest of teachers in the status quo:** The new system called for harder work from teachers but no special incentives were given for this, with the result that the main agent of reform, the teacher, remained unenthusiastic and even hostile.

6. **Linkages with the secondary stage were not forged:** Those who came out of basic schools did not know where to go. The post-basic schools, which were started, were too few and far between. This led to frustration. While innovation, change and development are essential for the growth of a dynamic system of education, citizens cannot be made guinea pigs. The state representing society as a whole has to pay the price-if any price is to be paid of experimentation and its accompanying uncertainties. Again, when any change is introduced at any point in the education system, its impact at other points should be visualized and provided for in time. A half-hearted bureaucracy cannot initiate and manage educational change.
7. **Unimaginative implementation:** Whereas Gandhiji started the experiment in rural areas because of the priority they had in his scheme of things, bureaucracy introduced it only in rural areas, in the spirit that while this type of education was all right for rural areas it was not good enough for their own sons and daughters, who continued to be sent to public schools. No wonder villagers perceived it to be an inferior type of education devised by elite to keep their own stranglehold on society intact. The scheme should have been implemented simultaneously in rural and urban areas and for the rich and the poor alike.

Education and Community Development

A most promising opportunity for promotion of the programme arose in 1952, when the Community Development and National Extension Service programme was launched, with education as the main instrument of rural development. Community Development was defined in the First Five Year Plan as "a comprehensive programme of community uplift, primarily through community action[7]." State aid was to stimulate, not to replace, community effort. This would be possible only if the entire programme was subordinated to and guided by an educational approach. This required, apart from training all extension officers in techniques of community organization, dynamic programmes of elementary education which would take care of the development of children and of adult education for adults. Fortunately by that time the country had already discovered such programmes in the form of basic education and social education. Both had been accepted as governmental policies and were spelt out in the First Five Year Plan itself.

A basic school was the epitome of life of the community with its various problems and constraints, and the entire educational process consisted of trying to understand "the why and wherefore" of these problems and to find solutions for them which would be immediately relevant to the community. Apart from the help that such schools would provide to rural community, they would be building up future generations. Trying to find the scientific basis and the reasons behind the practices and attitudes constituting daily living, students would start the process of innovating and effecting improvements. Schools were intended to become self-reliant, cooperatively organized producing and impacting communities and demonstrating effectiveness of that organization to local communities. They were to be self-governing, which would train future generations in the effective running of Panchayats and other institutions.

Social education programme[8] was also conceived as an instrument of building self-reliant communities, cooperatively organized, with men and women full of initiative, resourcefulness and self-confidence, imbued with a scientific temper that would enable them to direct social change, where that was not possible, to adapt themselves to such change, without being at a disadvantage.

A nation-wide programme was launched, main aim of which was to set rural communities on the path of self-reliance and development and educational instruments had already been forged which would enable the attainment of desired goal. But the expected success did not come. The C.D. programme became a programme of pumping government aid and attaining physical targets to an almost complete neglect of the education process. People, instead of being self-reliant and self-propelling, became only passive recipients or greedy snatchers[9] of government aid and when it was withdrawn, they were perhaps frustrated. We failed to grasp a great opportunity.

The reasons for this colossal failure may be summed-up as follows:

1. The weakness of communication between planning and implementation was most strikingly illustrated in this case. The Community Development Administration was located in the same building as the Planning Commission and yet what was implemented was quite different from what was intended as evident from various annual reports of the Programme Evaluation Organization – part of the Planning Commission itself. Subversion of its policy of an educational approach took place right under the nose of the Planning Commission. There were repeated discussions between the Administration and the Planning Commission – till the Administration became a Ministry and drifted further apart. And yet the message could not be got across!

   Or is it that the Planning Commission itself was not fully committed to what one Member had written in the Education Chapter? Or they were not fully aware of its implications? Or was education regarded only as a peripheral issue where the Planning Commission without conviction could say anything? It appears from examination of this programme, as of many others, that perhaps there is some truth in all these.

   If allocations are the acid test of the priority of a programme, education did not receive much importance. It was given only peripheral importance in the allocation of resources. The orientation programme was slow. While 22,000 new schools were opened between October 1952 to December 1956 only 8,448 were basic schools. The role of the social education organizer (SEO), who was to be the main agent for community organization was not properly understood and appreciated.
2. Disregard of the pilot stage. The desire to "spread like wild fire in the country-side" was so great that essential step of the programme being preceded by a stage was ignored. The awareness has yet to grow that general delineation of policy, without careful watching of the working out of its detailed implications on pilot basis is risky. Therefore, the Planning Commission has to be careful participant, at least careful observer at all

stages of implementation-chain, along with other implementation agencies. Planning will gain in substance, if close touch is maintained with field level in carefully designed and directed pilot projects to identify problems of implementation and their likely solutions.

3. Lack of coordination of educational agencies with extension machinery was evident as is indicated below:
   (a) While the school was declared as one of the three pillars of rural development, it was not formally given a specific place in the extension chain. It could have occupied a strategic intermediate position between the VLW at the level of 10 villages and the community
   (b) The school needed to be linked to the facilities created for agricultural extension, and production and training centers for cottage industries – production, demonstration and training centers, model and mobile units, and productive cooperatives for cottage industries; and demonstration plots and 25-acre farms, for the multiplication of improved seeds and demonstration. No such linkages were established with the result that potentialities of the schools to help community development were neither developed nor exploited. The entire programme of using school, as an important agency of community development, did not go beyond general statements.
   (c) Similarly, links of the SEO with other members of the extension team were not even clearly visualized, leave alone firmly established and practised. SEO, who was conceived as the kingpin of community organization and development, soon became redundant, and "an odd jobs man". Later on it was decided that the SEO would be under the technical guidance of the District Social Education Organizer, but for administrative purposes he/she would be under the Block Development Officer. This too was not a happy

decision as it had the effect of weakening his ties with other members of the extension team, especially as he/she was looking for promotion in the education department. Further, these links with education department ruled out the promising possibility of recruiting SEOs from the more enterprising and able of the VLWs, who had shown capacity for community leadership, because an SEO having aspirations for promotion in the education department had to have professional educational qualifications.

(d) A highly centralized and inflexible block budget made it impossible for helping the school to equip itself for discharging extension functions, although it was ideally suited to do so.

(e) A highly departmentalized and compartmentalized culture, consequences of a long tradition, and a highly centralized administration ruled out the possibility of growth of new approaches based on field experience.

(f) Wrong selection criteria were adopted and consequently unsuitable persons were recruited for jobs to be performed. The qualifications prescribed for an SEO was graduation. The large urban market for graduates and their general preference for urban areas, led to recruitment of rejects of other departments for a job, which required qualities of a community leader and a social worker. For him an understanding of and sympathy for rural community were the most important basic qualifications.

Similarly, in regard to basic education, no attempt was made to deploy in basic schools of project areas, teachers who had demonstrated their understanding of and commitment to it.

Both these cases illustrate that the elementary principle of administration of innovative programmes – that their implementation should be entrusted to persons who had shown initiative, resourcefulness and an experimental spirit – was not put into practice. The flexibility of procedures and freedom to experiment, which were essential, were nowhere in evidence.

4. Training provided was insufficient in duration and inadequate in content and quality for the objective to be achieved. No case studies were prepared as indigenous teaching material, which alone could be helpful. Much of the material used by teachers and available for training was written by foreigners and hence was of limited validity in Indian and local conditions. The techniques of community organization was not included as a subject either in the training programmes of SEOs or of basic teachers, even though that was the main challenge both types of workers were to face. Teachers were drawn in the work of social education but a short training course giving them a veneer of social education was hardly calculated to make much difference.
5. The concepts of basic and social education, as contained in the Plan document were not properly grasped, leave alone implemented. Social Education, as pointed out in the Programme Evaluation Organization reports, remained confined to the beaten track of adult literacy or mere recreation. The main idea of social education as the main instrument for community organization and mobilization and utilization of resources – local and state – to create self-reliant and self-propelling communities, was nowhere in sight. Not a single pilot project was conducted even to see what it implied.

   Basic education, as already explained, suffered a similar fate. Both the programmes were implemented in a routine fashion, both in the projects, as in the rest of the country. The opportunity to experiment and discover dynamic ways of doing things in the context of more favorable conditions, than had so far been provided in rural areas, was thus missed.

Rural Institutes

Another significant programme was that of Rural Institutes. The University Education Commission (1949) emphasized the need for developing higher education as an instrument of rural development, building on the work already done in basic and post basic education at the elementary and secondary stages. In one of its most brilliant chapters, the Commission recommended the setting up of the Rural Universities.

The Hindustani Talimi Sangh at Sewagram and Jamia Millia Islamia were also ready to implement the idea. The idea was perhaps too revolutionary and radical for the bureaucracy to grasp. As it happens usually in such cases, another committee was set up to examine the recommendations of the University Education Commission in regard to the Rural Universities. The Shrimali Committee, as it was popularly called, with a new set of international experts and their Indian counterparts, took months to make their recommendations. The Committee suggested a more modest proposal of setting up Rural Institutes. 14 such Institutes were set up. Some very dedicated voluntary organizations were given the charge of implementing the scheme. The Council of Rural Higher Education was set up. Two loopholes were left unplugged which ultimately led to the failure of the scheme. They included:

(a) No assured employment was provided to the products of these Institutes. While students were trained for a particular job market-rural development-they had to compete with products of other well-established universities. No attempt was made to educate employers in regard to special qualifications of the products of these Institutes, which suited them especially for jobs in hand. These products should have been given a protected or at least a sympathetic employment market and the courses should have been steadily improved to make them more relevant in the light of the feedback provided by their performance. None of these things happened. As a matter of fact, products of these Institutes steadily lost ground to products of established universities, as the prejudice against "new fangled" courses and their products, in the absence of a scientifically assessed feed-back collected from their performance, worked against them.

(b) Without being given a university status, as the University Education Commission had recommended, and their diplomas not having been accepted as equivalent to degrees, the products of these institutes were not admitted to universities for higher education. The products, therefore, had neither assured employment, nor opportunities for further education in the Institutes themselves, or in other universities.

No wonder the Institutes clamoured for linkage status and in the end all of them were affiliated to existing universities except Gandhigram, which was given the status of a deemed to be university. These Institutes, therefore, lost their independent status and orientation and were soon submerged in the sea of conventional higher education, bound by its rules and regulations. Even special monitoring of the programme was given up. The Council for Higher Rural Education was wound up. We do not know today whether any worthwhile remnants of the "dream" remain. The programme, which began with hopes, ended in frustration.

Lack of clear-cut orientation of these institutes in terms of specific tasks for which their students would be prepared was no doubt an important reason for their failure. It could also be surmised that an important contribution was the perception of rural youth about what knowledge and skills led to more gainful and remunerative employment. The preferences of the job market regarding the competencies that it will demand are important determinants of people's choices. Rural Institutes were conceived of and established at a time when the "conventional" competencies promoted by institutions of higher learning were preferred by employees. At the same time inadequate investment in rural areas did not throw up enough jobs for which competencies promoted by Rural Institutes were required.

National Adult Education Programme (NAEP)

The NAEP was one of the most ambitious programmes of mass education launched in the country. It began under very auspicious circumstances. The political will was solidly behind it. The plan allocations were raised to Rs. 200 crores under education, with the prospect of large funds flowing in from other departments and the promise of more funds, if needed. Rarely was a green signal given to a programme in such clear terms. Some of our most dedicated officers were directing it. The three documents: "Adult Education – A Policy Statement", "National Adult Education Programme – An Outline" and "Report of the Working Group on Adult Education for Five-Year Plan 1978-83" showed a wider degree of consultation with all concerned at the national and international levels than had ever been done before. Every effort was made to digest the lessons of available experience. Yet within two years – one of which (1978-79) was a year of preparation – serious doubts began to be widely expressed about the whole programme. A review committee was appointed, which called for a radical modification of the whole programme. The Committee – consisting of some of our top educationists called for a "considerable strengthening" of the central administration and organization. No immediate action followed about this recommendation.

Causes of Failure of NAEP

The causes of the failure of the NAEP were both political and technical; and were so typical of development implementation in a democracy that it would be fruitful to analyze them in some detail[10]. These are:

1. **Political:** A significant educational programme in a democracy gets associated with a ruling party and thus gets linked with its fortunes; if its period of power is short, an educational programme can get discredited, irrespective of its inherent worth, before it had had enough time to take root. As the NEAP was started during the Janata regime, its fate was virtually sealed with the Janata's fall, despite heroic bureaucratic efforts to save it. Those who had been earlier most anxious to clamber up the bandwagon were the first to come tumbling down and became the programme's most vociferous critics. Since it was impossible to attack the importance of adult education in a democracy the critics attacked its mode of implementation, especially the 'favoritism' shown to voluntary organizations. As these organizations were the main implementation agencies, their demoralization under persistent attack of the 'supporters' of the new government was most damaging to the programme.

   But for this political factor, one fails to understand the violence of the criticism against a programme of such magnitude after so short a period. In the implementation of the programme of this size, there had to be a considerable period of trial and error before it could reasonably be expected to get on to an even keel. It is also significant that the programme again started picking up rapidly after its inclusion in the 20 point programme of the congress party government.

2. **Technical:** To mention the political factors first is not to ignore the technical flaws-both of planning and implementation – but to enable them to be viewed in proper perspective and approach in a spirit of constructive criticism. The technical flaws in the programme may be broadly divided into: (a) defects of planning, and (b) defects of implementation.
   (a) **Defects of Planning:** They were pointed out by the author in an article entitled "NAEP – Beware of Reefs Ahead", published in the Yojana in its issue of October 1, 1978 and are summarized below as the observations therein have been borne out by subsequent events:
      (*i*) The content of the programme consisted of literacy, functionality and awareness – literacy including reading, writing and numeracy; functionality meaning skills and capacities to function effectively in his vocation, as a citizen and as a member of the family; and awareness implying knowledge of one's social rights and obligations including the knowledge of how the poor are deprived of the benefits of policies and programmes intended for them. It was a comprehensive package but priorities within this and the sequence of the various parts were not clearly indicated and the fear was – and this fear has been proved correct by subsequent events – that the programme would begin with and end up with literacy[11]. Preoccupation with literacy is understandable in view of the fact that *we house one third of the World's illiterates and that the number of illiterates in our country is increasing in spite of all our efforts, as the population increase of over 2% per annum is more than offset by our average rate of 1% increase*

of literacy. Literacy is also the easiest thing to impart and get recognition for. But literacy is not what an adult wants and is prepared to strive for. It is not a felt need and elementary principle of adult education is to begin with the felt need. The first felt need in the context of India's poverty where, as Gandhiji said, even God has to come with a rice bowl to be recognized, is economic betterment. That is why Gandhiji had said that our adult education centres must become "consuming and producing cooperatives." The advantage of beginning with a cooperatively organized productive activity is that it builds the confidence of the adult in himself and in his educator. The first step will also create resources – however small – for the next step. Having established his rapport with the client, the adult educator can move on to literacy to increase the impact of adult education programme by using this tool to pass on to the adult new prescriptions for his own improvement. The success stories of the first phase will also provide excellent and eagerly sought after reading material. Then one can move on to widening the area of felt needs through progressive sensitization of the adult and take up such activities like health, recreation etc. which can be taken up by group of learners as its capacity to help itself increases. This way, felt Gandhiji, a self-propelling adult education movement could be generated and built up, leading to development of self-reliant communities. There was no such vision in the NAEP. Secondly, all and sundry, who were proposed to be drawn into the movement could only contribute to literacy. Further, in the absence of any concrete plan for inter-departmental coordination and cooperation in the three documents referred to as the guides to action, skill formation could not be seriously attempted. Again, in the absence of any realistic plan for resolving social tensions that would be created by a frontal attack on existing power structure through "awareness" was dangerous and was likely to be ignored. The foregone conclusion therefore, was that the programme would almost concentrate solely on literacy, with poor chances of success even in that because of lack of motivation for it among the adults, as had been demonstrated again and again, not only in India but all over the world in the democratic context. That the programme remained largely confined to literacy was been borne out by the Review Committee (1980).

(*ii*) All and sundry-unemployed youth, students and teachers, cooperatives, Panchayati Raj Institutions etc. – with very different backgrounds and capacities were expected to perform a highly complex task – organization of a community for self-development, without an integrating agency like the Community Organizer or the Social Education Organizer of earlier times, who could take from each agency the help that it could give and integrate it with the help received from other agencies. The result, it was apprehended, would be a chaotic approach through which a comprehensive concept of adult education could not be concretized.

(*iii*) Too much reliance was put on voluntary agencies without taking into account their strengths and weaknesses and without developing methods by which grain could be separated from the chaff. For all sorts of voluntary organizations had grown up under political patronage. While much of the complaint against many voluntary organizations sparked off by the change of government could have been politically motivated, the possibility of misuse of funds by some organizations could not be ruled out. Also, as was brought out in the Report of the Review Committee, voluntary organizations, though being the second most important contributor to the programme, were far behind the government in their contribution. While the

Government ran 67% of the centres, voluntary organizations could run only 25% Good voluntary organizations, being a scarce resource could and should have been used for strategic and more challenging tasks, like research preparation of materials and work among the most disadvantaged groups.

(*iv*) By assigning only a supplemental role to other departments, instead of giving them the primary role in adult education of their own clientele, with Education Departments only as helpers with technical advice, the scheme as it was drawn up, could not be expected, to promote inter-departmental coordination and cooperation that was required for linking adult education with development, especially skill development.

(*v*) The scheme did not show any clear idea of the training required. It visualized large-scale training at the very outset instead of visualizing centres of in-depth study by some of our best men, the results of which would be allowed to grow through sharing and dissemination, and base large-scale training on indigenous and relevant case studies.

(*vi*) Approach to the problem of safeguarding interests of the poor through "awareness" was rather simplistic. The safeguards that were required to control tensions that the confrontation with the existing power structure would create did not receive any adequate attention.

(*vii*) The programme was too ambitious keeping in view the resources. Only Rs.200 crores were provided. Even if double the amount came from other Departments and other sources, the most optimistic calculation could not put the total resources available at more than Rs. 600 crores. So each of the 6 crore of adults proposed to be covered during the 1978-83 Plan would have received Rs.100, which would include administrative and follow-up expenditure. In each year the amount would be only Rs.20 per adult.

The programme on the other hand was a 10-month basic course followed by three years of follow-up. The programme of adult education included, as already stated, literacy, functionality and awareness.

(b) **Flaws of Implementation:** Implementation flaws as brought out by the Review Committee (1980) and reported by State Officers were:

(*i*) Inadequate preparation, haste to complete the overall quantitative targets somehow, were underlined by the Review Committee. The quantitative results achieved were spectacular. The Report says:

"Before the NAEP, the size of the adult education programme had a total enrolment of 675,000. In the preparatory year, this increased to 2,171,000 (or about three times) against a projected coverage of 1,500,000. In 1979-80, it rose to 3.6 million against the projected enrolment of 4.5 million. "The shortfall in performance was due to lack of interest by some State Governments, drought which had affected large parts of the country, and general elections" (Review Committee, 1980).

This hasty implementation and lack of preparation were shown in many ways. Firstly, there were no micro-plans at the district and community levels taking into account objectives and identification of needs of local and governmental resources. Secondly, the programme, while professing to be comprehensive was reduced to mere literacy and that too of poor quality. There was no time for the sort of in-depth studies that were necessary for generating awareness in realistic and fruitful manner. There was no detailed work done which was required for establishing inter-departmental coordination and linking adult education with development. The teaching material that was generated was too generalized to be of use in a situation where only a local need-based material could meet the diversified needs of local communities. Thirdly, no attention was paid to giving the programme, even the literacy part of it, the necessary research support. Fourthly, training was either not given or was provided late and was inadequate. No attempt was made to generate indigenous material through case studies, which alone could make training relevant and meaningful.

The article consequently concluded as follows:

"In conclusion, one would like to say that India is launching on a programme of adult education larger in size and under more propitious circumstances than ever before. In this vast adventure, there will be many things, which we will learn through trial and error. But as that is a costly course, though inevitable, it is desirable that every effort must be made to avoid and prepare for all the dangers and difficulties that can be foreseen. It may be worthwhile reconsidering the internal priorities of the package of programmes constituting adult education and keep the economic factor to the fore. This would require emphasis on resource generation rather than resource consumption. Secondly, the identity of the basic unit of adult education – the cohesive interest group in a local community – must be kept intact and all programmes must be directed to meet its precise needs. Thirdly, the change agent working with this cohesive interest group must be identified, trained and supported. Fourthly, the precise role of the voluntary organizations in this massive programme must be identified, keeping in view their strengths and limitations. Every effort is, however, to be made to identify and encourage new foci for voluntary action especially among the educational institutions. Fifthly the programme will have to be largely a programme depending upon the bureaucracy and any realistic programme – both in size and quality – must keep their capacity in view. Intra-agency and inter-agency coordination and cooperation must be ensured. As adult education is an interdepartmental activity, every department must make provisions in its plans, at the planning stage itself, for educating its own clientele. Sixthly, our best men should be put to work in the rural communities which constitute the laboratory of adult education, and arrangements must be made by which experience from the ground level can be exchanged so as to enrich available experience of different strategies, which could ultimately make a large scale training programme feasible. Seventhly, in-depth studies must be started from the very beginning to see how social tensions, which will inevitably be created by the adult education programme, are to be tackled. Finally, the self-communities will be the acid test of the reality of the programme of adult education." (Yojana 1978).

(*ii*) The qualities required of personnel for the task were not clearly identified nor methods of selection designed for choosing the right type of men required for an innovative and challenging programme. Though human ingenuity to defeat the purpose of whatever methods are adopted cannot be underrated, its effect can be minimized by clearly defining selection criteria and the methods required to apply them. The Review Committee stated:

> "In some States, the State and district level staff has been selected keeping in view the special requirements of the programme. This, however, does not hold for most of the other states. The latter have made appointments largely on the basis of seniority amongst officers of the education department. Such staff is unlikely to show initiative and qualities of leadership, so essential for the success of a programme of this kind."

(*iii*) The motivation of the instructor was severely strained. He was paid a much lesser amounts per month that the amount paid to the Supervisor and Project Officer.

(*iv*) Inordinate publicity was another bane of the programme. To some extent publicity is essential. For, people must understand what is happening before they can cooperate and get involved. But when publicity far exceeds actual performance, it arouses false expectations and, sooner than later leads to frustration and cynicism. Quiet publicity, however does not suit democratic temper of the politician, who has to create an impression and build up an image somehow within the five year period. The bureaucrat, who very often links his fortunes with the politician in power, also becomes excessively target conscious.

(*v*) There was very little coordination between the state government, which was responsible for the programme, and the Resource Centers, which were to generate materials for them.

(*vi*) Follow-up was weak. Follow-up literature was not ready in time.

(*vii*) There was too much arbitrariness in the method of teaching. As the Review Committee pointed out, the "atmosphere of joint learning which must pervade the teachers and the learners in adult education was nowhere in evidence." Further: "There is hardly any awareness of this aspect among the functionaries of the programme and it was hardly reflected in the working of the Centres." In such a mood experimentation and research, so necessary for a new programme like the NAEP, generally gets neglected.

In the light of the above, no wonder that while the Committee was in favour of the continuation of the programme and anxious that nothing should be done to weaken its momentum, it called for a "radical modification" of the programme.

Lessons of the Past: Problems and Remedies

Innovations are at the centre of development but to perfect an innovation and implement it is an extremely difficult and complex task-especially in the case of educational innovations, because the educational process involves almost all citizens as students, parents, planners and administrators, employers or employees, or in many other capacities. *The analysis of some cases in the post-independence period, presented in the preceding pages, brings out difficulties due to both political and technical factors.* These, along with some possible solutions, are indicated in the paragraphs that follow:

Political Factor

Education is by its very nature a slow process and because of the large and highly diverse interests, educational reform is very difficult to put through. Hence pilot projects, national debate etc. are an inevitable part of the implementation of an educational innovation. The politician, however, is in a hurry and so is the bureaucrat, who has to "deliver the goods," to his Minister. Inadequately conceived and tested ideas are often put through in an atmosphere of high publicity. Results, which cannot he achieved, are cooked. On the other hand, the opposition, anxious to discover flaws of the Government exaggerates, the flaws as it happens in a drain inspector's report. This confuses the public, whose understanding and support is required for educational reform. Voluntary organizations, who could play a very important role in experimental and pilot project stage, rightly or wrongly, get dubbed as pro or anti government and are either pampered or starved of necessary support. Many politically sponsored voluntary organizations spring up and soon over-shadow genuine voluntary organizations, who consequently tend to become indifferent to rendering government the honest help, which the government badly needs.

The following measures may help in keeping impact of political processes on education within manageable limits:

(*a*) Policies in education should be national rather than partisan and the opposition should be fully associated with decisions in regard to educational reforms.

(*b*) A national forum of students, teachers, educationists, intelligent citizens and social workers should be established, devoted purely to educational matters (leaving out the questions of salaries, promotions and other trade union activities) to educate public opinion in regard to educational reform and secure for government public support for right policies; and to inform government and the public of any failings of educational policies and implementation through the press, debates and discussions, and the media like the radio and the T.V. It should draw its financial support only from the public to retain its independence.

(*c*) Parent-teacher associations should be formed in every institution; where educational programmes and policies and discussed and the feeling encouraged that education was a joint responsibility of teachers and parents. Education, it should be realised, is everybody's duty, and according to his capacity, he should understand the educational process.

(*d*) Accrediting professional bodies should be encouraged to grow. Their services should be available to voluntary organizations for evaluating their work on payment of a small fee. Voluntary action is of the essence of democracy and it should be a central principle of public policy to encourage it. The problem, however, is that there has been a mushroom growth of voluntary organizations under political patronage which has overshadowed genuine voluntary organizations; the problem is how to separate the wheat from the chaff. An impartial, professional body's evaluation should be welcomed by genuine voluntary organizations; academic community, who should be interested in optimum use of the critical institutions that voluntary organizations can become; and the government, as a professional opinion, universally respected, enables them to resist political pressures. It will also assist the honest bureaucrat.

Initiative for setting up these accrediting bodies could be taken by the National Forum mentioned above or by philanthropists. But the aim should be to make these bodies independent and self-supporting.

(*e*) The pilot project approach, which is required by technical considerations should be made politically more acceptable and even technically more profitable by so arranging that those ideas of the pilot project which have passed the pilot stage test, are injected into the general system, after due preparation, without waiting for results of the entire pilot project.

(*f*) Selection of the right man for the right job is essential for success of innovative programmes. It is very often made impossible by political pressures. Though human ingenuity to nullify the intended effect of any methods that may be adopted cannot be underrated, mischief can be minimized by carefully defining job requirements selection criteria.

The above is by no means a condemnation of the political system. We have opted for democracy as the best available form of government. Political processes are part of life, and like everything else they have both their good and bad points. It is necessary, however, to optimize the good and contain the evil.

Technical Factor

While it is essential to ensure that the political factor does not sabotage imperatives of the technical factor, the first task is to ensure soundness of the technical exercise of innovation management. The prime necessity is that, as education is at the heart of socio-economic transformation, its natural connections with other sectors must be clearly understood and its linkages with them actually established so that education reform is clearly understood in its comprehensiveness. It should, therefore, be formulated in discussion with all concerned and should be accepted by the political authority with full knowledge and commitment.

Technically, innovation planning and implementation chain, in continuous interaction, must be compact, consisting of the following stages:

- Emergence of an idea;
- Pilot project to spell it out and test it in situation which are representative;

- Enlarging the pilot project to include typical areas/cases;
- Planning large scale programme based on the findings through the pilot project (s) with careful working out of inputs required in men, materials and procedures;
- Monitoring implementation for correcting the plan on the basis of feedback; and
- Impact evaluation

As a matter of fact planning and implementing would be related to monitoring, evaluation and correction at every stage and, in case of every operation, through backward and forward loops. The continuous monitoring of operations under implementation and almost simultaneous correction is enjoined by cybernetics, which is the science of the future. Evaluation will provide information on the adequacy and viability of the innovation.

The second requirement of technical efficiency in the management of innovations is to have the right type of persons, materials and procedures. As innovation management throws up highly complex, difficult and exacting tasks, it is essential to have people who understand their jobs, have the competence to accomplish them and are enthusiastic about doing so. The qualities required should be carefully identified and scientific processes brought to the aid of the administrator to design appropriate selection criteria. Research and innovation management is an area, which has to be kept strictly out of external pressures. This requirement must be realized in the highest quarters and utmost attempt made to ensure it. Seniority cannot be used as a selection criterion. Similarly, favoritism, masquerading as "hand-picking" and merit-based, selection would be suicidal.

The third imperative is the motivation of the people selected for the purpose. People engaged in research and innovation management need to be compensated for any loss of power and prestige, which is at present reserved for administrator of large-scale routine operations. It has to be remembered that innovators are a rare and select breed, needing special nurture. There should be appropriate plans for career management to ensure adequate channels of promotion while the State continues to make use of their special and comparatively rare qualifications and aptitudes.

The fourth imperative of technical efficiency is appropriate training. As innovation management means breaking new ground everywhere, it requires generation of indigenous material based on case studies. Foreign and readymade case studies will not meet the situation in education, which is the main agent of social transformation. And our social situations, as almost every social situation, have their own unique character.

The duration of training and even its character and form will have to be designed, keeping each in view the requirements of the programme. Training should include practical work in the community around and social engineering as an essential component.

The fifth requirement of effective innovation management is flexibility of approach and decentralization of authority to enable the man on the spot to make decisions so that there is little delay in implementing new solutions to existing problems.

The sixth requirement is the production of guidebooks and large-scale training in their use at the time of the propagation of the innovation.

In regard to financial procedures, the annual budgeting leads to much unplanned expenditure, most of which is hurriedly spent, before 31st March, to prevent lapsing of allocated funds. This is bad enough for ordinary programmes. This is doubly so where the course of expenditure cannot be ordered. In research and innovative programmes, the organization should be generally allowed to carry over the unspent balance. Otherwise, funds asked for these programmes should be the first charge on the next year's budget. When cuts become necessary due to shortages, funds for research should be regarded as a core of the plan. Since funds for research are usually small, they will not seriously affect the budget. Similarly, in any fund allocation, highest priority should be attached to research and innovation in view of their critical importance in any development.

Again, when introducing an educational reform, its impact preceding and succeeding stages must be visualized and prepared for simultaneously, so that when children pass out of the reformed stage, they do not find doors of the next stage barred, as it happened in case of basic education and rural institutes. If an innovation fails, its price must be paid by the state and not pupils/students who go through an innovative programme. If any attempt is made to make any section of citizens guinea-pigs, they would legitimately resist it; that would considerably limit the power of society to experiment and innovate which is a basic necessity for healthy growth of an educational system.

It is also necessary to inject into the preceding stage the lessons of an innovative programme at a later stage regarding the requirements of pupils coming to it from the preceding stage. This will help pupils making a smooth transition since the later stage would have taken into account their needs. In short, a systems approach is necessary in promoting educational innovations.

Again, not only have the rights of admission to higher stage of those who enter innovative programmes to be safe-guarded, their employment prospects have also to be clearly stated before hand. For, if their employment prospects are restricted in any one direction, they should get specific preference on the basis of the special features of their education. For example, a boy who took rural engineering in a Rural Institute as an area of study should have got a definite preference over another boy trained in other engineering institutions, where he did not study a similar course. If the course was not specifically designed to really make him better qualified for work in rural areas, fault was that of the state and it must pay the price.

Another aspect of innovation management is training/orientation of supervisors and senior administrators. As was seen in the case of basic schools, lukewarm attitude of the inspectors towards new practices, and the general lack of competence to provide guidance to basic trained teachers tended to demoralize teachers of basic schools.

A sympathetic understanding of the new processes involved and a little pat on the back of enthusiastic teachers will go far in determining the success of an innovative programme. This is not only necessary for inspectorate but also for the officers of the Directorate. For, in our hierarchical administration, top level sets the fashion.

Again, educational innovation-especially those linked to development – require a very high grade person to work at the basic institutional level, where most of linkages with other departments and the community have to be established and the delicate tasks of social engineering dealt with. The existing practice of putting in that situation a person who is at the last rung of the administrative/technical ladder would need radical alteration. Some of our best men with requisite aptitude should be especially selected for these tasks and their career prospects duly safe-guarded.

Perhaps, the most difficult and the most important concern is the question of inter-departmental coordination, which is essential in all innovations airing at linking education with development, the theme of the present study. Coordination is in the interest of all departments as it optimizes results from investment through exploitation of the mutually reinforcing capabilities. Yet the tradition of departmental exclusiveness is so entrenched that wherever it has been attempted – whether in Community Development or the NAEP, it has not succeeded. And yet if education is to help develop linkages with other development departments, it is the inevitable pre-requisite. The basic conditions for success of inter-departmental coordination seem to be the following:

(*i*) The Chairman of the coordinating team must be senior enough to assign tasks and effectively pull up defaulting department.

(*ii*) Each department must know its specific role in the joint venture and get credit or discredit for efficient performance on its failure. The part of the programme allotted to it must be officially owned by the department on the basis of a memorandum of understanding, if necessary and planned with as much meticulous care as their usual duties. They should not be regarded as mere helpers and their role regarded as departmental personnel "supplemental" as was done (for example) in the NAEP. Allocations required for performing its role in a coordinated venture should also be made in the plan of each department. Otherwise, expressing the vague hope that funds would be coming forth from other Departments, as was done in the case of the NAEP, for example, leads us nowhere.

(*iii*) The policy, having been decided upon at the highest level and also spelt out to the extent possible at that level must trickle down the line to appropriate levels of implementation.

(*iv*) The representative of each of the coordinating departments must know the role of his counterparts of other departments before he can effectively coordinate his activities with theirs.

(*v*) Coordination being an innovative practice would inevitably require new initiatives and certain changes in procedures, for which the man on the spot should have the necessary freedom. Some decentralization and delegation of authority would be inevitable.

(*vi*) Above all, a culture of coordination will have to be promoted right from the highest level. For, it is holding up work not only in government but also in our universities where the need of the hour is inter-disciplinary research to which departmental exclusiveness is the strongest impediment.

Lastly, to optimize benefits from an experiment, it should be documented in detail so that other people in different situations can also benefit from it by suitable adaptation keeping in view their own situation.

In the light of these tasks, the study goes on to examine the changes that would be required in the existing structures at the Central, State, District, Block and Community levels, through which these tasks have to be accomplished and these challenges met.

Structural Reorientation

Having identified the tasks required to be performed for efficient innovation management, next step would be to study the extent to which these tasks are being performed by structures already available at various levels and the way in which functioning of these structures needs to be reoriented for more efficient performance. Education[1 2], according to the Constitution is, by and large, a State subject but Economic and Social Planning is a central responsibility. Education, which is one of the most important components of this planning, becomes a central responsibility. The levels at which the problem in hand needs to be studied are:

Central level,
State level,
District level,
Block level, and
Community or village level.

Central Level

At the central level, a number of institutions/organizations are concerned with education. they include: Planning Commission, Ministry of Human Resource Development and its subordinate offices like the Directorate of Adult Education, the autonomous organizations created by the Ministry –Research Councils, Academies, National University of Educational Planning and Administrations (NUEPA), the National Council of Educational Research and Training (NCERT) and so on. There are also various National Advisory Boards of which the most important is the Central Advisory Board of Education (CABE). Obviously, if optimum results are to be obtained and a chaotic approach is to be avoided, there has to be coordination among their policies and programmes. There is considerable scope for improvement in that direction. There are also other Ministries of the Government of India, with whom the Ministry of Human Resource Development must coordinate its functions, either because they are also engaged in educational activities like the Ministries of Agriculture, Health, Labour etc. or they are economic Ministries whose programmes have educational implications.

Planning Commission

Obviously, being responsible for designing plans for over–all development, establishing and maintaining of inter-sectoral linkages is the responsibility of the Planning Commission. In this regard one finds that there is no specific point in the Planning Commission where social imperatives and implications of development are looked at in depth and in an integrated way. The Divisions in the Planning Commission work more or less in an isolated manner and function as counterparts of Ministries. There is insufficient interaction between them, and especially with social services and social engineering divisions like Health, Education etc. With education, interaction of other divisions is confined to balance manpower availability with its demand since technical institutions train manpower which other Divisions utilise. Even this coordination is very imperfect at the moment. There is little realization that contribution of education to development is much more comprehensive than provision of skilled manpower. It has to provide the social climate, promote attitudes of people and their social organizations and reflect their aspirations. The result may be illustrated by one or two examples. The setting up of an industrial plant in an *Adivasi* area leads to building of rail and road transport and coming in of a large number of outsiders; destruction of forest, which was the main source of livelihood for the local people; and coming in of new systems of values and social norms held by intruding hordes, which seriously disturb the social life of the tribals. Industrial life again requires a tempo of life different from the one which is familiar to locals. Therefore, if the plant is set up – as such plants frequently are – without taking into account socio-economic changes that will accompany it and without enabling the people, through education and other measures, to adjust to these changes, to face new challenges and grasp new opportunities, the establishment of an industrial plant would be a disaster and not a boon. For, on their own, mass of the people, whom these development projects deeply affect, are incapable of withstanding the shock of change. Similarly, large river dams have been built without adequate plan for all round rehabilitation of thousands of displaced people with their social and economic life disrupted*.

Another closely linked weakness of the Planning Commission is insufficient interaction among human resource development Divisions or wings of Divisions themselves. This departmental isolation exists in entire Government of India. It could be at least removed to some extent if the Planning Commission could take a coordinated and integrated view of human resource development. Some of the elements of human resources development would include:

- Food,
- Health depending upon food, healthy environment, healthy occupational conditions, leisure time

utilization, healthy social climate with a system of values preferring cooperation to cut-throat competition, thereby avoiding tension, etc.

- Education and training, and
- Social and political organization as would be conducive to a healthy environment.

It will thus be seen that human resources development is a much more comprehensive issues than mere manpower planning with which it is often equated. And an integrated view of development policies in this regard would reduce some of the absurdities, where we spend hundreds of crores on education, while giving insufficient attention to nutritional deficiencies of children of ages five years and below, which make them permanently mentally deficient. Again, while there may be an advantage in keeping agricultural education with the Ministry of Agriculture, and medical education with the Ministry of Health etc., there are policies, which are as valid for agricultural and medical education as for the rest of education. Therefore, at least in the Planning Commission, there should be close interaction among Education, Health and Agriculture Divisions and it should be the responsibility of the Education Division to take an integrated view of education "from the moment (a child's) of conception to the moment of death".

To remove these deficiencies, it may be worthwhile to have a Member incharge of Social Planning Human Resource Development. A high-powered Social Planning and Human Resource Development Cell, consisting of very highly qualified social scientists, should assist him. Divisions of Education, Manpower, Health, Social Welfare, Labour and other Social Service Divisions should work to him/her through this high-powered cell. Similarly, economic divisions like Agriculture, Irrigation, Power, Industries etc. should secure views of this cell in regard to the social implications of their policies, programmes and projects and the safeguards, if any, which are needed while implementing them. Their requirements of manpower and other matters of human resource development pertaining to their sectors would be referred to this cell for advice. It would be the responsibility of the Member (HRD & SP) to bring up various issues of social policy for consideration before the Planning Commission.

Another difficulty pertains to insufficiency of discussion in the Planning Commission on different chapters of its report. The member in charge of a sector is responsible for drawing up the chapter pertaining to that sector, in consultation with the concerned Ministry, it passes muster with the Commission without sufficient scrutiny and, consequently, commitment. The result is that each Division and the corresponding Ministry tend to think that they are concerned only with their own sectoral chapter; if there are any suggestions of policy or programmes pertaining to them in some other chapters, they are not taken into consideration nor are allocations, wherever necessary made at an appropriate time. For example, in the Fifth Plan the recommendation in the Education chapter was that other sectors/programmes involving large mass of men as participants or beneficiaries should make provision for adult education and literacy with focus round their programmes. None of the sectors did so and later on when the question was taken up with them, they simply pleaded inability to accommodate these provisions in their plans. The Planning Commission was in no position to provide additional funds. The matter was, therefore, dropped for all practical purposes.

Therefore, it is essential that before plan is finalized, various suggestions in different chapters are identified and discussed with concerned ministries and where it is decided to implement a recommendation, precise role of each coordinating sector be defined and definite allocations made for its fulfillment at the planning stage itself.

The third difficulty at the Planning Commission end is the insufficient technical support, which a division can provide to its Member as compared to the large organization, which a Ministry commands. Under the circumstances, Members tend to follow the Ministry concerned rather than take an independent view, necessitated by their responsibility to view things in a wider perspective than it is possible for a Ministry. It would not be administratively feasible and it will adversely effect the compactness of the Commission, if the Divisions were made too large. They can and should, however, be assisted by expert panels on a continuing basis. At present these panels are ad-hoc bodies hastily constituted and hastily wound up. Each Member should, however, be only for a limited period so that the bodies retain their flexibility. A member may be reappointed after the expiry of his term.

Another weakness of the Planning Commission is its lack of involvement in working out the details of an innovative idea. Planning and development are a continuously evolving process. Today new ideas are put in Plan documents and the responsibility of working them out is left to implementing agencies. Not being originating agencies, they either pass by an idea or only half understand it and are not committed to it. Thus, if an idea is implemented, it turns out to be something very different from what the originator had in mind. If full advantage is therefore to be taken of an innovative idea, the Planning Commission must guide various stages through which an idea passes to the stage of implementation. It is only after it has been worked out, on an experimental scale and perfected, that the idea should be passed on to various implementing agencies. It was very encouraging to see that the involvement of youth and universities in eco-development was undertaken on an experimental basis under direct guidance of the Planning Commission. Three projects – the Himalayan, the Ganga and the Western Ghats – were identified. Universities of these regions, State Governments etc. were involved and experiment was moving forward, with the Planning Commission's promise that if experiment was a success it would be enlarged in scope and coverage subsequent plans. Unfortunately, however, the entire project was passed on to Department of Environment, where the Planning Commission had no control and responsibility to develop its appropriate thrusts.

As regards the Education Division of the Commission, it must:

(a) Look at educational imperatives of development programmes, for which they should be consulted so that they can ensure that educational programmes reflect these demands;
(b) Define the help that education would need from the other sectors and help determining the required allocations for the sectors concerned;
(c) Ensure that manpower demands of various sectors will be met by the Education Plan;

(d) Make its own contribution towards ensuring internal coordination in the Education Sector. Ministries are so big and their parts work with such "independence" that they very often fail to project a coordinated view of education; this view is not reflected in the plan of the Education Ministry. The Education Division accustomed to look at the sector as a whole and not burdened with details of implementation is in a favorable position to assist remove this deficiency; and

(e) Take, as already stated, a coordinated view of all education, irrespective of the Ministry in which it is represented.

The most important and basic requirement is the realization of the pivotal role of education in development. Education chapters in the Plan underline this role; it is not reflected in various sectoral plans. It is another case of departmental functioning in the Planning Commission and insufficient discussion and commitment of the Commission as a whole to various ideas contained in individual chapters. For otherwise, one fails to understand the clubbing of education with social services in the Plans and of the residual approach in determining allocations, which are the "acid test" of the priority attached to any sector, as well as almost complete neglect in practice of innovative programmes which alone could help education to play its developmental role. Instead of being regarded as the core of the plan, innovative programmes are often the first to be sacrificed in case of shortage of funds.

Ministry of Human Resource Development (*M/HRD*)

The Constitution limited the role of the central ministry to a few subjects like the maintenance of standards in higher education, technical and vocational personnel etc. It became obvious that without a national policy on education, one could not build a nation. This need for a national policy on education was further reinforced with launching of planned development. As socio-economic planning was a central responsibility, according to the Constitution education, being an important component of the process of socio-economic development, could not be left out of the central government's list of responsibilities.

The only way that responsibility could be discharged within the framework of the Constitution was to evolve a national policy through discussicn. As a matter of fact the need was so patent that even before Independence, the Central Advisory Board of Education (CABE) had already come into being. The Constitutional position underwent change with 1976 amendment to the Constitution. With education in the Concurrent List centre was made equally responsible for educational development.

The main function of the CABE is to evolve and review national education policies. Unfortunately, however, the Central Ministry has tended to use the CABE as a pressure group for increasing the number of centrally-sponsored schemes and thereby its own operations. The State Education Ministers, not very hopeful of generous allocations for education in State Plans, are always willing to support the Ministry. On the other hand, the state Chief Ministers anxious to have as large a share of the available plan resources as possible, look askance at any expansion of the Central Sector. This tends to result in virtual neglect of or at least insufficient attention, to policy matters. It is suggested that the CABE should concentrate its attention on substantive issues of policy, leaving discussion of programmes to Committees of Education Secretaries and Directors of Public Instruction.

In the context of development, it should be the prime responsibility of the Ministry of Human Resource Development to interpret and spell out educational imperatives of socio-economic development, indicated by the Planning Commission in somewhat general terms, and ensure that they are reflected in the national policy for education. For this purpose, there should be frequent discussions between the Planning Commission and a small but compact agency of the CABE, led by the Education Minister. At present there is hardly any contact between the CABE and the Planning Commission. The Deputy Chairman or the Member for Education is generally invited to impress him with their united demand for more funds than for any serious discussion of the development imperatives for education and vice-versa.

Again, educational policy formulation becomes fragmented – the CABE confining itself mostly to school education – leaving higher education to the University Grants Commission (UGC), technical education to the All India Council for Technical Education (AICTE), youth and sports affairs to the Sports Council (now under a separate Ministry), Cultural affairs to various Academies and State Ministers of Culture and so on. While each of these bodies has an important role to play, there should be a single place where all educational programmes can be viewed in integrated manner. The only appropriate body for the purpose is the CABE, where all interests should be represented. The CABE should be the forum where national educational policy is evolved, periodically reviewed and reoriented to keep pace with the tasks of socio-economic development.

It is only in the context of national policy that activities of various organizations created by the Central Ministry can be coordinated and a chaotic approach avoided, so that their capacities can reinforce national objectives and priorities. Research programmes of various Councils have practically no set of priorities, no policy frame; this provides a fertile ground for many unhealthy practices. The key questions needing investigation are neglected while considerable duplication takes place. No national effort is made. Hence no nationally relevant findings emerge. There is no mechanism for ensuring that recommendations emanating from research studies are considered and brought to the notice of concerned organizations. In most cases, studies, meticulously done by researcher, adorn the forgotten shelves of research bodies.

Even within the Ministry of Human Resource Development, organic integration of educational programmes under its control is lacking. It is a sprawling Ministry. Various demands are added up by its Statistical and Planning Division and with such pruning as is possible, with insufficient understanding of the programmes put forth by its various Bureaux. A judgment is arrived at about the need for funds of each Bureau, depending on pressure it is able to exert rather than on the basis of the inherent worth of the programme. It is suggested that Statistical and Planning Division be considerably strengthened so that it can take a coordinated view of educational policies, relate them to the needs of socio-economic development and effectively discuss various programmes of the Ministry in their proper perspective with the Planning Commission. A full time senior educationist, of the Status of Additional Secretary, who can competently assist the Education Secretary and the Minister, should head this Division.

State Level

At State Level, machinery for planning and implementation of development policies and programmes is more or less similar to that at the Centre. It consists of:

- The State Planning Commission or Board or a Cabinet Committee for drawing up and reviewing the State plan, and
- A Committee of Secretaries under the Chairmanship of the Chief Secretary or a very Senior Secretary called the Development Commissioner or Planning Secretary to coordinate action of various Departments.

The machinery suffers from similar problems from the point of view of inter-sectoral linkages and management of educational innovations resulting therefrom, although the position might vary from state to state. These problems are almost similar to those at the central level. They include:

- Insufficient reflection of development imperatives in educational policies, programmes and methods;
- Insufficient appreciation of the developmental role of education and indifference of the development departments to help education to develop its potential to assist them;
- Absence of the culture of coordination and predominance of departmental exclusiveness; and
- Absence of a suitable mechanism for interdepartmental coordination.

Education Departments do not operate all education programmes. As a matter of fact, scatter of educational activity in different departments is even greater in the States; and there is no place where an integrated view of education in respect of both policies and programmes – is taken except in the Planning Department, where many of these scattered activities are brought together for purposes of presentation of the State Plan to the Planning Commission. The exercise is primarily in the nature of an aggregation of outlays rather than a coordinated view of policies and programmes.

Even in the Education Department, as it is, there is little coordination. There may be a Director of school Education, a Director of College Education, a Director of Adult Education, a Director of Technical Education etc. Their work is supposed to be coordinated at the Education Secretary's level, who may be incharge of other portfolios also. His secretariat, consisting of Deputy Secretaries, under Secretaries etc. cannot coordinate educational policies at technical level. For this purpose, a strong Planning and Statistical Cell, headed by a senior educational administrator and capable of taking a coordinated view of educational policies and programmes in the plan and their relationship with other sectors of development, should assist the coordinator. Such a cell would also be in a position to assess the impact of any administrative innovation introduced at other points of the educational administrative system and warn the coordinator thereof, so that change can be prepared for.

Another point for consideration is whether the division of responsibility between the Directorate and the Secretariat – with the former dealing with all technical matters and the latter concerning itself with broad issues of policy, which should be in line with the government policy in the various other departments – should be altered. From this broad division of functions followed that the Director should be an educationist while the Secretary should be from the general civil service, with very broad experience and perspective. With large-scale induction of the IAS as Directors of Education, this broad division of functions and the qualifications of the cadres intended to discharge them is getting obliterated. It may be useful to retain the old division of responsibilities and the type of personnel intended to discharge them, with such modifications in their system of training as may be needed by the present situation.

Another difficulty in the State Education Department – and this applies to other Departments as well – is the highly centralized character of administration and the consequent inflexibility of procedures, which adversely affect innovation management.

Innovative and research programmes themselves are given low priority in the plan and in spite of the fact that funds they require are very modest, allocations for them are the first to undergo a cut in case of any shortage of available funds. And this happens in spite of the brave words said about them in plan documents. The average administrator and the average politician do not understand them. Nor is there any pressing demand for them from any strong pressure group.

Research support to educational policies and programmes is intended to come from the State Councils for Educational Research and Training (SCERT), training colleges and university education departments. Here again, there is no policy frame and carefully defined list of priorities. Research tends to be ad-hoc and superficial. Secondly, seniority alone determines the choice of the head of the SCERT and not his/her aptitude, even an understanding, of research. Belonging to the administrative cadre and yet denied the power and influence enjoyed by officers of his status in the Directorate, the head of the SCERT is anxious to get back to a normal administrative post – with obvious implications for leadership he/she can provide to major research organization in the State. His qualifications, selection procedure and service conditions need a careful review. The question of recruiting his team also needs a review. Thirdly, there is no linkage between the SCERT and research in the Education Departments of the universities in the state. Fourthly, there is very little involvement of teachers in research. The potential of teachers for research remains unexploited. Also in the matter of developmental linkage of education – as it requires school community interaction and the interaction of a school with local representatives and institutional units of other departments/organizations, which has to take place in field situations and the innovative ideas as to how to improve that interaction can also largely emerge only at the field level – it is most important to utilize and develop the capacity of the teacher, who is the field agent of the education department. It is then for the senior administrators and higher research bodies to refine these ideas, so that they can be generalized and introduced over a much larger area.

In this connection, the recommendation of the Planning Commission in their Draft Fifth Five Year Plan about experimental schools – which incidentally is a good illustration of how valuable recommendations remain buried in the plan documents and the poor communication and interaction between planning and implementing bodies – is worth considering:

"Experimental schools – The plan visualizes many changes in the content and methodology of elementary education. These will involve a considerable amount of work by the National Council of Educational Research and Training, the State Institutes of Education and selected training schools. These institutions are being strengthened. The results of their work will be made available to improve the practices in the large majority of the training schools who will work intensively with one school attached to or adopted by each of them. In order that its experience becomes relevant to the large majority of the schools, the schools chosen for innovative purposes must be representative. The effort will be to try out such new ideas as depend largely on the imaginative utilization of local resources, both material and human. The practices found feasible in this school will be demonstrated to 10-15 schools in the surrounding area and through them to a larger belt of elementary schools. They will also be provided such additional financial inputs as are found to be essential. Through appropriate linkages with the state institutes of education and through them with the NCERT, on the one hand, and on the other, with the district administration and the subject teachers' associations, which exist or can be promoted, the chain of stimulation from above and feedback from below will be completed."[17]

The Commission recommended the idea of experimental schools and their linkage with research bodies and the district administration at the secondary stage[18] as well. The idea of experimental schools is even more relevant in the context of linkages with development and the possibility and importance of innovative ideas emerging at the field level, which will need to be refined and generalized with assistance from higher levels.

The situation is more or less similar in all states. As an example, the position in the Haryana State has been studied in somewhat greater detail*.

With the Planning Board being practically a defunct body, the state plan is presented to the State Cabinet for all practical purposes by the Planning Department. Their exercise, however, is really an aggregative exercise, putting together the Departmental Plans, with an eye to a certain over-all plan ceiling, which appears feasible within likely resource availability – both state and central. The cabinet at its level can only address itself to certain overall questions in a very general and broad way. There is a committee of Secretaries of Development Departments under the Chairmanship of the Chief Secretary. But it is more of a monitoring body for plan implementation than an agency for establishing close coordination between various departments and for reinforcing their mutually reinforcing capabilities, thereby maximizing returns from investments. However, if there was a culture of coordination detailed proposals of coordination could be worked out by Departments and if there was a hitch or a procedural or financial difficulty, existing arrangements could prove sufficient to remove it. In the absence of such a culture, existing arrangement proves insufficient to break departmental isolation. In addition, the agreement to take common action does not go beyond the meeting room; even various departments invite representatives of other concerned departments to their appropriate meetings.

Even in the Education sector itself, various activities are too scattered to ensure effective coordination. There is a Secretary for Education, a Secretary for Technical Education, a Secretary for Sports and a Secretary for Culture. Being in different Departments, possibilities of exploiting their mutually reinforcing capabilities are left unexplored. There are different Directorates for School Education, Higher Education and Adult education. As the Secretary is supposed to deal only with policy issues, machinery for technical coordination virtually does not exist.

The scattering of educational activities in different departments very often takes place not on technical grounds but for accommodating political and administrative aspirants to higher positions. In quite a few states there are ministers dealing with different aspects of education. This makes coordination of educational programmes quite difficult, if not impossible.

District and Sub-District Level

The District level is in a way the most important level in a multilevel planning system. It is largely here that planning impulse from above gets translated into implementable projects, keeping ground level conditions – both human and material – constraints and resources in view. At this level, national and state imperatives have to be reconciled with local imperatives hopefully for the emergence of the country's planning perspective. At this level planning and implementation interact and provide necessary feedback to state and national levels which help to present a national plan. The plan of the district emerges from files and becomes a full blooded perspective of development, involving people, institutions, financial resources, social attitudes, fields and factories, etc. At this level, we enter the realm of micro-planning, where the unit is not too big to allow a national view of objectives, juxtaposed with resources and constraints; and, at the same time, it is not too small for using the expertise of technical personnel required for effective planning. At the sub-district level – sub-division, block and community – planning and implementation is possible only under the umbrella of the district together with which these various levels constitute an integrated whole. The district was a very important unit for administering law and order under the British. Its importance has increased many fold since it has become the unit of development as well.

To understand the situation in regard to plan implementation at the district level and below – problems, possibilities and strategies – two districts of Haryana State – Mohendergarh and Hissar – were chosen for a more detailed study. Findings from the study have been made use of in relevant sections of this document. In this section findings referred to are in regard to: inter-departmental coordination, required for inter-sectoral linkages, of which linking education with development is a part; flexibility of procedures, decentralization of decision making powers; selection and utilization of personnel required for effective innovation management; and research support necessary for progressive change in methods, procedures etc.

Coordination

There is no well-coordinated development administration, required for area development, in the District. There are parallel departmental activities, which are coordinated in a general and very loose manner by the Deputy Commissioner (DC). The D.C.

is the coordination officer at the District level. Coordinator is generally ensured through:

a) Monthly meetings,
b) Letters by departmental officers to the DC requesting him to arrange help of other departments, and
c) DC initiating coordinated administrative activity.

The D.C., belonging to the Indian Administrative Services, commands sufficient prestige to be able to coordinate in a general way the working of various departments except in the case of a recalcitrant department. It will considerably add to the effectiveness of coordination if the coordinating officer has the authority both to reward and punish. The power with the coordinating authority to write the confidential reports (CRs) of officers, whose activities are to be coordinated, should serve the purpose. This practice was in vogue in early days of community development but has been discontinued in most cases. There is a steady assertion, although undeclared, of departmental isolation – "independence" as it is called. In this connection, the developmental role of the superintendent of police needs special mention. The D.C no longer writes his/her CR. The process of social transformation and economic development, however, creates social tensions and conflicts and without the understanding and sympathetic attitude of the forces of law and order, forces of change are considerably handicapped. It is important, therefore, to represent police in the development teams at various levels.

To strengthen the DC's effectiveness as a coordinator, following steps seem to be called for:

(1) He must get back the authority to write CRs of all district level officers. That is the only way in a government organization by which the coordinator can be given indispensable power to reward and punish those whose activities he is supposed to coordinate. The specific attributes in member of his team that the DC could most appropriately comment on, are developmental attitudes and capacities – initiative, resourcefulness, capacity for leadership etc. – as well as flexibility and capacity for teamwork. The demands of internal cohesion of individual departments and

inter-departmental coordination within an area can be reconciled by the administrative competence of departmental officers being reported on by the area coordinator while their technical competence is reported on by their supervisors in the technical departments.

(2) His competence as a coordinator should be augmented. At present departments – with some justification perhaps – complain that under the plea of coordination, their energies are diverted to non-departmental work. To remove any legitimate grievance and to optimize results in terms of development, it may be useful to:

(a) Educate the coordinator as well as various members of the team in the concept of area development and its advantages even from the departmental point of view;

(b) Put every new incumbent, before he assumes charge of the district, through a short but intensive training course in basic government policies and the technique of coordinated area development; and to follow this up with refresher courses at not too long intervals;

(c) Send to him copies of all important governmental policies so that the intent of government can be kept in view by him when issuing instructions to various departments in his capacity as coordinator; and

(d) Give him a highly competent planning and implementation cell under the charge of an Assistant Deputy Commissioner (Development) – an IAS Officer – already appointed to assist, in many districts. The object of the cell, composed of qualified technical persons, would be to draw up the district development plan, monitor its implementation, evaluate and apply corrective feedback. In a way, it will act as the Secretariat for the District Development Planning Committee. It may be considered in what manner this cell could take advantage of the District Statistical officer and the Statistical Unit of the District Rural Development Agency (DRDA).

Effective coordination would require progressive decentralization of decision-making authority so that mutual adjustment, which teamwork requires, can be smoothly effected. More powers should be delegated to both team members and the team leader.

Sub-Divisional Level

The SDO's role in revenue and law and order maintenance is supportive of his role in development. For law and order problems, especially those centring round land disputes are an inevitable part of rural development. The sub-division is an important administrative and development unit. The SDO's authority has, however, been seriously eroded. The following departments are outside the sphere of the SDO (Civil): PWD, Irrigation, Public Health, Electricity and Police. Even in regard to departments, that he coordinates, his sole advantage is his status as Class II Officer. Apart from the BDOs, who work to him on development side, he does not write the CR of any other officer. In context of the area development approach, Sub-Division is an important level to guide and coordinate plans of blocks, monitor implementation, evaluate and provide the necessary feedback. For this purpose, the authority of SDO (Civil) should be strengthened and he should write CRs of all officers from administrative point of view, leaving the technical aspect of their work to be reported upon by their technical department superiors. Both people and the authorities instinctively look up to SDO for tasks to be done in his area and very often he is blamed for lapses even though he has no direct responsibility for them. There is, therefore, need for an area coordinator; a focal point for administration.

Financial powers delegated to him are very inadequate. Delegation of financial powers also needs a serious consideration.

The responsibility of the SDO in regard to personnel that he controls has increased very considerably. Short, but intensive, management courses, departmentally arranged, are very necessary. No such training arrangements exist at present. Short refresher courses arranged at not too long intervals would also be helpful.

The position at Block level is even worse. The Block Development Officer's (BDO's) authority as the coordinator of overall development has been seriously eroded. In case of education, even functional areas of Block Education Officer (BEO) and that of the BDO do not coincide. The operational area of an education block is slightly different from that of the revenue block. BDO is at present only incharge of Panchayats. Most development, however, takes place through the Panchyats and as such the BDO's role becomes important.

BDO's position vis-à-vis other extension offices in block is made anomalous by the fact that many of latter draw higher salaries than the BDO (e.g. Agricultural Development Officer and Inspectors of Cooperative Societies). The salary of the Social Education and Panchayat Officer (SEPO), who is second in command to the BDO, is less than that of a Head Clerk of the BDO's office.

The competence of BDOs – except those directly recruited, who are graduates with farm experience – also leaves much to be desired. They are promoted from VLWs.

The BDOs are frequently exposed to serious political pressures and are too quickly transferred unless they are in league with local politicians.

By freeing them from the control of the coordinating officer – BDO, SDO etc. – departments have created a vaccum in regard to supervision of their personnel. It is not financially feasible for each department to appoint its own supervisor to replace the supervisory role of the coordinating officer.

In view of the poor facilities – educational etc. – available at Block headquarters, BDOs keep their families in towns and are therefore frequently absent from headquarters.

The key task in strengthening developmental administration is to strengthen the BDO. He should be a class I Officer and his salary should be higher than that of other extension officers, whose CRs, on their administrative he must write.

Earlier his salary and position were so attractive that some Tehsildars opted for the post of BDOs. Later, however, their scales and that of other extension officers were made higher than that of the BDO.

Block agency, as well as the number of police thanas in villages, have not increased along with the increase in population. Consequently tasks have become unmanageable and developmental work and maintenance of law and order have suffered. The "food for work" programme which relies on Panchayats is hamstrung by the inadequate staff that the BDO has to plan it and execute it properly. There has, therefore, been inevitable wastage.

At village level, there is not even a semblance of inter-departmental coordination. All departments have their own representatives in the village or a group of villages. The elected Panchayat has no control over these officers although it performs a number of development tasks for which it gets government grants. There is first of all the need for placing all developmental agencies under a coordinator. The need at this level is for integration rather than coordination; the umbrella for that integration can be provided by only the Panchayat, without which the drawing up of village plans, mobilization of local resources and matching of effort with local aspirations are not possible. At the lowest level, planners and the implementers, producers and beneficiaries, are the same; and they have to be given full responsibility through the medium of their elected Panchayats.

The main task of effective development administration is to strengthen the Panchayat. Today village has been torn asunder by elections and most of the time of the panchayat is spent in helping their 'friends' and punishing their "foes". Local factions get linked to State and national parties. Some regulations can be formulated to mitigate the effects of this evil. For example, it may be laid down that nobody would be elected as a Sarpanch unless he worked as a Pancha for 15 years. If people of the village as a whole have consistently voted for him for that period, one may presume that he has solid qualities and is not a mushroom political favourite. Certain educational qualifications may also be laid down. It would also be useful if conventions are established to keep out national and State level political parties. Preferably, office bearers of the Panchayat should be unanimously elected and decisions on major issues also taken unanimously. A substratum of the old community feeling still exists and can be made the starting point of building up community cohesion on new basis. Old ties are vanishing. New common interests are, however, emerging in relation to technical, economic and social services that the village community needs. This sense of common destiny, institutionalized and strengthened by village planning process should be developed. Within that context and with an appropriate system of education, existing divisions and tensions can also be steadily resolved. This would be the surest way of strengthening Panchayats.

Till such time that an effective, coordinated or integrated development agency is set up at village level, it may be pertinent to promote the capacity of each of the departmental local agent for development under the guidance of their block-level guides. In case of education, following steps can be taken to strengthen its linkages with other departments or with the people:

(1) There is a large-scale development of Parent Teacher Associations (PTAs). For example, in the Hissar Block out of 46 schools, 43 have PTAs. The position, however, varies from block to block. A nominal fee is charged as admission fund from every pupil and the money is placed at the disposal of the PTA for development of the school. The PTAs also help to mobilize local resources for schools. The local people in Haryana construct all school buildings. It is by any standard a magnificent feat. PTAs should be set up everywhere.

(2) If general instructions for policy of coordination can be issued from all departments, local teacher can get in touch with his counterpart in another department and work out cooperative action on some projects – planting trees, developing kitchen gardens, health check up, instructions to teachers in regard to simple, identifiable diseases – can be taken. At present, there is hardly any help available from other departments. In spite of an afforestation policy, in schools the grounds are bare. Nor is there a kitchen garden. Even a hedge round the school is not visible. There is a District Health Officer (DHO) (Schools) but there are hardly any visits to village schools except for vaccination.

The question of inter-departmental coordination was discussed in a meeting at the Girls' Government Middle School, Goad (Narnaul Teshil), where Panches and teachers of Goad and Balaha Kalan were present. It was the unanimous opinion of all that there was hardly any inter-departmental coordination.

Although the Government Middle School, Goad, was quite close to Balaha Kalan rural dispensary, the doctor never visited the school, even when requested, except for purposes of vaccination. The forest department had an ambitious programme of increasing forest cover and they had succeeded in convincing and inspiring farmers to such an extent that the 1981-82 target of planting 26 lakh saplings in Haryana had been raised to 40 lakhs. But so far as the schools were concerned there was hardly any contact established by the Forest Department. Considerable land around schools was bare. Nor had agricultural extension officer, who came to demonstrate to villagers improved methods of cultivation, ever visited the school and encouraged setting up of even a small kitchen garden even when all facilities required were available. As a matter of fact an enterprising teacher set up such a kitchen garden and it continued to flourish during 1978-81 till the teacher left and boys of the high school nearby (Goad High School) ate up what was there. That was the end of the kitchen garden activity.

Vacations and the syllabus should link school activities with local environment and local problems. Once that is done, sources of help from within the community should be tapped. All teachers and Panches who gathered at Goad as well as teachers at Krishna Nagar High School, Narnaul Tehsil, complained of the absence of local colour in the syllabus. Activities like agriculture, first aid, elementary nursing etc. could be introduced in schools and teachers trained therein in training colleges. Local farmers can help in guiding agricultural operations. The present position is, however, exactly the reverse of what it should be.

It was reported at the meeting (4.5.82) with the Panches and teachers at the Goad Girls' Middle School that vacations were not linked with harvesting, with the result that during the season there were lot of absentees in school. On the day of our visit only 25 per cent of girls were present while at Krishna Nagar High School, Narnaul Tehsil, the attendance was only 33 per cent. As regards the syllabus, teachers at the Krishna Nagar School pointed out serious absence of the local environment. For example, in textbook on social studies for class IV, while there was a lot of talk about the United Nation (UN), there was no mention of the Panchayat and its significance. (As a matter of fact the UN becomes intelligible and interesting to pupils, especially at that stage, only when it is linked to local institutions, which they can see and understand.) In Hindi textbooks, while we hear all about the wide world, we have very little of India, leave alone Haryana. In Geography, while we do not hear much about Indian rivers, we hear of the Nile. The absence of local colour is a serious matter in textbooks. For, it reverses the rational learning process – from the known to the unknown. Moreover, intense involvement in immediate environment is the first pre-requisite for developing a development temper. Even when environment is reflected in the textual material or activities, they are not examination subjects and are consequently neglected both by students and teachers, although they are a part of the internal assessment, marks for which are shown along with the result of the public examination.

REFERENCES

1. Analysis of Budged Expenditure on Education, 2005-06, Government of India, Ministry of HRD, New Delhi.
2. Nayar, Dev Parkash (1952), *Building for Peace*, Atma Ram and Sons, Delhi.
3. Dewey Stated this in a discussion with Shriman Narain, a former member of the Planning Commission, Government of India.
4. Reference his experiments of the Tolstoy Farm.
5. University Education Commission Report (1949), Government of India, p. 559.
6. In a letter to G. Ramachandran, the President of the Hindustani Talimi Sangh.
7. First Five-year Plan, Government of India, Planning commission, p. 542.
8. Ibid. pp. 542-548.
9. Government development aid enabled the more advantageously placed classes to appropriate all the benefits for themselves and thereby still further strengthen themselves vis-à-vis the weaker sections.
10. The observations in this section are based largely on interviews with the officers of the National Institute of Educational Planning and Administration, New Delhi who conducted a large number of training courses on NAEP for the State Officers; and the Report of the Review Committee.
11. Yojana, Vol. XXII/18, Planning Commission, Government of India, new Delhi.
12. Before 1976, education was the exclusive responsibility of states.

The Constitutional amendment of 1976, included education in the concurrent list. The substantive financial and administrative implications required a new sharing of responsibility between the Union Government and the States. While role and responsibility of the states in education remained largely unchanged, the Union Government accepted a larger responsibility of reinforcing the national and integrative character of education, maintaining quality and standards including those of the teaching profession at all levels and the study and monitoring of education requirements of the country *India, A Reference Annual*; Research, Reference and Training Division, Ministry of Information and Broadcasting, Government of India, 2006. (p. 215).

* The development at Nandigram in West Bengal are a pointer to the disastrous impact of industrialization without seeking the cooperation of the effected people.

17. Draft Five-Year Plan 1974-79, Government of India Planning Commission, pp. 195-196.
18. Ibid p. 197.

* The situation relates to 1980's.

Chapter 7
Conclusions

Perspective and Priority

Mankind stands terror-stricken, being at the brink of a nuclear holocaust. Nuclear terror is, however, only the tip of the iceberg. The present situation is spiraling levels of violence from individual upwards through the institutions of a highly competitive and acquisitive society. If society is to be saved, the trend has to be reversed all along the line. It may appear to be a desperate attempt but desperate situations call for desperate remedies. A desperate attempt is better than none at all. Humanity, to survive, must move towards the goal of a cooperative rather than a competitive society - "a caring society" where individuals are bound by ties of mutual concern. The imperatives of this global perspective must be worked out in terms of international, national and local institutions that may bring out the best in humans instead of their worst, as at present. The existing gross inequalities and injustices-not only between nations but also within nations – need to removed to usher in a non-exploitative global society.

Rural areas and rural communities constitute perhaps the largest and most glaring example of inequity. They need most concern and attention of the world. On account of their large number, they pose the most serious potential threat to world peace and stability; yet they could become a potent force of world prosperity, given the efforts of the developing world, where most of these populations are concentrated, and the enlightened self-interest of the developed world.

Working out imperatives of this global perspective in the Indian context, we have to strive for a decentralized economic and political order. The principal aim of the economy should be maximizing employment and progressively moving towards the goal of "work for all". It will also achieve a significantly more equitable distribution. The economic system will need to be highly efficient and decentralized, relying mainly on cottage, small and medium-sized industries, with large industries confined to meeting certain essential needs, supported by a large-scale and appropriate R & D effort to devise appropriate technology and a wide-spread extension service to propagate it. The development, spread and effect of large industries – to the extent that they are needed for their employment potential – should be maximized by development of ancillaries and through spacing. For maximum efficiency, A coordinated policy of cooperation by operational analysis will be needed so that each operation is performed on the scale most suitable to it. To feed the population, vigorous family planning and population control programmes, a powerful land reform movement and programmes to create the climate of just social order is required. Considerable stepping up of R & D effort concerning the problems of small and marginal farmers and of dry land farming will be required. Mechanization of agriculture should be resorted to only in those cases where there is a sizeable addition to production or where there is a net addition to the labour force. The development of industries or vocations allied to agriculture should aim at reducing or removing under-employment. The other features of the required economic order would include: highest priority to production of goods and services to meet the minimum needs of the mass of the people; sizeable and progressive reduction of disparities in income; creation of an atmosphere of austerity where ostentatious living is frowned upon; and the organization of space on "growth centres" model to create a balanced and mutually supportive relationship between cities, the small towns and villages. The system will require an appropriate administrative, credit and marketing support.

A decentralized political system with full involvement of people-participatory democracy-alone can ensure growth with justice, which is, among India's declared goals of development. Building of strong self-governing communities is the inevitable corollary of a decentralized economic and political order. While modern forces have destroyed the earlier basis of local communities, delivery of ever-increasing social and technological services has created a new rationale for strong, cohesive local communities-self reliant and self-propelling.

National integration and cultural harmony, will necessitate satisfaction of minimum needs of all; participatory democracy; organization of space and the establishment of mutually supportive relationship between the city, the small towns and the villages; and, above all, support of an appropriate educational system.

It is against the back drop of these global and national perspectives that rural development in India, and elsewhere, has to take place and the problems of rural areas solved through numerous projects within the constraints of each local situation; making full use of locally available resource. While each local situation will have its own specific character, certain general features of rural areas and society can be summed up. Rural areas face tremendous problems of development – poverty, search for alternative sources of energy etc. - requiring large resources, appropriate technologies and institutions and effective methods of energizing the poor. Against this, there are serious constraints of resource availability and serious limitations of democratic governments, having to face democratic pressures. To provide effective help to the poor against the design of well-entrenched vested interests, on whom the powers that be have themselves to rely for continuing in power, is no easy task. It is in this context that widening gap between the rich and the poor, despite an impressive array of professions, legislation and investments since impendence to reduce it-becomes explicable. The remedy lies in developing and organizing the poor through a radically oriented system of education, which would strengthen them as individuals and organize them into effective communities capable of creating resources out of the scattered natural resources around them, appropriation of state help intended for them, becoming aware of their own rights and responsibilities, and capable of taking their own decisions and getting them respected-in short, masters of their own destiny. In this silent revolution main activities would be performed by individuals and voluntary organizations, which it should be the state policy to encourage and support. The creation of an appropriate system of education would also be a state responsibility with the help of enlightened sections of the public and bureaucracy. It will be the function of activists to identify their supporters at various levels in the established order, which does not consists only of black and white but of many shades of gray as well. The politics of numbers should also enable them to establish relationships with centres of power. Learning the art of building their own strength, the poor would command increasing respect, which will lead to a slow and steady change in the existing balances in rural society towards an increasingly equitable balance of power.

Educational Imperatives

The chief features of educational system, which would be capable of assisting us to move towards our social, political and economic goals in development, have been identified as follows:

1. It must, above all, be a **character building education** for, without discharging this basic function, education becomes a socially disruptive force and enables only the 'haves' to increases their exploitative power. Increasing violence in the world is an inevitable corollary of moral decay. The crisis of character is much deeper than economic crisis.
2. **Methodologically,** education must centre around life's problems and activities, which provide foci for the integration of knowledge. It must also be a production-centred education to generate resources, create strong motivation for acquiring education in a poor country and effectively promote self-reliance among people. To teach cooperative living and the democratic way of life, institutional life-especially in residential institutions – must be organized on the basis of cooperative community living. It must build in pupils developmental personality traits and leadership qualities-initiative. resourcefulness, enterprise, managerial capability, team spirit, social commitment etc. and capacity for organizing the community.
3. **Content** must reflect major issues: energy; ecological balance; population management and the problem of health; technology transfer and up-gradation of skills; and community cohesion and the cooperative way of

life in both, the local and the global perspective – the relative proportion of the two perspectives being determined by the stage of education.

4. The following stage-wise inter-sectoral linkages can be and need to be established:

   (a) **Pre-school Centre** (age group 3-6) should confine itself to making up nutritional deficiencies of the child-through a community-contributed and a community-organized mid day meal programme-and the formation of orderly and clean personal and social habits, through simple activities-both physical and imaginative suitably organized. The programme should be linked with the programme of adult education, integrated Child Care programme of the Social Welfare Department, programmes of food and agriculture departments and those of health departments etc.

   (b) **Elementary School** is ideally situated to be developed into the most effective agency of socio-economic extension through which ideas and techniques of social and economic development can reach every rural family. For this, various extension agencies should help the school with material inputs and technical guidance. The curriculum should include knowledge and skills required for basic health, employment and cooperative living. Subject knowledge will be integrated around the problems thrown up by these major concerns, That will improve problem-solving capability of the child and promote his/her active interaction with environment. Subjects should be handled in such a way that if a child enters life at the end of the elementary stage, he/she is able to deal with problems of family and community life more efficiently than those who have never been to school. If he/she chooses to go further, basic knowledge and skills will serve as a good starting point for the next stage.

   (c) **Secondary Stage**, consisting of the lower secondary (classes IX and X) and the higher secondary (Classes XI and XII) stages will continue processes of building the total personality of the students, using individual and community problems as Centres of Interests, in close cooperation with and with the full assistance of extension agencies. There will be a progressive increase in emphasis on the vocational skills especially at the higher secondary stage, where, however, vocations should be selected after a careful survey of manpower needs of local areas. Correlated teaching will be deeper; more sophisticated and will link the local environment with an ever-widening environment within the country and the world outside.

(d) **Universities** in India represent a very large potential for helping the cause of development. They have the prime responsibility towards development of rural areas, which contribute very largely to the highly subsidized university education at great sacrifice. Any denial of this responsibility – by profession or action – would be so iniquitous adding insult to injury and will constitute the most vulnerable point in our social and political system. Universities, cut off from the vast mass of the rural people, cannot produce leadership steadfastly loyal to the people, which a democracy requires. Leaders that emerge from universities – intentionally or unintentionally - can and do considerable damage to social and political health and stability. Hence, if planning of university education is to have any meaning, one of its major objectives should be to establish firm links between universities and rural communities, which will have the additional advantages of getting university men into touch with virgin soil, research in problems of which will get them international recognition, because they will be the first in the field, as well as solve urgent national problems.

The main findings of the Study in the section on university institutions include:

(*i*) Participation in rural development and responsibility towards rural people should figure prominently in laying down the objectives of higher education. These objectives should be frequently repeated to increase the awareness in the academic community of their basic responsibility.

(*ii*) New universities, as far as possible, should be opened at District headquarters and there should be a phased programme of shifting existing universities also to District headquarters, where they should be linked with development machinery. They should also have their extension and research centres in the interior to interact with typical rural situations. They should further establish close linkages with voluntary organizations in areas where they operate.

(*iii*) Restructuring of the curriculum in order to make it problem-centred and inter-disciplinary, with the problems of rural areas figuring prominently therein, and integrating theory and practice should receive very high priority.

(*iv*) Improvement of the general atmosphere in universities should be taken up as the basic requirement for getting any worthwhile thing done in the universities.

(*v*) Establishment of Departments of Continuing Education, Adult Education and Extension Work, and Universities' Involvement in Bio-development represent significant programmes and, to exploit their educational potential fully, activities they represent should become a part of the curriculum. Technical efficiency of activities undertaken and the services rendered should be improved with appropriate help from development agencies, with which necessary linkages should be established. Further, they should be organized on the basis of maximum possible self-reliance. Wherever possible, nationally significant programmes should be preferred.

The control of NSS and its direction should be transferred to the University Grants Commission.

(*vi*) To break conservatism and inertia of the university

bodies in restructuring of courses, the UGC should mobilize the opinion already created in its favor by exposure of students and teachers to programmes of involvement in community work, as well as expertise created by the favourable beginnings in a few universities, and, with their help, launch a vigorous programme of seminars on the subject, give financial help to those wanting to frame and try out reformed curricula, and bring out detailed reports on the work being done.

(vii) General universities have considerable potential for helping development and linkages must be established with development departments to exploit and develop this potential. In turn, universities would gain pedagogically, for these linkages will give them opportunities for concretizing what is taught in class room and integrating theory with practice. It will also enable them to generate original teaching material as well as develop in students some social commitment at an impressionable and idealistic age.

(viii) Apart from including materials relating to various aspects of rural development in particular subjects, a Department of Rural Development should be set up. It should design and introduce courses in rural development after carefully ascertaining the need for products of such courses. This Department would draw/enlist the help of other Departments, while itself acting primarily as a catalyst and a coordinator.

(ix) Rural orientation of agricultural universities should be enhanced, especially in regard to their Home Science programmes and their choice of research subjects.

(x) Work of the IITs should be further strengthened in evolving and transfer of appropriate technology to the rural areas not only for its own inherent worth but also because of the inspiration it would provide to other technical institutions. Further, it needs remembering that even the highest knowledge is

gained by establishing and maintaining its links with the ground realities.

(*xi*) Institutions of higher learning of varying types need a forum for interaction among themselves.

(*xii*) The potential of colleges of arts, science and commerce for rural development should be developed both in the interest of society and their own pedagogic necessity. For pedagogic reasons, a study of the local environment should be an essential part of their curriculum.

Keeping in view their constraints of time and academic commitment, such programmes should be taken up by every department which pertains to its disciplines; do not require too much time or resources; and do not bring any section of the community served into conflict with another.

Apart from sectional programmes, a number of departments or a college as a whole must also take up some area development programmes, which provide excellent training in inter-disciplinary approach.

(*xiii*) For a phased programme of college involvement in development work and its sequel, and reconstruction of syllabi, should be drawn up and implemented by the UGC, the Ministry of Education and the Ministry of Rural Development.

(*xiv*) Science and technology are the basic instruments for rural development. Technical institutions will, therefore, have to play a critical role in rural development. The major capacities they should develop would include: upgrading of skills, evolving and transferring of appropriate technologies, fabrication of new machines till their manufacture is picked up by industry, and installation and maintenance of machinery.

(*xv*) The above jobs require competence at various levels and so a hierarchy of institutions, linked through a referral system, would be necessary.

(*xvi*) While all institutions should participate in and assist rural development, a major share of responsibility in this regard will have to be borne by institutions located in rural areas. For this, they should be adequately equipped. It should be a major policy to open a polytechnic at each district headquarter, with the specific responsibility of assisting rural development-apart from its other normal responsibilities-unless that is ruled out by the overall manpower demand and supply situation. In that case, some existing institutions should be equipped to discharge this responsibility.

(*xvii*) The basic policy should be to so reorient curriculum as to give a prominent place to local problems and their solutions. Articles required for workshop practice could also be picked up from the environment.

(*xviii*) As evolving and transfer of appropriate technology has to be done in the total socio-economic situation, technical institutions will need the assistance of, and to cooperate with, other developmental governmental and non-governmental agencies. These institutions should further have a definite and important place in the development teams at the District and Block headquarters, apart from at state and national levels.

(e) **Non-formal Education** in the context of rural development, the study identifies following overall objectives for non-formal education, in the inter-linked local, national and international perspectives:

- To improve economic condition of the people through the promotion of knowledge and skills-both technical and organizational (required as the first essential objective in view of mass poverty);
- To build cohesive strength of the community to meet the demand of economic and social development, to provide an effective receiving mechanism at the local level for the delivery of services and to forge a peaceful alternative to confrontation as means of social transformation;
- To create a scientific temper in the people so as to enable them to critically examine the life around-

social, political, economic – and participate more effectively in rationalizing it; and

- To enable people to see the global problems of energy, ecology, population etc.-in their local perspective and to develop in them the capacity to solve them at the local level, thereby making their specific contribution towards the solution of the global problem.

The criteria for an effective programme of **Adult Education** are then suggested. These are:

- Strict relevance to life's problems;
- High degree of efficiency; and
- Low cost.

The main target groups in rural areas would be:

i. School going children who have missed going to school or have dropped out;
ii. Those who have completed classes I-VIII of schooling and have entered life as farmers, artisans etc.; and
iii. Vast and amorphous group of those beyond the school going age, i.e. from the age of 15 onwards with the most important component being the 15-35 age group.

While some beginnings have been made in India in regard to groups: (i) hardly anything has been done for group, (ii) There is, however, considerable experience in regard to Group, and (iii) On the basis of an analysis of past experience there study, suggests the outline of an effective strategy:

In regard to Group (i) where the problem is to effectively link their education with curriculum of the formal school on the one hand and the occupational problems of the children involved on the other, the only remedy possible is the reform of the elementary school to make it life-centered and problem-oriented, which is even otherwise a crying necessity.

In regard to group (ii) it is recommended that the approach should combine-through inter-departmental coordination-extension – the introduction of short contact courses. The Study emphasizes that the group represents the most important foci in labour force, which could be developed as progressive farmers and artisans. This reform could include elements of skill training useful for school leavers/dropouts who settle down in parental/community occupations.

In regard to group (iii) the elements of an effective strategy are summed up below:

(*i*) The pivot of the programmes would be the Community Organizer who has knowledge of community organization and social commitment.

(*ii*) While an activity, depending on prevailing situation, could provide entry point into the community, the organizer must quickly move to a cooperatively organized economic activity, which should lead to economic benefits. That would build self-confidence of the local community, confidence in and rapport with Community Organizer and also provide funds for further group action.

(*iii*) The second step would be to impart literacy through the medium of local dialect to remove the hiatus between learning of the alphabet and getting of useful practical knowledge through the written word. Reading material provided should be based, as far as possible, on their own experience, with further "prescriptions" for improvement added thereto.

(*iv*) Having developed the means of building resources as well as an effective tool of communication, community could move on to other aspects like health, recreation etc. in its progressively enlarging area of felt needs.

At this stage, mass media, and even more importantly, our own cultural agencies would be useful in preparing software for the mass media it would be helpful to use as much of local context as possible.

Implementation Challenge

Linking education with rural development will call for many radical changes in the system of education. While it will be an up-hill task, but the challenge has to be met. To ignore it would be disastrous. The Study analyses four major innovative programmes, linked with rural development, implemented since independence, the hurdles experienced in innovation management and some suggestions, as to how they could be overcome in the future. A brief discussion follows:

Political Factor

Education by its very nature is a slow process. Because of the large and highly diverse interests involved, educational reform is very difficult to implement. Hence pilot projects, a national debate and other measures are an inevitable part of implementation of an educational innovation. On the other hand, politician is in a hurry because of his limited time in office; so is the bureaucrat, who has to "deliver the goods" to his Minister. Often therefore inadequately conceived and tested ideas are implemented in an atmosphere of high publicity. Results, which can not be achieved, are cooked. On the other hand, the opposition, anxious to discover flaws of the Government, exaggerates if not invent, flaws in the programme and in their implementation. This confuses the public, whose intelligent support is required for successful implementation of an educational reform. Voluntary organizations, who could play the most important role at experimental and pilot project stages, rightly or wrongly, get dubbed as pro or anti government and are either pampered or starved of necessary support. Many politically sponsored voluntary organizations spring up and soon over-shadow genuine voluntary organizations, which consequently tend to become indifferent to rendering the honest help, which the government badly needs.

The following measures may keep the impact of political processes on education within manageable limits:

(a) Policies in education should be national rather than partisan and the opposition should be fully associated with decisions in regard to educational reform.

(b) A national forum should be established. It should comprise students, teachers educationists, intelligent citizens and social workers devoted purely to educational matters (leaving out the questions of salaries, promotions and other trade union activities). The forum will educate public opinion in regard to educational reforms, secure for government public support for right policies to inform government and the public of any failings of educational policies and implementation through press, debates and discussions, and media like the radio and T.V. It should draw its financial support only from the public to retain its independence.

(c) Parent-Teacher Associations should be formed in every institution, where educational programmes and policies are discussed and the feeling encouraged that education is a joint responsibility of teachers and parents and it is everybody's duty, according to his/her capacity, to understand and participate in educational processes.

(d) Accredited professional bodies should be encouraged to grow. Their services should be available to voluntary organizations for evaluating their work for a small fee. Voluntary action is the essence of democracy and it should be a central principle of public policy to encourage it. The problem, however, is that there has been a mushroom growth of voluntary organizations under political patronage which often over-shadow genuine voluntary organizations. The problem is how to separate wheat from the chaff. An impartial professional body's evaluation should be welcomed by genuine voluntary organizations, public whose funds are involved, academic community who should be interested in optimum use of critical institutions that voluntary organizations can become; and the government, since professional opinion, universally respected, enables them to resist political pressures. It will also assist the honest bureaucrat.

Initiative for setting up these accrediting bodies could be taken by the National Forum mentioned above or by philanthropists. The aim, however, of including these bodies in the forum should be to make these bodies independent and self-supporting.

(e) Pilot project approach which is required by technical considerations should be made politically more acceptable-and even technically more profitable-by so arranging that those ideas of pilot project which have passed the pilot stage test, are injected into the general system, after due preparation, without waiting for final results of the completed pilot project.

(f) Selection of right men for right job-so essential for the success, especially of innovative programmes-is very often made impossible by political pressures. Though human ingenuity to nullify intended effect of any methods that may be adopted cannot be underrated, the mischief may be minimized by carefully defining job requirements and selection criteria for every job.

The above is by no means a condemnation of the political system. We have opted for democracy as the best available form of government. Political processes are a part of life, and like everything else they have both their good and bad points. It is necessary, however, to optimize the good and contain the evil within manageable limits.

Technical and Administrative Factor

While it is essential to ensure that political factor does not sabotage imperatives of technical factor, the first task is to ascertain soundness of the technical features of innovation management. The Study identifies the following requirements for technical soundness:

(1) As education is at the heart of socio-economic transformation, its natural connections with other sectors must be clearly understood and its linkages with them actually established, so that an education reform is clearly understood in its comprehensiveness. The reform should, therefore, be formulated in discussion with all the concerned and should be accepted by political authority with full knowledge of its nature and implications.

(2) Technically, innovation planning and implementation chain, in continuous interaction, must be compact, consisting of the following stages:
   - birth of an idea;
   - pilot project to spell it out to include typical areas/cases;
   - planning a large scale programme based on findings of the pilot stage with careful working out of inputs of men, materials and procedures required;
   - implementing the large scale programme;
   - monitoring for effecting midway corrections; and
   - Evaluation of the impact.

As a matter of fact, planning and implementation would be connected at every stage with monitoring, evaluation and correction and in case of every operation, through backward and forward loops. The need for continuous monitoring and evaluation of operations under implementation and almost simultaneous correction is now a well accepted principle in management science.

(3) We should have the right type of men, materials and procedures. As innovation management throws up highly complex, difficult and exacting tasks, it is essential to have men who understand their assignments, have the competence to carry them out and are enthusiastic about doing so. The qualities required should be carefully identified and scientific principles brought to the aid of administrator to design appropriate selection criteria. Research and innovation management is an area, which has to be kept strictly immune from external pressures. This has to be realized at the highest quarters and utmost attempt made to ensure it. Seniority cannot be used as a selection criterion. Similarly favouritism, masquerading as "hand-picking" and "merit-based" selection, would be suicidal.

(4) The man selected must be highly motivated through appropriate encouragement. People engaged in research and innovation management need to be compensated for the loss of authority and prestige, which is at present reserved for administrator of the large-scale routine operations. It has to be remembered that innovators are a highly rare and select breed, needing special nurture. There should be appropriate plans for career management to ensure adequate channels of promotions for them while the state continues to make use of their special and comparatively rare qualifications and aptitudes.

(5) Appropriate training of men selected is the most essential requisite. An innovation management requires breaking new ground everywhere; it requires generation of indigenous material through case studies. Foreign and ready-made case studies will not meet the

needs of the situation in education, which is the main agent of social transformation. And our social situations-as almost every social situation-have their own unique character.

The duration of training and even its character will have to be designed, keeping each case in view. The training programmes will also need to have practical work in the community around and social engineering as an essential component.

6. Effective innovation management requires flexibility of approach and decentralization of authority to enable the man on the spot to take decisions required to put through new solutions to existing problems.
7. Another requirement is the production of guidebooks and large scale training in their use at the time of the propagation of the innovation.
8. In regard to financial procedures, annual budgeting leads to much unplanned expenditure, most of which is wasted to prevent the lapsing of allocated funds. This is bad enough for ordinary programmes. This is doubly so where the course of expenditure cannot be precisely ordered. In research and innovation programmes, an organization should be generally allowed to carry over the unspent balance. Otherwise funds asked for these programmes should be the first charge on the next years' budget. When cuts become necessary due to shortage of funds, those for research and innovation should be regarded as the core of the plan. As such funds are usually small and they will not seriously affect the budget. Similarly, in any fund allocation, highest priority should be attached to research and innovation in view of their critical importance in any development.
9. When introducing an educational reform, its impact on preceding and succeeding stages must be prepared for simultaneously, so that when children pass out of the reformed stage, they do not find the doors of the next stage closed to them, as it happened in the case of basic education and the Rural Institutes. If an innovation fails, its price must be paid by the state and not pupils/ students who got through an innovative programme.

If nay attempt is made to make any section of the citizen guinea-pigs, they would legitimately resist it and that would considerably limit the power of society to experiment and innovate which is a basic necessity for the healthy growth of an educational system. It is also necessary to inject into the preceding stage, lessons of an innovative programme at any stage regarding the requirements of pupils coming to it from the preceding stage.

In short, a system's approach to educational innovations is necessary.

10. Not only have the rights of admission of those who enter innovative programmes, to the higher stage, to be safe-guarded, their employment prospects have also to be clearly stated before-hand. If their employment prospects are restricted in any direction, they should get specific preference on the basis of special features of their education. For example, a boy who opted for rural engineering in a Rural Institute should get definite preference in rural engineering over another boy trained in an other engineering institution. This he did not get, because, perhaps, the course was not specifically designed to really make him better qualified for work in rural areas. The fault was that of the state. It must pay the price.
11. Another aspect of innovation management is training/ orientation of supervisors and senior administrators. As was seen in the case of basic schools, luke-warm attitudes of inspectors towards new practices that the basic trained teachers were trying to adopt demoralized them. A sympathetic understanding of new processes involved and a little pat on the back of enthusiastic teachers goes far in determining the success of an innovative programme. This is not only necessary for Inspectorate but also for the Directorate. For, in our hierarchical administration, the top ladder sets the fashion.
12. Educational Innovations – especially those linked to development-require very high-grade persons to work at basic institutional level, where most of the linkages

with other departments and the community have to be established and the delicate task of social engineering handled. The existing practice of charging the man on the last rung of the administrative/technical ladder with the task would need radical alternation. Some of our best men with requisite aptitude should be especially selected for these tasks and their career prospects duly safe-guarded.

13. Perhaps the most difficult and the most important issue is that of inter-departmental coordination. This is essential in all innovations which aim at linking education with development. Coordination is in the interest of all departments as it optimizes results from investment through exploitation of their mutually reinforcing capabilities. Yet the tradition of departmental exclusiveness is so strong that wherever coordination has been attempted-whether in Community Development or the NAEP-it has not succeeded. And yet, if education is to help development, its linkage with other development departments is the inevitable pre-requisite. The basic conditions for meaningful inter-departmental coordination seem to be the following:
    (i) The Chairman of the coordinating team must be senior enough to assign tasks and expect performance. Any defaulting department must be pulled up. In universities, where the need of the hour is inter-disciplinary research, departments should be made to fall in line.
    (ii) Each department must know its role in a joint venture and get credit or discredit for efficient performance or for failure. That part of the programme allotted to a department should be officially owned by it – if necessary – and planned through a Memorandum of Understanding, the memorandum should be drawn up with meticulous care. Departments should not be regarded as mere "helpers" and their role regarded as, for example "supplemental", as was done in the NAEP. Allocations required for performing its role in a

coordinated manner should also be made in the plan of each department. Expressing a vague hope that funds would be coming forth from other Departments as well-as was done in the case of NAEP, for example-leads us nowhere.

(iii) A policy having being decided upon at the highest level and also spelt out-to the extent possible at that level-must be communicated down the line to different levels of implementation. Intra-departmental coordination is basic to inter-departmental coordination.

(iv) Representative of each of the coordinating departments must know the role of his counterparts of other departments before he can effectively coordinate his activities with theirs.

(v) Coordination, being an innovative practice, would inevitably require new initiatives and certain changes in procedures, for which the man on the spot should have the necessary freedom and authority. Some decentralization and delegation of authority would, therefore, be inevitable.

(vi) Above all, a culture of coordination will have to be promoted right from the highest level. For, lack of it is holding up work in government is the strongest impediment.

To optimize benefits from an experiment, its nature and implementation should be documented in detail so that other people in different situations can benefit from it by suitable adaptation, keeping in view their own situation.

In the light of these tasks, the Study goes on to examine the changes that would be required in the existing structures at the Central, State, District, Block and Community levels, through which these tasks have to be accomplished and challenges met. These are indicated below:

Central Level

(1) The most important and basic requirement is the realization by the Planning Commission of the pivotal role of education in socio-economic development and their commitment as a body to reflect this priority in

allocations and in the establishment of appropriate inter-sectoral linkages.

(2) To ensure that social implications of various developmental programmes are fully taken into account, the Planning Commission should have a Member in charge of Social Planning and Human Resource Development. A high-powered Social Planning and Human Development Cell, consisting of highly qualified social scientists, should assist him. Divisions of Education, Manpower, Health, Social Welfare, Labour and other Social Service Divisions should work through this high-powered cell. Similarly the Economic, Divisions like Irrigation, Power, and Industries etc. should obtain views of this cell in regard to social implications of various policies, programmes and projects and the required safeguards, while implementing them. The requirements of manpower and other matters of human resource development pertaining to their sectors would be referred to this Cell for advice. It would be the responsibility of the Member (HRD & SP) to bring various issues of social policy before the Planning Commission.

(3) To ensure better inter-sectoral coordination, it is essential that before the plan is finalized, suggestions in different chapters of the plan are identified and discussed with the Ministries where it is decided to implement a recommendation, precise role of each coordinating sector, defined and definite allocations made for its fulfillment.

(4) To bridge the communication gap between it and the implementing agencies, in regard to innovative ideas, the Planning Commission must guide various stages through which an idea passes from conception to the stage of implementation. It is only after it has been worked out, on an experimental scale, and perfected, that an idea should be passed on to various implementing agencies.

(5) Member in Charge of education should be technically strengthened by the appointment of expert panels on a continuing basis.

(6) Education Division of the Planning Commission must be strengthened to look at educational imperatives of development programmes; define the help that education would need from other sectors and help in determining the allocations required to be made in various sectors as also to ensure that man-power demands of other sectors are met by the Education Plan; make its own contribution towards ensuring internal coordination in the Education sector; and take a coordinated view of all educational programmes, irrespective of the Ministry in which they are located.

(7) To help evolution of a national policy on education, the Central Advisory Board of Education should concentrate on substantive issues of policy, leaving discussion of programmes to Committees of Education Secretaries and Directors of Public Instruction.

(8) In the context of development, it should be the prime responsibility of the Ministry of Education to interpret and spell out educational imperatives of socio-economic development, indicated by the Planning Commission in somewhat general terms, and get them duly reflected in the national policy of education, which should in turn be duly reflected in the State and Central Plans. For this purpose, there should be frequent discussions between the Planning Commission and a small but compact delegation of the CABE led by the Education Minister.

(9) To reverse the present trend towards fragmentation of educational policy formulation, the CABE must be strengthened by representation of all interests to become the focal point where national educational policy is evolved, periodically reviewed and reoriented to keep pace with the tasks of socio-economic development.

(10) Within the framework of a national policy for education, a national policy of research should be drawn up for guidance of various research councils so that a well directed national research effort can be mounted to support the implementation of the policy.

(11) To ensure that an organically coordinated view of the Plan of the Ministry of Education is taken, the

Statistical and Planning Division of the Ministry of Human Resource Development should be considerably strengthened so that it can take a coordinated view of educational policies, relate them with the needs of socio-economic development and effectively discuss various programmes of the Ministry in their proper perspective with the Planning Commission.

State Level

The lack of inter-sectoral and intra-sectoral linkages at the Centre are to be found at the State end also. Steps recommended for removing them at the Central level are required to be taken at the State end as well. A culture of, and effective machinery for, coordination are urgently required. In addition, the Study makes the following specific recommendations:

(1) The traditional division of responsibilities between the Education Secretary-belonging to the general administrative service and responsible for broad policies of government-and the Director of Public Instruction-an educationist, responsible for technical aspects of educational planning and administration-needs to be kept intact and strengthened. While overall coordination of the education plan and its tie-up with other sectors of development should be the responsibility of the Education Secretary, detailed working out of this coordination would have to be the responsibility of the Director of Public Instruction, who should be senior and knowledgeable enough to be able to coordinate all sub-sectors of education. He should, in turn, be assisted by a strong Planning and Statistical Cell, headed by a senior educational administrator, capable of taking a coordinated view of educational policies and programmes in the Plan and their relationship with other sectors of development.

(2) To allow for the initiative required at various levels for effective management of innovative programmes, it would be necessary to decentralize decision-making.

(3) High priority should be given to research and innovative programmes and in case of budgetary cuts, funds

required for them should be treated as the core of the Plan.

(4) To improve research support to educational policy and programmes:
   (a) there should be a policy for research within the framework of the state education policy, which may require that the national educational policy is modified, where necessary, in the light of the peculiar conditions in the State, and key problems, requiring research, should be clearly identified;
   (b) the personnel for research organizations should be carefully selected keeping in view their capabilities and aptitudes, and they should be duly compensated so that their rewards compare well with those of their compeers in the administrative services; and
   (c) the work of the SCERT should be coordinated with that of the Department(s) of Education in the State universities.

District Sub-District Level

Inter-sectoral coordination at District level needs improvement. The position at the sub-Divisional and Block levels is unsatisfactory. And there is practically no coordination at the village level. The authority of the coordinator at these levels has been steadily eroded after the hey-days of the Community Development Programme. To improve the situation, authority of the coordinator at each level must be strengthened through a salary higher than those of the other team members and by giving him the duty to adjudge the administrative capacity (through the CRs) of all officers constituting the development team. These teams should include all officers working at that level, especially those entrusted with the maintenance of law and order. Similarly, the competence of the coordinator must be improved by training and refresher courses in development-administration, man-management, area development, basic governmental policies etc. Technical support for discharging his functions as a coordinator of development programme is also essential. Coordinating machinery also needs to be evolved at village level under the umbrella of the Panchayat.

To strengthen the Panchayat, process of election, qualifications of the sarpanchs, existing power structures etc. need a careful review. Conventions need to be evolved to keep national and state level political parties out of Panchayat elections; to have Panchayat elections on the basis of consensus; to decide major issues again by consensus; to select sarpanch only from those who have been sarpanch for a sufficiently long period to establish their credentials with the people etc. The most important step to build the strength of the Panchayat would be the creation of strong cohesive local communities in response to the challenges of new situation arising from an expanding delivery system for social and technical services.

Till such time as an effective coordinating machinery is put in place, the initiative of the local representative of each department to get in touch with his counterparts in other departments should be encouraged through decentralization of the decision-making powers, developing a culture of coordination through a policy pronouncement conveyed all down the line in each department, making each functionary aware of the roles of his counterparts in other departments etc.

So far as the Education Department is concerned, its links with the community can be strengthened through curriculum and rescheduling of vacations as well as setting up of Parent-Teacher Associations.

Apart from coordination with other development departments, there is the question of strengthening and development orientation of the educational administration itself.

Education Departments can strengthen and orient themselves for innovation management, that linkages with development would demand, through increasing their own efficiency and basic integrity; by introducing flexible procedures and effective decentralization of decision making authority; by developing a forward looking, intelligent and appreciative supervision; by establishing a close tie-up between syllabus, training of teachers and evaluation; by careful planning of transition from the experimental stage of an innovation to that of general applicability; and provision of an adequate research support.

Index

Academic institutions, 126
Access with equity scheme, 106
Activity-centred education, 83
Administration
centralized, 178
educational, 247
Administrative innovation, 43
Adolescence Education Programme (AEP), 107-08
Adolescent education open schooling system, 109
Adult education, 4, 93, 130, 150, 155-59, 161, 163, 174, 182, 184, 186-90, 199, 202, 208, 211, 229, 233
concept of, 157, 185
linking, 186-87
programme of, 161
Adult literacy, 96, 157, 179
Afforestation
policies, 218
programmes, 129
Agencies
centralized, 111
educational, 177
implementing, 203, 243-44
non-governmental, 133, 232
voluntary, 92, 125, 128, 131, 170, 185
Agricultural development paradigm, 44
Agricultural marketing, 138
Agricultural practices, 101, 120
improved, 159
modern, 109
Agricultural predominance, 61
Agricultural processing industries, 34
Agricultural revolution, 31
Agricultural universities, 31, 120, 139-40, 149-50, 230
Agriculture
broad-based, 28
improved, 165
mechanization of, 37, 164
modern, 61
All India Council for Technical Education (AICTE), 140, 144, 149, 206
All India Educational Survey, 104, 114
Alternative and innovative education, 96-97
Anganwadi centres, 93
Anti-poverty programmes, 21
Apprenticeship scheme, 148
Assistance
educational, 164
governmental, 27
Association of Indian Universities (AIU), 143
Autonomous institution, 113, 138

Back-to-school camp, 97
Badheka, Gijubhai, 91
Bal Shree Camp, 114
Balaha Kalan, 218-19
Balwant Rai Mehta Committee, 30
Basic education, 80, 82, 95, 114, 167-73, 175, 178-80, 195
Basic National Education, 169
Bhave, Vinoba, 58, 72
Bihar Education Project (BEP), 96
Block and Community levels, 4, 198, 242
Block Development Planning Committees set, 142

Capabilities, 85-86, 155, 158, 222-23, 246
managerial, 103, 152, 226
problem-solving, 227
Capacity
administrative, 246

decision-making, 79
economic, 102
excess, 147
growing, 70
Central Advisory Board of Education (CABE), 199, 205-06, 244
Central Board of Secondary Education (CBSE), 106
Central Social Welfare Board, 91
Central Tibetan School Administration (CTSA), 106
Centrally sponsored scheme, 106-07
Character building education, 226
Children with Special Needs (CWSN), 99
Children
challenged, 109
creative, 114
malnourished, 25
rearing, 52
young, 77
Colleges
affiliated, 124
junior, 104
medical, 116
professional, 131
rural, 125
technical, 116, 141
Communication technology, 106
Community Cohesion, 90
Building of, 90
Community Development Administration, 176
Community Development Programme, 29, 246
Community learning centre, 114
Community organization, 87, 90, 174, 176-77, 179, 234
Community
academic, 123, 127, 130, 137, 140, 148, 192, 229, 236
adopted, 131
adult, 158
cohesive, 152
effective, 225
self-propelling, 179
self-reliant, 184
spatial, 151
vigorous, 158
well-organized, 153
Computer Aided Learning (CAL), 99
Computer literacy, 107
Co-relation technique, 78
Cottage industries, 38, 43, 59-60, 141, 177
Council of Rural Higher Education, 180-81
Cow dung gas plants, *see* Gobar gas

Decentralized society, 66
Department of Adult and Continuing Education, 132
Department of Women and Child Development (DWCD), 92
Developing countries, 5-6, 13-16, 25, 29, 34-35, 37, 70, 88, 118, 135, 165
helping, 13
importing, 34
Development planners, 57
Dewey, John, 169
District Primary Education Programme (DPEP), 96
District Rural Development Agency (DRDA), 214
Dropout, 98, 102, 112, 151, 160, 165, 234

Early Childhood Care and Education (ECCE), 91-92, 94-95
Eco-development, 132-33, 150, 203
Economic betterment, 152, 184
Education Commission, 103, 111, 167, 170
Education for All (EFA), 95-96, 114
Education Guarantee Scheme (EGS), 96-99
Education
activity-centred, 83, 134
agricultural, 201
character building, 226
compulsory, 95-96
computer-aided, 107
environment-based, 71
life-centred, 78, 80, 136
medical, 201
need-based, 135
physical, 113
political, 161
pre-school, 91-93
problem-centred, 55, 137
production-centred, 85, 226
stage of, 92, 105, 227
Educational libraries, 107
Educational policies, 192, 206-09, 236, 245-46
Educational reform, 6-7, 80, 171, 191-92,

195, 235, 239
Extension agencies, 110-11, 223, 227-28

Family planning, 60, 89, 141, 224
Farmers Functional Literacy Project, 157
Fertility replacement level, 23
Five Year Plan, 45, 157, 166, 182, 221
First, 157, 170, 174-75, 220
Third, 157, 170
Fourth Plan, 157
Fifth Plan, 128, 137, 157, 202, 209
Sixth Plan, 132, 157
Tenth Plan, 44, 95-96
Food and Agriculture Department, 94, 114
Food for Work Programme, 21
Foreign exchange constraints, 29
Formal school system, 165
Fuel-wood, 34-35

Gandhi, Mahatma, 91
Gandhigram, 181
Geographic Information Technologies (GIS), 99
Gestation programme, 155
Gobar gas, 36, 38, 87
Gram Shiksha Mohim, 159
Green revolution, 30-32, 37, 40, 45, 49
Gross enrolment ratio, 105
Growth rate, 15, 22, 30-31, 33, 105

Hindustani Talimi Sangh, 169-70, 180, 220
Human resources development, 26
Hussain, Zakir, 171

Inclusive education, 99
India Council for Technical Education, 206
Indian Council of Social Science Research (ICSSR), 135
Indian Institute of Management, 54, 144
Indian Institute of Science, 140, 144
Indira Awas Yojna (IAY), 21
Indira Gandhi National Open University (IGNOU), 135-36
Inequalities, 5, 13, 15-16, 19, 22, 39, 44-45, 48, 50, 69
inter-country, 16
international, 16-17
Information Computer Technology (ICT), 106-07
Integrated Child Development Services (ICDS), 92-94, 96
Integrated Education for Disabled Children, 106

Jamia Millia Islamia, 180

Kendriya Vidyalaya Sangthan (KVS), 106-07, 112

Leadership qualities, 86
Library research, 4
Life-skills, 96, 108, 127
Literacy campaigns, 156-57
Literacy programmes, 142, 159

Mahila Samakhya (MS), 96, 160
Malnutrition, 25-26
Marginal Farmer and Agricultural Labour Development Agency (MFALD), 44
Marginal farmers, 20, 51, 60-61, 76, 120, 224
Mid-day meal scheme, 96, 101
Millennium Development Goals (MDGs), 77, 114
Montessori, Madame, 91

National Adult Education Programme (NAEP), 167, 181-84, 187, 190, 197, 220, 241-42
National Bal Shree Award Scheme, 114
National Centre for Advocacy Studies, 45
National Charter for Children (NCC), 95
National Council for Teacher Education (NCTE), 113
National Council of Educational Research and Training (NCERT), 71, 104, 106, 113, 199, 210
National Employment Guarantee Act, 91
National Extension Service, 29-30, 43, 49, 174
National Food for Work Programme (NFWP), 21
National Institute of Basic Education, 170
NIEPA *see* NUEPA, 113, 118, 220
National Institute of Open Schooling (NIOS), 106, 109
National Institute of Rural Development, 46, 143
National Literacy Mission (NLM), 159-60
National Policy for Children, 93

National Policy on Education (NPE), 92, 95, 104, 106, 170
National Rural Employment Guarantee Act, 21
National University of Educational Planning and Administration (NUEPA), 113, 118, 143, 199, 220
Navodaya Vidyalaya Samiti (NVS), 106-07
Nayar, Sushila, 52
Nayee Taleem (New Education), 27, 66, 69, 78, 85-86
Nehru, Jawahar Lal, 113
Nutritional standards, 22, 28, 88, 94

Open Basic Education Programme (OBE), 109
Open schooling, 106, 108-09
Out-of-school youth, 131
OXFAM, 121

Panchayati Raj Institutions, 49, 62, 67, 97, 185
Parent Teacher Associations (PTAs), 94, 101, 192, 218, 236, 247
Personality traits, 86, 110
    development of, 86
Physical proximity, 117, 120-21, 126, 148
Planning Commission, 3, 44-46, 132-33, 137, 166, 176, 199-207, 209, 220-21, 243-45
Preschool education centres, 91, 227
Problem-based curriculum, 83
Problem-based textbooks, 83
Problem-centred and life-centred education, 78
Production-centred education, 85

Quality improvement in schools, 106

Referral centres, 144
Regional disparities, 20
Residual illiteracy, 160
Resource centers, 190
Rural development report, 18, 45-46
Rural institutes, 167, 179-81, 240
Rural-urban conflict and partnership, 49

Sangha Yogins, 160
Sarva Shiksha Abhiyan (SSA), 94-99, 112
Saxena Committee Report, 156
Secondary Education Commission, 103
Self-employment, 24, 103, 110, 134
Sergeant Report, 170
Shiksha Karmi Project (SKP), 96
Shrimali Committee, 180
SMART schools, 107
Socially relevant education, 134
Special education, 134
State Councils for Educational Research and Training (SCERT), 209, 246
Student-centric learning, 107
Sustainable development, 77

Tarabai Modak, 91
Teacher Education Programme (TEP), 96
Teacher-pupil ratio, 105
Tribal development agency, 44

UNESCO, 3, 96, 114, 156-57
United Nation (UN), 219
University Education Commission, 11, 44, 168-69, 179-80, 220
University Grants Commission, 3, 128, 137, 205, 229
Uttar Pradesh Basic Education Programme (UPBEP), 96

Vidya Mandir Scheme, 170
Vigyan Mandirs, 94
Village adoption, 127
Village Education Committee (VEC), 97, 101
Vocational institutions, 150

World Bank, 14, 25
World Declaration on Education, 95

Yoga and Population Education, 107

Zila Saksharta Samiti, 109